THE
PIG WAR

THE

PIG WAR

THE MOST PERFECT
WAR IN HISTORY

E. C. COLEMAN

The
History
Press

First published 2009
This paperback edition published 2018

The History Press
The Mill, Brimscombe Port
Stroud, Gloucestershire, GL5 2QG
www.thehistorypress.co.uk

British Library Cataloguing in Publication Data.
A catalogue record for this book is available from the British Library.

ISBN 978 0 7509 8918 3

Typesetting and origination by The History Press
Printed and bound in Great Britain by TJ International Ltd

Contents

A New Nation Flexes its Muscles

On the obverse of the Great Seal of the United States of America, a spread-winged bald eagle clutches in one of its talons an olive branch; in the other, thirteen arrows. The eagle's body is hidden behind a shield, whilst above its head a circle of light-emitting clouds enclose thirteen stars. A ribbon streams from the bird's beak, bearing the words '*e pluribus unum*' ('out of many, one'). It is a fine – indeed, noble – image that threatens firm retaliation, but offers peace.

The reverse of the seal shows a quite different design. The main feature is an unfinished pyramid with its top layers and cap missing. As if to take the place of the missing section, a matching triangle, containing a light-emitting eye, hovers just above the incomplete structure. Above the design, a Latin motto reads '*annuit coeptis*,' which is usually translated as 'God has favoured our undertaking.' Along the bottom another Latin motto states '*novus ordo seclorum*,' which is taken to mean 'a new order for the world' (or 'of the ages'). Taken together, however, the mottos can be read as 'grant the beginning of a new world order.'

The fathers of the American Revolution were not long in attempting to set the beginning of this new world order in motion. Dr Benjamin Franklin, who was the leading designer of the unfinished pyramid of the Great Seal, had the following as the thirteenth of his Articles of Confederation of 21 July 1775:

Any and every colony from Great Britain upon the continent of North America and not at present engag'd in our Association shall upon

Application and joining the said Association be receiv'd into this
Confederation, viz. West India Islands, Quebec, St Johns, Nova Scotia,
Bermudas, and East and West Florida; and shall thereupon be entitled
to all the Advantages of our Union, mutual Assistance and Commerce.

As the negotiations for the recognition of the United States began in
September 1782, the American side (John Adams, Benjamin Franklin
and John Jay) began by demanding that Great Britain surrender Canada
(then consisting of the two colonies of 'Upper' and 'Lower' Canada) to
the United States. It was a bold thrust that would have set the missing cap
onto the pyramid. The British negotiator, David Hartley, backed by the
Prime Minister, rejected the suggestion with such vigour that it quickly
became clear to the Americans that to continue with such an outrageous
demand would jeopardise the whole negotiation and risk subjecting the
fledgling nation to an unwanted continuation of hostilities. Consequently,
the national border between Canada and the United States, fishing and
property rights, and the withdrawal of the British from American soil
were all negotiated and settled. The northern border of the United States
would, it was agreed, reach from the Atlantic, through the Great Lakes, 'to
the most northwesternmost point' of the Lake of the Woods, and 'thence
on a due west course to the River Mississippi.' The principle, however,
of obtaining all the land in North America for the United States had
taken root, and so began the longest cold war in history: that between the
United States and Great Britain.

Beyond the Mississippi, Louisiana – the land as far west as the Rockies
– had belonged to the Spanish since 1763, when it was taken from the
French. In 1801, by treaty, France regained control of Louisiana and, as a
result, the United States found itself staring at a golden opportunity. By
the end of that year, the French Revolutionary War had fought itself to
a stand-still. Both France and Britain were exhausted. The Royal Navy
dominated the seas, while the French Army, under Napoleon Bonaparte,
continued to grow more powerful. But a larger, more powerful army is
expensive, and Napoleon was keen to raise the necessary funds. The
Treaty of Amiens, signed in 1802, provided a pause in the conflict,
but Britain had not done well out of the treaty and, when the French
began to disregard parts of the agreement, Britain refused to abandon
Malta and began an aggressive blockade against French shipping. In this
atmosphere, the Americans approached Napoleon with a remarkable
suggestion. They would like to buy part of Louisiana. The bait worked.
The French offered not just a part, but all of Louisiana, in return

for which the United States would pay 60 million francs and cancel 20 million francs' worth of debt (a total of $15 million). At a stroke, the French economy was raised to a war footing, the Americans had doubled the size of their country and the British were, once again, embroiled in a continental war.

As the combatants took up their positions, the Americans could afford to await the outcome. If the British came out on top, nothing would have changed; but if the British were defeated, it would be an easy task to walk into their possessions in North America and take them over.

Across the Atlantic, the war had taken on a significant change on its resumption. The Royal Navy, especially after Nelson's great victory at Trafalgar, continued to sweep all before it, but the British Army was occupied in removing the French from Spain. By 1812, the United States of America felt it could make moves of its own. It did not have to look far for an excuse. As far back as 1807 an incident had occurred which had threatened to bring the Americans into the war.

Against a background of blockading that had badly affected American trade, the Royal Navy insisted on continuing its practice of raising men by pressing them into the service. In Britain itself, any man 'used to the sea' was at risk of being pressed. There were exemptions, but being on board a foreign vessel was not one of them. Many seamen had deserted to American ships, usually for the better rates of pay rather than for any greater principle. Consequently, the Royal Navy assumed the right to stop any American ship and to search it for His Majesty's subjects who would be better employed in the ships of war of their own nation – or hanged as an example if desertion could be proved.

On 22 June 1807, Captain Humphreys of HMS *Leopard* sent a boat across to the USS *Chesapeake* with a demand that Humphreys' men be allowed to search her for British seamen. Captain Barron of the *Chesapeake* refused the demand and was seen by the men in the *Leopard*'s boat to be preparing for battle. On learning of the American's action, Humphreys promptly gave the order to engage the *Chesapeake*. Within minutes, three Americans had been killed, eighteen had been injured and the British were searching their ship.

In response to the incident, the Americans passed an Embargo Act forbidding any merchant vessel to leave American ports with cargoes for foreign destinations. The effect on the British war effort was significant, but not crippling. The same, however, could not be said about the American merchants, who saw the United States' export trade fall dramatically. The Embargo Act was repealed in 1809.

The United States took its revenge for the *Chesapeake–Leopard* incident in May 1811, when HMS *Little Belt* of 20 guns ran into the 44-gun USS *President*. The *Little Belt* hailed the *President* to ask who she was – the reply came in the form of a full broadside. For half an hour the tiny British corvette tried to close with the American vessel, but, whenever her captain, Commander Arthur Bingham, tried to get alongside the *President*, Commodore John Rogers kept out of range and used his much heavier guns to bring down the *Little Belt*'s mizzen mast. Unable to steer or bring his guns to bear, Bingham ceased firing. The American also stopped his cannonading and sailed away after signalling his regret at the incident. The British ship had eleven killed in the action and twenty-one wounded. The *President* had one boy slightly injured.

The incident had no effect on American attitudes, which, in some quarters, had already hardened. By now, Congressman Henry Clay – a leading 'War Hawk' – was demanding the invasion of Canada. Clay was not alone, and he was able to muster enough support to have war declared against Great Britain on 18 June 1812. Congressman Daniel Webster was appalled: 'Public opinion, strong and united, is not with you in your Canada project.' But it was too late, and the 'cold' war was about to become hot.

The prospects of another war on a second front were not too good for Britain. The military forces in Canada were weak and thinly spread. Less than 5,000 soldiers, supported by a poorly trained militia, were supposed to guard against invasion along a thousand-mile border. It was not, however, on land that the main shocks were to be felt, but at sea.

The Americans possessed a number of very powerful 44-gun frigates (actually mounting 54 guns), against which the Royal Navy was expected to deploy frigates mounting 38 guns. The swift capitulation of the *Chesapeake* in 1807 had sent out the wrong message, and the British people were stunned into disbelief when the *Constitution* tore the masts from HMS *Guerriere*, leaving her dead in the water and unable to continue the fight. Disbelief then turned into outright alarm when Lieutenant Chads, the first lieutenant of HMS *Java*, found he had the 'melancholy task' of informing the Admiralty that, with his captain seriously injured and his ship dismasted and helpless, 'our colours were lowered from the stump of the mainmast.' Matters became even worse when HMS *Macedonian* was not only pounded into a wreck by the USS *United States*, but was actually returned to an American port as a prize. Being outgunned was not an excuse acceptable to a nation – or a navy – that had seen someone like Horatio Nelson serving beneath its flag. Consequently, a new strategy saw the American frigates blockaded in port as British ships, more than capable in strength or in firepower, waited outside.

In the case of the *Chesapeake* (nominally a 38-gun vessel, but actually mounting 48), a different tactic was used. The 38-gun HMS *Shannon* managed to tempt her out of Boston harbour. The American ship was not only captured, but had the ignominy of her timbers ending up as the framework for an English flour mill. The *President*, in attempting to escape from New York during a snow-storm, fell in with a British squadron. After a chase, she was captured and also taken to England. A third American frigate, the *Essex*, was to meet her destiny off the coast of South America.

On land, matters had not fared so well for the Americans. Almost a dozen attempts to invade Canada had fizzled out and what had been achieved amounted to little more than vandalism involving the destruction of private and public property. In revenge, the Royal Navy invaded the nation's capital and burned the presidential mansion (now known as the White House) and the Capitol. Nearby, the town of Alexandria, faced with a bombardment from two frigates and five smaller vessels, promptly surrendered, turning over all its stores to the British.

Nevertheless, much of the British military involvement suffered from incompetent leadership. At Plattsburgh, Lieutenant-General Sir George Prevost, despite having tough, eager veterans who had fought against Napoleon lined up ready to advance against the enemy, and despite the Americans managing to burn down their own buildings whilst using heated shot, refused to launch the attack and ended up lamely retreating across the border. In the south, at New Orleans, Major-General Sir Edward Packenham, ignoring the opportunity to allow part of his force to outflank the Americans, advanced over open ground towards a wide, muddy ditch and an enemy sheltered behind breastworks of cotton bails and sugar barrels. Needless to say, the British suffered a defeat of catastrophic proportions.

Three days after the debacle at New Orleans, Captain Robert Barrie of HMS *Dragon* captured Cumberland Island, off the coast of Georgia. Using the island as a base of attack, Barrie crossed to the mainland on 13 January 1815, captured the fort at Point Peter, took the nearby town of St Mary and sent two captured ships to join his squadron. Then, no doubt much to his chagrin, Barrie found he had to retire to his ships and leave the area. News had reached him that a peace treaty had been signed on Christmas Eve 1814. Consequently, both the Battle of New Orleans and Barrie's invasion of the United States had taken place after the treaty had been signed (as did a further United States surrender to British forces at Fort

Bowyer, Alabama, exactly one month later). Barrie, who had already had a spectacular career against American shipping along the east coast, and had helped in the capture of part of Maine, later became the senior naval officer in Canada and had the town of Barrie, Ontario, named in his honour.

At the start of the war, Great Britain owned vast areas of land in North America. Not only Upper and Lower Canada, Nova Scotia and Labrador, but also Rupert's Land, the huge area controlled by the Hudson's Bay Company which reached north to the Arctic Sea, the known lands of the North Western Territory and the lands west of the Rocky Mountains as far south as the 42nd Parallel, known as Columbia Country.

The latter territory had fallen to the British as a result of their victory in the Seven Years' War (1756–63), and was administered by the North West Company, the main commercial rivals of the Hudson's Bay Company. However, between 1804 and 1806 an American 'Corps of Discovery' expedition led by Captain Lewis and Lieutenant Clark had crossed the continent (the second to do so north of Mexico), giving the Americans – in their opinion – a claim on the land. In 1811, to underline this claim, the wealthy fur-trader John Jacob Astor sent a ship to the north-west Pacific coast to build a fort on the banks of the Columbia River. With the outbreak of war, the existence of 'Fort Astoria' on British territory became, at last, an affront to British sensibilities. Something had to be done.

The answer to the problem arrived in the form of an order to Captain James Hillyar of the 36-gun HMS *Phoebe*. On passage in company with a North West Company ship, the *Isaac Todd*, Hillyar was to enter the Pacific, make his way to Fort Astoria, capture it and hand it over to the North West Company, who, in turn, would use it as a base to establish a settlement at the mouth of the Columbia River.

The *Phoebe* and her consort left Portsmouth in March 1813 and arrived at Rio de Janeiro three months later, only to learn that the purpose of the mission was already known to the Americans. Of even greater interest to Hillyar was the news that a 38-gun frigate, the USS *Essex* (like the *Chesapeake* actually armed with 48 guns), under the command of Captain David Porter, had entered the Pacific and was doing considerable damage amongst British whalers and other shipping in the vicinity of the Galapagos Islands. If the *Phoebe* and the *Isaac Todd* fell in with the *Essex*, there was every chance that Hillyar would be overwhelmed. Even if the *Phoebe* was sacrificed, the North West Company ship would not be able to escape the speed of the American. To even the odds, Hillyar was given two smaller ships to add to his squadron: the 18-gun sloop HMS *Cherub* and the 16-gun *Raccoon*.

After a stormy passage around Cape Horn, the *Isaac Todd* was discovered to be missing and, when she failed to appear at a rendezvous at Juan Fernandez Island, Hillyar was forced to assume she had been lost. Under the changed circumstances he chose to ignore the main thrust of his mission and sent the *Raccoon* on alone to take Fort Astoria. Why bother with the trifling business of taking a fort manned by fur-traders, when there was much better game afoot? Hillyar intended to go after the *Essex*.

Unbeknown to the *Phoebe's* captain, news of his mission had already reached the *Essex*, and Porter took measures accordingly. One of the whalers the American had captured was converted into a 20-gun man-of-war with a ship's company of ninety men and re-named the *Essex Junior*. Both sides were now hunting for the other.

They met by accident: not at sea, but in the harbour of Valparaiso. As the *Phoebe* and the *Cherub* prowled up and down outside the harbour, Porter, who had promised his men 'an abundant supply of wealth, and the girls of the Sandwich Islands,' remained under the protection of Chilean neutrality: a precarious policy as Britain, by now allied with Spain, had shown no signs of recognising Chilean independence or such neutrality.

It was, however, not the question of neutrality that decided the issue, for, after six weeks secured in the port, a violent storm caused one of the *Essex's* mooring cables to part. Forced to sail from the harbour or risk the likelihood of being driven aground, Porter suddenly realised that the high winds were actually in his favour. With the wind astern, there was every chance that he could race out of the harbour and leave the slower British ships in his wake. But it was not to be. As he cut his remaining cable and left the harbour entrance, the main-topmast snapped, reducing both his speed and his manoeuvrability. Unable to return to the refuge of the harbour, Porter turned to what he hoped would be his salvation – the neutrality of Chilean waters. The *Essex* retreated to the coast in the expectation of sanctuary, but Hillyar was not impressed. Even if Chilean neutrality had been expected, it could not last indefinitely. The British ships bore down upon their enemy and, knowing that the American could throw out a broadside of 676 lbs compared to the 476 lbs of the *Phoebe* and the 248 lbs of the *Cherub*, Hillyar kept well away from the range of the *Essex's* 32-lb carronades as he poured in fire from his long 18-pounders. Before long, men were to be seen jumping from the *Essex* in an effort to swim to the shore and, after just two and a half hours, Porter was forced to haul down his flag. The balance of power in the Pacific now lay with the British, and one of the much-vaunted American 38-gun frigates was on its way to becoming a convict hulk in an English port.

The *Raccoon*, on the other hand, had faced a much less glorious outcome as she reached Fort Astoria. Much to the outrage and disappointment of her captain and ship's company – who had been looking forward to the prize money which would have been theirs at the imminent capture – the fur-traders, knowing that the British were coming, and showing true American initiative, had sold the fort to the North West Company. The only light in the gloom came when the battered – and given up for lost – *Isaac Todd* made its way up the Pacific coast with much-needed supplies.

With the signing of the Treaty of Ghent on 24 December 1814, the Canadian economy boomed from the resources spent during the war, the disparate parts of the country had earned the respect of each other and every American attempt at invasion had been repulsed. The question of pressing men from American ships was not even raised in the peace treaty, and not a single American enterprise existed on the north-west coast of North America.

2

The Boundary Settled?

After the war of 1812 there still remained a number of inconsistencies and general bones of contention regarding the border between the United States and the lands of British North America. Under the Treaty of Ghent a series of four joint commissions, with one commissioner from each side, would examine different sections of the eastern end of the border with a view to arriving at an amicable agreement as to the final line. All went well for two of these surveying commissions, but the question of the border with the state of Maine proved difficult, as did the boundary from Lake Huron to the Lake of the Woods. Both reported back to their governments as having 'disagreed.'

For both parties the border difficulties in the east appeared to be little more than a tidying up of the line. There was some land to be lost or gained, some access to resources to be denied or achieved, but all agreed that the answer to the difficulties lay only in diplomacy. Such was not the case in the west.

Another look at the borders came six years after the war, when a treaty known as the 'Convention of 1818' was signed by both sides. After the usual jostling for position over fishing rights, Article II re-examined the border running along the 49th Parallel. Not only was it discovered that the 49th Parallel did not run from the 'most northwesternmost point' of the Lake of the Woods, but closer to the south-west corner, but it was also learned that the line of latitude did not meet the Mississippi at any point of the river's length. The latter problem was dealt with after some difficult negotiations by continuing the line westwards until it met the 'Stony (i.e. 'Rocky') Mountains.' The question concerning the line's starting position on the Lake of the Woods, however, fell into farce.

In drawing the line southwards from the 'most northwesternmost point' of the lake, a section of Canada (modern Ontario) was sliced off. Covering an area of about 130 square miles, the land – known as the Northwest Angle – remained suspended above the 49th Parallel, unconnected to the United States and accessible by land only by going through Canada. A far more logical solution would have been to have given to the United States the land bordering the south-east corner of the lake until the 49th Parallel made contact with the water, and then taken it straight across the southern end of the lake following that latitude. However, as will be frequently seen, common sense and diplomatic negotiations often prove to be uncomfortable bedfellows in a cold war. They were just as uncomfortable when the treaty turned to the question of British possessions in the north-west.

There was never any doubt regarding Great Britain's rights to the ownership of Columbia Country. South from the southern border of Russian North America at 54° 40' N, to the northern border of Spanish Mexico on the 42nd Parallel, and extending as far east as the Rocky Mountains, the area had been taken from the Spanish in 1763 at the end of the Seven Years' War. Britain's claims could go back even further. The coast had been sailed by the Spanish as far back as 1542, but no land claims had been made. Nor were any claims made until the region was visited by Francis Drake during his voyage of circumnavigation. It is known for certain that he landed and claimed 'New Albion' (probably Upper California), but there was the mystery of the question concerning 'a certain truth concealed.' Some open-minded historians have come to the conclusion that Drake sailed much further north, beyond even the Straits of Juan de Fuca. This could be based upon the report of the expedition in which it was noted that, after a dash to the north, '… the men being thus speedily come out of the extreme heat, found the air so cold that, being pinched with the same, they complained of the extremity thereof.' Drake then headed east to the coast (where he may have landed, at least for water), and then south, probably towards San Francisco. If far enough to the north, the southerly voyage would have taken them past the Straits of Juan de Fuca. Seeing the wide waterway, and realising that it might be a western outlet of a north-west passage across the top of North America, Drake – and, on his return, the Queen – decided not to publicise any claims in the area and thus forestall any foreign commercial competition. Whilst such a theory cannot be proved, it would, at least, account for the surprising discovery by later expeditions of northern American Indians of unusually large stature, with pale skins, lighter-coloured eyes and hair, and – most surprising of all – facial hair.

Between the southern border of the territory and the Straits of Juan de Fuca, the Columbia River reached the Pacific Ocean. Although guarded at its entrance by a treacherous series of sand bars, once these had been safely negotiated the river proved to be a natural highway for the delivery of stores and the receipt of furs. The North West Company's Fort George (previously the American 'Fort Astoria') was situated on the southern bank of the river close to the entrance. The question of the fort had proved to be contentious during the negotiations of the peace treaty at the end of the war of 1812, when the Americans demanded its return on the grounds that it had been in their possession at the outbreak of hostilities. Had the fort been taken by enemy action, there may have been a case for its return, but as the Americans had sold the fort to the British it was felt (at least by the British) that its acquisition had been entirely legitimate. However, as someone pointed out, on closer examination it could equally be shown that at least one British organisation had, in consequence, been guilty of trading with the enemy. As a result, the fort was handed back to the Americans in a ceremony more pantomime than sincere. No Americans were present during the handover as, with full formality, the Stars and Stripes was run up the flagpole to replace the Union Flag, and the British continued to live in, and operate out of, 'Fort George.'

During the negotiations leading up to the Convention of 1818, the Americans had provided a proposal that the border line along the 49th Parallel should be continued until it reached the Pacific Ocean on the western coast of Vancouver Island. Such a proposition was, to the British, unthinkable. Not only would thousands of square miles of prime land be lost along with the entrance to the Straits of Juan de Fuca, they would also lose the southern access to the Pacific provided by the Columbia River. But in an effort to show good will, they submitted a counter-proposal in which the line would be extended along the 49th Parallel to the point where it met the western loop of the Columbia. From there it would follow the river until it reached the sea. It was an eminently sensible compromise that would release a massive amount of land to the United States, allow both sides passage on the river, and allow Great Britain access to the Pacific south of the Straits of Juan de Fuca. The Americans refused. Finally, an uneasy compromise was reached. The territory (by then known as the 'Oregon Territory') would be settled by both sides. The joint occupation would continue for ten years, after which time the problem would be looked at again.

There were problems for both America and Britain in the compromise. The British were not keen to start mass settlement of the region (colonies meant defence, defence meant cost), whereas the Americans had long planned a westwards expansion of their population. On the other hand, all American attempts to start fur-trading in the territory met with failure, as the British interests had so tightly secured the industry that no opportunities remained for outsiders. The British, however, did eventually have to give up Fort George, and moved their headquarters upstream to a newly built 'Fort Vancouver.'

In 1823, Great Britain, delighted at seeing the success of the revolutions in South America, and already profiting from the trade with the newly independent nations, proposed to the American President, James Monroe, that the two countries form an alliance intended to prevent Spain and Portugal, along with other European allies, from attempting to regain their former colonies. Monroe refused and countered with his own policy. Eventually to be known as the 'Monroe Doctrine,' the President declared that no European country should ever again establish a colony anywhere in the Americas. From one point of view, this suited Britain, as the policy would appear to ensure that the United States would be allied with Britain should any European power try to take possession of any part of British North America – although whether or not that was Monroe's intention is unclear. The only likely problem to arise for Britain would be if she made any arrangement with Russia to take over Russian North America. Monroe's policy expressly forbade the trading or purchasing of colonies by other powers. Great Britain could not settle too comfortably into the apparent acceptance of the current position of British North America. Monroe's Secretary of State, John Quincy Adams, also asserted in 1823 that the world should become familiar 'with the idea of considering our proper dominion to be the continent of North America.' And that included Canada.

After almost ten years of joint occupation it was time to revisit the 1818 treaty. Once again, there was no agreement regarding the ownership of Oregon Territory. The United States, now under the presidency of the same John Quincy Adams, pushed forward and obtained agreement on the proposition that the 1818 Convention should continue indefinitely, with the provision that either party could withdraw from the Convention upon giving twelve months' notice.

For another decade the Oregon Territory went about its business without too much difficulty. Protestant missionaries arrived from the east and began their work among the Native Americans. They were followed by a trickle of settlers, but nothing to cause alarm amongst the representatives of the governing Hudson's Bay Company. Then, suddenly, the attention of both nations was switched dramatically to the north-east.

In 1837, an American-backed rebellion broke out in Upper Canada (Ontario). A Scotsman, William Lyon Mackenzie, leading a band of dissident farmers and demanding a republican government, broke into an armoury and began to march on Toronto. They, and a group of supporters near Hamilton, were quickly defeated by British troops. Fleeing across the border into the United States, Mackenzie found eager support for his rebellion amongst the people of Buffalo, who supplied him with arms and ammunition, including two artillery pieces. Thus encouraged, he set sail across the Niagara River and established himself and a few dozen men on Navy Island, declaring themselves to be 'The Republic of Canada.' Supplies continued to be ferried out to the rebels in the steamer *Caroline*. To cut this supply line, British soldiers landed at Fort Schlosser in New York State, boarded the ship, towed her into the middle of the stream, set her on fire and, in a spectacular underlining of their achievement, sent the blazing vessel plunging over the Niagara Falls. Just weeks later, the rebellion collapsed and the leaders fled into the United States. Matters, however, did not end there. In retribution for the taking and destroying of the *Caroline*, twenty-two members of the Canadian Refugee Association – a New York-based organisation dedicated to the overthrow of British power in Upper and Lower Canada – boarded the Lake Ontario passenger steamer *Sir Robert Peel*, landed the passengers and set the vessel on fire, causing her destruction. Even worse, one of the men who been part of the *Caroline* attack was arrested in America and put on trial. If found guilty, he would hang. At this, Great Britain demanded his release on the grounds that the man had been a member of the British Army. If he was executed, it could – and probably would – mean war. The United States Government agreed with the British demand, but had no power to stop the trial in the State of New York. The trial went ahead, only – to everyone's relief – to end in acquittal. Nevertheless, tension remained high and strong feelings continued to exist between the two governments – a situation not about to be helped when lumberjacks from the British colony of New Brunswick spent the winter of 1838–39 cutting timber in Madawaska District.

The area chosen by the lumberjacks was claimed by the State of Maine, a claim not supported by the British Government. The problem arose as a result – not for the first time – of poor boundary decisions in 1794 and in the Treaty of Ghent. At that time the surveyors had placed the northern border between Maine and New Brunswick along a range of 'highlands.' Later surveys revealed that there were two ranges of highlands, one to the north that followed the southern banks of the St Lawrence River, and another further south that ran across the state broadly in an east–west direction. Naturally, the British claimed the more southern range of hills as the border, whilst Maine insisted that the original treaty had meant the northern range. As far back as 1832, King William I of the Netherlands had been asked to arbitrate in the matter and he had come up with a compromise that took the border along the St John River, a waterway that roughly bisected the region between the two ranges of hills. The British Government reluctantly accepted the decision, but Maine, and the United States Government, refused. Consequently, when it was learned that the lumberjacks were at work to the south of the Maine-favoured border, an American Land Agent was sent to remove the invaders. The lumberjacks, however, kidnapped him.

The reaction was astonishing. The Governor of the State of Maine called out the 10,000 men of the local militia and persuaded the United States Congress to approve a force of 50,000 men and allocate $10 million to fund the emergency. In New Brunswick, where many families were descended from 'Loyalists' who had opposed American independence in 1776, thousands of militiamen, desperately keen to assert their rights, were called up and funded by the colonial legislature. Many were veterans of the war of 1812.

The President, Martin Van Buren, was aghast at the thought of an impending war with Britain. A kindly, asthmatic man who was more interested in rescuing the waning fortunes of the Democratic Party than in getting involved in armed conflict, he knew just the man to send to the region.

General Winfield Scott was the son of a Virginia farmer who had fought in the War of Independence. After studying law, Scott entered the army and had distinguished himself during the war of 1812 and during the fighting against the Indians. At well over six feet tall and heavily built, he could hold his own physically as well as in debate – and it was to be the latter attribute that came to the fore on the border between Maine and New Brunswick. Instead of simply taking command of the American forces and squaring up against the colonists, he persuaded the leading officials of both sides to agree to calm the situation down and allow the dispute to be dealt with through negotiation.

In 1842, meetings were held between the United States Secretary of State, Daniel Webster, and his personal friend, Alexander Baring,

Lord Ashburton. The negotiations were highlighted by elements of farce in which both sides tried to persuade their own people to accept their decisions by means of discredited evidence, and by a whiff of corruption.

Having come to the conclusion that the Dutch king had probably come to the best conclusion in his compromise proposal of a border along the course of the St John River, both Webster and Ashburton knew they would meet opposition from their own sides. Webster dealt with this by the 'discovery' of a map in France which purported to show the border delineated by Benjamin Franklin during the negotiations at Paris in 1782. Much to everyone's surprise (except, that is, Webster's), the border apparently agreed by Franklin was along the more southerly range of hills. It followed, therefore, that if Maine, pretending ignorance of the map, was to agree to the St John River compromise, the state would gain more than had been agreed during the Treaty of Paris – and be seen, in consequence, to be the winner in the negotiations.

Astonishingly, on the other hand, in the library of King George III, another map was discovered, one marked, no less, than by the King's Geographer. This time the border line traced almost exactly the line demanded by the Americans – along the northern range of highlands. For the British, therefore, again pretending ignorance of their map, the St John compromise would make them winner in the negotiations.

The 1842 Treaty of Washington (or the 'Webster–Ashburton Treaty') finally put the seal on the north-east border between the United States and British North America. But not everyone was happy. Lord Palmerston, who had been Secretary of State for Foreign Affairs during the Dutch king's arbitration, criticised the treaty on the grounds that too much had been given away to the Americans. Of greater concern to some people was the fact that Lord Ashburton was married to an American woman, and owned several million acres of land – in Maine.

The avoidance of hostilities in the country's north-east gave the United States a chance to concentrate on activities along its southern borders. Texas had become an independent republic in 1836 and, after refusals by America to grant annexation as a state, decided to go for full-blown nationhood. British influence had been involved since the earliest days of the republic (a large percentage of the heroes of the Alamo had been British), and Great Britain was soon allowing Texans to trade at British ports, supplying loans and offering to help in negotiations with Mexico. Treaties were signed and a chargé d'affaires appointed.

An illustration of how sensitive this made the Americans over British involvement may be found in the curious incident of the United States

Pacific Fleet commanded by Commodore Thomas Jones. Moored with his fleet in the Peruvian port of Callao, Jones watched as HMS *Dublin*, the flagship of the Pacific Station, sailed into the port before promptly returning to sea. The reason this had happened was that, on her arrival, it was discovered that there was no room for her in the harbour. Jones convinced himself that the British ship had seen his vessel and had left on some secret mission that the British did not want him to know about. Even more strange, Jones came to the conclusion that the British were about to invade California in lieu of Mexican debts. Consequently, Jones took his and other American warships to the port of Monterey, aimed his guns ashore and demanded the surrender of the authorities. When this happened, Jones promptly annexed California in the name of the United States. It was, therefore, with some embarrassment, that he had to give up his conquered territory when he learned that not only had the British no intention of taking California, but Mexico and the United States were still at peace. In compensation, Mexico demanded payment of 1,500 complete military uniforms, enough musical instruments to form a military band and $15,000. Nothing, however, was ever paid.

In 1843, with the help of the chargé d'affaires and the British Minister to Mexico, an armistice was agreed between the Mexicans and Texas. Alarmed at the prospect of increasing British influence in the region, the United States Government agreed to the annexation of Texas. Then, through a demand for more territory, it engineered a war against Mexico which resulted in the United States obtaining Texas as far south-west as the Rio Grande, along with California and New Mexico to the west. Among those who had shown great courage and leadership during the war was General Winfield Scott, who had entered and taken Mexico City itself.

The President, James Polk, now found himself with a problem. The newly acquired Texas was a slave-owning state with the right – if it so wished – to divide itself into four smaller states. Even the acquisition of a single slave-owning state caused grave concerns among the Northern non-slave-owning states, who could see themselves being out-voted in the nation's legislature. The answer was obvious. The Oregon Territory would have to be acquired as a non-slave-owning state to keep the balance.

There was no lack of support for such an idea. During his election campaign, Polk's supporters had taken up the chant of 'Fifty-four Forty or Fight!', referring to the southern border of Russian North America which was set at 54° 40' N. Great Britain, on the other hand, had perfectly sound claims to the 670,000 square miles of the whole territory. What she had not gained by war she had achieved through the surveys of Captain George Vancouver. The area had been under the benign stewardship of the Hudson's Bay Company, who had fostered a continuing good relationship with the Native American tribes. Nevertheless, there had been important changes in the region and, alert to the possibility of new pressure from the United States, the Company had moved its headquarters from Fort Vancouver to Fort Victoria, on the southern tip of Vancouver Island.

There was still the need for good access to the Pacific. The Columbia, despite the dangerous shoals at the entrance, remained a vital part of the Company's operation, while to the north, still to be developed, was the magnificent deep-water harbour on Puget Sound (named after Vancouver's first lieutenant). All of which, of course, was known to the United States, who could argue that the priority of discovery of the Columbia was, in fact, theirs, as the entrance to the river had first been made in 1792 when the American Captain Robert Grey first entered the river in his ship *Columbia Rediviva*. Grey did not go upriver as Vancouver was to do later, but the priority still remained an American achievement.

The most important change, however, was the number of Americans who had made their way to the Oregon Territory. The migration had caused the Company employees to be considerably outnumbered. The newcomers had, for the most part, settled south of the Columbia, mainly in the Willamette Valley. There they had formed an elected provisional government, which provided for the security of land ownership and the introduction of a legal system. Of even greater importance, the legislature barred the introduction of slavery. Consequently, the pressure on the United States Government to take a closer look at the question of the Oregon Territory became almost irresistible, and could not be ignored by either them or the British.

At the Democratic Party national convention of 1844 there had been an absurd demand for the 'reoccupation of Oregon' (just as there had been a demand for the 'reoccupation of Texas'). Those making the demand were firmly of the view that, as the United States had made a treaty with Russia which stated that the Russians would not expand further south than 54° 40' N, it must follow that that was where the northern boundary of the Oregon Territory must be. Nothing less would be acceptable. What they overlooked was that Great Britain had also made a treaty with Russia under exactly the same terms, giving Britain the same rights as the United States. In addition, the Americans were demanding that, under the Monroe Doctrine, to leave any of the Oregon Territory in the hands of the British would inevitably lead to the creation of a European colony on the continent – something expressly forbidden under the doctrine. The threat of war, however, could be dangerous. The First Opium War (1839-41) had shown that the British could transport an army to the Pacific and challenge and defeat a far larger force. Furthermore, they not only had the most powerful navy in the world, but, as a result of the war, they now had a base at Hong Kong. Any aggression on the part of the Americans would meet a full and vigorous response – and this time the Americans could not depend upon the French to help them out, as had been the case in 1776 and 1812.

At about the same time, more rational and, at first, more reasonable discussions were taking place between American officials and the British Minister in Washington, DC, Sir Richard Pakenham (who had previously been Minister to Mexico). The Americans returned to their offer of the 49th Parallel as the boundary. Packenham turned the offer down and countered with the offer, once again, of a line along the 49th Parallel to the Columbia, then down the river to the Pacific. When the Americans turned that down, Pakenham suggested that the question be put to international arbitration, such as had been tried in the difficulty with the Maine–New Brunswick border. Again, the Americans turned the idea down. Matters then took a more critical turn when, in his inaugural address, President Polk referred to 'the whole of Oregon,' a reference which created palpable anger in Britain. This rise in temperature led the new Secretary of State, James Buchanan, to return to the offer of the 49th Parallel – an offer which was rapidly withdrawn when news of it got out and created a storm of protest from the 'Fifty-four Forty or Fight!' faction.

In December 1845, Congress was faced with resolutions demanding that 'the whole of Oregon' belonged to the United States and that the President should give the British notice that, under the Convention of 1827, the joint occupation agreement would end in twelve months. Across the Atlantic, Britain began to arm and prepare herself for war against the United States.

In America, the response was to take up a two-word phrase that had first appeared in the *United States Magazine & Democratic Review* at the time of the attempt to annex Texas. Those foreign governments who opposed the annexation were, according to the editor, attempting to prevent 'the fulfilment of our manifest destiny to over spread the continent allotted by Providence for the free development of our yearly multiplying millions.' Six months later, the New York *Morning News* used the phrase 'manifest destiny' when referring to the movement of settlers to Oregon.

The phrase moved rapidly into public, then political, usage. God – in the shape of 'Providence' – clearly intended that the Americans should inhabit the entire continent of North America.

In an effort to forestall an impending conflict, Sir Richard Pakenham returned to the negotiating table with an offer to accept the proposed line along the 49th Parallel that had been drafted by the Foreign Secretary, Lord Aberdeen. Provisos insisted that the Hudson's Bay Company should be able to use the Columbia to reach the Pacific, and that property rights would be respected. Chief of the provisos, however, required that the line, on reaching the coast of the continent, would extend to the middle of the Gulf of Georgia, and then proceed southwards along the centre of the gulf until it swung westwards through the middle of the Straits of Juan de Fuca to the Pacific. With the line following such a route, it would ensure that the whole of Vancouver Island would remain in British hands. Polk, in the certain knowledge that the United States was not prepared for a war, passed the responsibility for a decision to the Senate. By a vote of 38 to 12 the Senate passed a resolution advising the President to accept the proposal. Pakenham wrote to Lord Aberdeen at the Foreign Office, saying the draft Treaty had been 'accepted by the Government of the United States, without the addition or alteration of a single word.' The *Liverpool Times* was in a congratulatory mood:

> The people of the two countries owe this happy result to the wisdom and moderation of the British Government and the American Senate, both of which have acted in the difficult matter with a temper and judgement which entitle them to the thanks of their fellow-country-men, and of all civilised nations. After the extreme rash conduct of President Polk, it required extraordinary firmness on the part of the American Senate, and great self-command on the part of the British Government to bring the question to a peaceful settlement.

The *Morning Sun*, however, felt that a little gloating was more appropriate:

> … it is certain that the American Government has conceded in all important particulars to the requisitions of the mother country.

The 'Treaty between Her Majesty and the United States of America, for the Settlement of the Oregon Boundary' was signed by Pakenham and Buchanan at Washington, DC, on 15 June 1846 and ratified by both governments a month later. War had been averted, America now had an open doorway to her westwards expansion, Britain had been relieved of the burden of colonisation and had retained 'New Caledonia' (as the British mainland north of the line was to be called) and all of Vancouver Island with Fort Victoria at its southern end. No one had actually won, and no one had emerged with an unmatched loss. There was, however, one small problem which had either been missed – or deliberately ignored.

Article I of the Treaty read:

> … the line of boundary between the territories of Her Britannic Majesty and those of the United States shall be continued westward along the said 49th parallel of north latitude to the middle of the channel which separates the continent from Vancouver's Island; and thence southerly, through the middle of the said channel, and of Fuca's Straits to the Pacific Ocean …

What no one admitted noticing, was that a group of islands cluster around the lower reaches of the Gulf of Georgia. Which passage through the islands would provide the 'channel' of the treaty? A small matter, perhaps? But, then again, perhaps not.

3

Defining a 'Channel'

The island group that is clustered at the junction of the Gulf of Georgia and the Straits of Juan de Fuca are formed from the tops of ancient mountains. The largest islands of the archipelago are San Juan, Orcas and Lopez; others are Blakely, Decatur, Cypress, Sinclair, Shaw, Stuart and Waldron. Taken together with the dozens of smaller islands they are known simply as the 'San Juan Islands,' or even the 'San Juans.' To the east lie the islands of Whidbey, Guemes and Fidalgo, while to the north other small islands are sprinkled about the Gulf of Georgia.

In their geography, the islands are modest and unassuming. There are no great mountains or deep harbours. Clad for the most part in pines and red cedars, the islands have areas of open grassland that dry off in the late summer due to the lack of rainfall. Above the forest and grasslands fly bald eagles and hawks whilst, in season, seals and whales ply the surrounding fish-laden waters.

The islands had been the home of the Lummi Tribe and a summer base to other Indians who fished off the beaches, but the archipelago held too little large game to provide year-round subsistence for a large population. The first westerners to reach the islands were probably the Spanish under the command of Manuel Quimper around 1789. Believing the islands to be part of the mainland, Quimper looked briefly at a north-trending waterway which he named after his ship's pilot, Gonzalo Lopez de Haro (variously known as 'Canal de Arro,' 'Channel de Arro,' 'Haro Channel' or 'Haro Strait'). Shortly afterwards, another Spanish expedition, led by Francisco Eliza, probed the islands before arriving at the broad waters to the north which he named 'Rosario Strait.' Then the British arrived on the scene in the shape of Captain George Vancouver.

Vancouver had been one of Captain Cook's midshipmen and had learned his navigation under the stern eye of Cook's sailing master, Mr William Bligh (of later *Bounty* fame). He had also developed a high level of skill in surveying, and it was chiefly this achievement that resulted in his appointment to lead an expedition to the north-west coast of America to look for a seaway that could mark the western end of a north-west passage. And, while he was about it, he could put an end to a certain unpleasantness concerning the Spanish and their claim to territory at Nootka Sound.

With HMS *Discovery* and HMS *Chatham*, Vancouver entered the Straits of Juan de Fuca in 1792. Taking the *Discovery* down Puget Sound, Vancouver ordered Lieutenant Broughton, commander of the *Chatham*, to carry out a survey of the San Juan Islands. When the ships were once again in company, Vancouver sailed northwards, keeping the majority of the islands to his larboard (port or left-hand) side and probably passing between Blakely and Cypress islands. On reaching Eliza's 'Rosario Strait,' Vancouver renamed the waterway the 'Gulf of Georgia' after King George III, and relegated the name 'Rosario Strait' to the eastern island passage he had just taken (previously named 'Canal de Fidalgo' by the Spanish). Then, in the name of the king, Vancouver took possession of:

> the coast, from that part of New Albion, in the latitude of 30 degrees 20' north, and longitude 236 degrees 26', to the entrance of this inlet of the sea, said to be the supposed straits of Juan de Fuca; as likewise all the coast islands etc. within the said straits, as well on the northern as on the southern shores; together with those situated in the interior sea we had discovered, extending from the said straits, in various directions, between the north-west, north, east, and southern quarters.

On his return to England, after having completed a magnificently detailed survey of the coast of north-west America, Vancouver produced his charts. The chart showing the San Juan Islands showed both the Canal de Arro and Rosario Strait with a line indicating that the latter was the route taken by Vancouver.

The question concerning the identification of which channel the 1846 treaty had meant was not long in being closely examined. Even before the treaty had been signed, the Foreign Secretary, Lord Palmerston, had asked Sir John Pelly, the head of the Hudson's Bay Company, for his opinion.

Pelly replied that:

> ... the water demarcation line should be from the centre of the water in the Gulf of Georgia in the 49th degree along the line coloured red as navigable in the chart made by Vancouver till it reaches a line drawn through the centre of the Strait of Juan de Fuca. The only objection to this is giving to the United States the valuable Island of Whitby [sic]; but I do not see how this can be avoided in an amicable adjustment.

Later, when Palmerston asked Pelly to give him his 'opinion privately on questions that might arise out of the Oregon Treaty,' Pelly informed him that:

> ... in the space below 49 degrees to 48 degrees 20' (when you open the Straits of Juan de Fuca) there are numerous islands and I believe passages between them – I know there is one close round Vancouver's Island, but I believe the largest to be the one Vancouver sailed through, and I think this is the one which should be the boundary.

The Americans thought differently. The United States Minister to Great Britain, Louis McLane, who had been involved in the negotiations, wrote to the Secretary of State a month before the treaty was signed, saying:

> The proposition most probably will offer substantially ... To divide the territory by the extension of the line on the parallel of forty-nine to the sea; that is to say, to the arm of the sea called Birch's Bay: thence by the Canal de Haro and Straits of Fuca to the ocean ...

In a letter published in the *Baltimore Sun* of 23 July 1846, McLane removed the words 'most probably' but included 'thence by the Canal de Arro' in his report on the treaty, despite the fact that those words did not appear in the treaty itself. Even at the ratification meeting of the Senate, Senator Thomas Hart Benton addressed the house with the words '[the line] proceeds to the middle of the channel, and thence, turning south, through the Channel de Haro to the Straits of Fuca, then west through the middle of that strait to the sea.' Again, the words are not in the treaty, but they show, nevertheless, that the Americans were thinking of a quite different – and importantly different – channel.

In late 1847, Palmerston wrote to the splendidly named Sir John Fiennes Twistleton Crampton, the Minister in Washington, DC – who had taken over from Pakenham – with a proposal that 'A naval officer of scientific attainment and conciliatory character' be appointed to survey the boundary and particularly look at the question of the channel. After having completed the land survey in company with an American officer, he was to mark the point where the 49th Parallel met the Gulf of Georgia 'with a substantial monument.' They were then to 'carry on the line down the centre of that channel and down the centre of the Strait of Fuca to the ocean.' With that much completed, Palmerston added, '… it may be asked what the word "Channel" was intended to mean.'

Just in case there was any doubt over what was meant, Palmerston laid out his (and the fortunate naval officer's) intention:

> Generally speaking the word 'Channel', when employed in Treaties, means a deep and navigable channel. In the present case it is believed that only one channel, that, namely, which was laid down by Vancouver in his chart, has in this part of the Gulf been hitherto surveyed and used; and it seems natural to suppose that the Negotiators of the Oregon Convention, in employing the word 'channel' had that particular channel in view … The main channel marked in Vancouver's chart is somewhat nearer to the Continent than to Vancouver's Island and its adoption would leave on the British side of the line rather more of those small islets with which part of the Gulf is studded, than would remain on the American side. But these islets are of little or no value; and the only large and valuable island belonging to the group, namely, that called Whidbey's would, of course belong to the United States.

Crampton approached James Buchanan, the Secretary of State, with the proposal. Buchanan, however, appeared to have been caught unprepared. Writing to Palmerston, Crampton noted that, rather surprisingly, the Secretary of State:

> … admitted that he had never himself examined, nor did he ever recollect ever seeing Vancouver's chart: and altho' he did not seem prepared to contest the probability of the channel marked with soundings by Vancouver in that chart being in fact 'the main navigable channel', he evidently hesitated to adopt that opinion without further geographical evidence.

As it was, the Americans proved very reluctant to submit the question to a joint survey and, for the time being, nothing further was heard.

Instead of the proposed joint survey, the United States Navy was ordered to carry out a survey of their own (the Royal Navy had carried out a survey under the direction of Captain Henry Kellett in HMS *Herald* some months earlier). The officer commanding the American survey was Captain Charles Wilkes – a man whose expeditionary and surveying skills might be illustrated by his having spent a considerable time in Antarctic waters naming icebergs as land. His most significant discovery of land in the Antarctic has been searched for several times since he fixed its position, but it has never been seen since. It was not long after the Royal Navy's Captain James Ross reported that he had sailed over Wilkes's 'land' that George Bancroft, the new United States Minister in London, sent Lord Palmerston a copy of Wilkes's survey. Accompanying the chart was a somewhat smug note from Bancroft pointing out that the chart 'contains the wide entrance into the Strait of Arro, the channel through the middle of which the boundary is to be continued.'

The Foreign Secretary was deeply unimpressed, and replied to Bancroft thanking him for his communication and airily suggesting that 'the chart would be of great service to the Commissioner by assisting them in determining where the line of Boundary described in the first article of that treaty ought to run.' Palmerston then returned to keeping his eye on Russian expansionism in Afghanistan and India. But at least one other individual was keeping a very close eye on the situation on the north-west coast of America.

James Douglas had led a life of ambition and achievement structured around a rigid sense of duty. Born in British Guiana in 1803, the illegitimate son of a Scottish planter and a 'free coloured' or 'native' woman, he was, for the most part, self-taught, although he had some schooling in Scotland. Joining the North West Company at the age of sixteen he climbed slowly but surely through its ranks, and then those of the Hudson's Bay Company when the 'Nor'westers' were bought out. In 1828 he married Amelia, the daughter of a chief factor, and earned a reputation for directness when, after two of his colleagues were murdered, he simply went out and shot the murderer dead. Douglas moved to Fort Vancouver and stayed there for nineteen years, serving the final four years as Chief Trader. He was appointed Chief Factor in 1840 and the following year was sent to Vancouver Island to set up a new trading post: Fort Victoria. With that successfully completed, the fort became the headquarters of the western region of the Hudson's Bay Company, and suggestions were floated in London that the Colonial Office might consider giving the whole of Vancouver Island to the Company.

Immediately, there was an outcry, for it was well known that the Company had little – if any – interest in colonisation, a fact appreciated by the British Government, who had an equally small interest in taking on yet more colonies. Others, however, especially James Edward FitzGerald, the Assistant Secretary at the British Museum, took the opposite view. With William Gladstone in support, FitzGerald wrote to the Colonial Office with plans for a large and vigorous settlement on Vancouver Island. 'There is,' he wrote, 'a deep and active conviction awake, that the great task of this generation allotted to the English race is colonisation.' On the other hand, 'The agents of the Hudson Bay Company have discouraged settled habits among the Indians, and communicated to them the worst vices of civilised society without its redeeming qualities.' In the end, a lease was made out to the Hudson's Bay Company for the princely sum of seven shillings a year. Colonisation, though, was not forgotten, and part of the agreement stated that the Company had to create a colony. Douglas showed willing and offered land for 100 people made up of twenty families. The new head of the Company, Sir George Simpson, refused permission, but the situation changed abruptly when coal was discovered on the island. Then, warned by powerful sources such as the Admiralty and the steamship owner Sir Samuel Cunard that such a vital resource must be protected from American attention, the idea of colonisation was given a more favourable wind.

To help towards making the island a colony, Douglas was appointed Acting Governor until the arrival of Richard Blanshard, who took over as Governor in 1850. Blanshard, however, was not the right man for the job and resigned after just a few months. Douglas was then confirmed as the Governor of the Colony of Vancouver Island on 1 September 1851.

Just over a year later, concerns about the possibility of American expansionism in the region were given solid ground. Douglas wrote to the Foreign Office to inform them that 'some American citizens have set up a claim in the name of the United States' to the islands in the Canal de Arro. He continued:

> I shall assert the sovereignty of Great Britain to all the Islands in the Arro Archipelago, situated to the Eastward of Strawberry Bay, so named by Vancouver, which is the usual channel into the Gulf of Georgia.

The letter was somewhat confusing, as Douglas appeared to be claiming American islands that were not in dispute. He almost certainly meant 'to the Westward of Strawberry Bay,' as the ownership of Cypress Island (which has Strawberry Bay on its western coast) was not disputed. Nevertheless, the Foreign Office seemed to know what he meant.

Douglas's letter was passed on to the Colonial Office, which replied with suitable, and essentially unhelpful, vagueness:

> With respect to the violation of territory which is undoubtedly British, and to which there is no disputed claim of sovereignty, Lord Clarendon [the Foreign Secretary] is of the opinion that the Governor of Vancouver's Island should take such steps as the Duke of Newcastle [the Colonial Secretary] may think proper for asserting and maintaining British rights in such territory from foreign aggression.

Despite Douglas's efforts to 'assert the sovereignty of Great Britain' over the islands, American 'squatters' continued to arrive. In November 1853, the governor found an American on Lopez Island claiming that he was on United States territory. Douglas wrote to Archibald Barclay, the Secretary to the Hudson's Bay Company, explaining that he had 'undeceived him on that point.'

In the same letter, Douglas, clearly warming to his task, explained a further reason why the boundary line should go through the Straits of Rosario (or 'Vancouver Strait,' as he referred to the waterway):

> Again, we observe that the Treaty provides 'that the navigation of the whole of the said channel and straits [of Juan de Fuca] south of the forty ninth parallel of latitude remain free and open to both parties.' Now what object could there be for leaving the navigation of the whole of the Straits of Juan de Fuca as far east as Whidbey Island and Deception Passage free and open to British vessels unless it was intended that 'Vancouver Strait' should be the boundary channel? To assume that any other passage was intended is to suppose that the American Plenipotentiary, so tenacious on all other points affecting the interests of his Country, has made in that instance an important concession in favour of British commerce, a concession affecting the navigation laws of the United States, without any positive necessity, arising from the nature of the navigation, and without securing thereby any reciprocal advantage for his own country.

Three months later, Douglas came up with another reason why the Rosario Strait should be the channel in question. Writing to the Duke of Newcastle, he informed the Colonial Secretary that:

I would further take the liberty of remarking that the Canal de Arro is not properly part of the 'Gulf of Georgia', nor of the channel leading from it into the Straits of Juan de Fuca. It is considered here to be a separate and different channel, running parallel to the 'Gulf of Georgia' from which it is divided by the numerous islands of the Archipelago De Arro.

Unfortunately, all the good work done by Douglas had fallen far down the list of British Government priorities – war had been declared against Russia and troops were landing in the Crimea.

With the outbreak of war in March 1854, the British Minister to Washington, DC, Sir John Crampton, used his initiative and invited any Americans who wanted to see action to volunteer to fight on the British side. The American Government effected outrage and, eventually, Crampton and three of his consuls were dismissed. At the same time, some Americans – including thirty surgeons – volunteered to fight and serve alongside the Russians. When the fall of Sebastopol signalled the end of the war, a celebratory dinner held by the British at San Francisco was ignored by American guests and the dinner itself was interrupted by a mob smashing the building's windows.

4

The Americans Begin
their 'Molestation'

With Britain's gaze directed to the conflict in the Crimea, Colonel Isaac Ebey, the United States' Customs Collector for Washington Territory, decided that it would be a good time to test his powers against the Governor of Vancouver Island. The Hudson's Bay Company had, several years earlier, established a fish-curing station on the south end of San Juan Island, an enterprise that had, ever since, remained undisturbed. Douglas, however, had since found another use to which to put the island.

Although blessed in many ways, Vancouver Island was not considered to be prime agricultural land. In his report of his survey in 1846, Captain Henry Kellett of HMS *Herald* had noted, with true naval bluntness:

> The Americans have certainly done us in that territory – with the exception of Victoria there are not a thousand acres of ground capable of cultivation on the south side of Vancouver's Island, that is to say, as far as we were able to penetrate; and as far as we could see, the hills were rocky and barren. There is also a great scarcity of water without a single commodious port, for Victoria is only a drain or gutter, whereas on the American side there are many fine anchorages and harbours and abundance of water. Many considerable rivers, or should I say rapids, fall into the sea on that side.

On the other hand, San Juan Island had many areas of open grassland that could sustain large numbers of sheep.

Consequently, on 15 December 1853, the Hudson's Bay Company paddle-wheeler *Beaver* discharged 1,300 sheep, along with a few pigs, on to the island. The operation was under the charge of Charles Griffin, a newly appointed agent for the Company, who was assisted by a dozen Hawaiian herdsmen. Basing himself on open land close to the southern tip of the island, Griffin erected a small group of buildings to which he gave the name 'Belle Vue Farm,' and settled back to enjoy a quiet life looking out across a bay that, before long, was to take on his name. Griffin, however, was not to enjoy his peace and quiet for long.

Colonel Ebey, who had had a gallant career as an Indian-fighter, and a less hectic one in local government, had been ordered to augment his tax-collecting duties with an investigation into the causes behind an upsurge in Indian raids into Washington Territory (the former northern part of the United States' Oregon Territory, which had been created in March the previous year). The British and American attitudes towards the native Indians were markedly different. As far as the British were concerned, the Indians were a useful means of enhancing their trading business. The natives were employed as guides, hunters and 'voyageurs,' who supplied the Company forts with furs and other necessities. Where possible, the colonists and the Company people looked after the local tribes, if only on the grounds that it was in their best interest to do so. Nevertheless, if the Indians did mount raids against the white population, or against each other, the remedy was a swift and devastating response – usually by the Royal Navy – that would leave the miscreants in no doubt that such behaviour would not be tolerated. The Americans, on the other hand, saw the natives as an impediment to expansion and took every opportunity to push them aside in their desire for land. Inevitably, the tribes took exception and their reaction led to many bloody skirmishes in which the weak and innocent on both sides suffered greatly.

Leaving Puget Sound, his normal area of tax-collecting responsibility, Ebey sailed in the Revenue Sloop *Sarah Stone* and probed among the northern islands on the outlook for Indian bands. What he found was sheep – lots of sheep – enjoying the pastures of San Juan Island.

Ebey landed on the bay beneath Griffin's accommodation in the late afternoon on 3 May 1854, and had barely set up his tent before he was confronted by the Company's agent. Griffin demanded of Ebey the reason for his presence on the island. The colonel, rather weakly, replied, 'I guess I've done nothing, c'est vrai.'

It may have been the truth, but Griffin was determined to make his point and replied, 'You have as yet done nothing, but I merely warn you in time, the consequences, be what they may, my instructions from

Mr Douglas shall be strictly adhered to.' What those instructions were can only be surmised, but they would almost certainly include an order not to allow any Americans to establish any claims on San Juan.

Ebey then tried to find out from Griffin the extent of the animal farming that was being undertaken on the island. The agent gave 'evasive replies' before wishing the American a good evening and, turning on his heel, returned to his farm, noting as he did so 'the star-spangled banner lying in a prominent place inside of the Collector's tent.'

A message was immediately dispatched to Governor Douglas, informing him of the situation. The response was not long in coming.

The Hudson's Bay Company vessel *Otter*, flying the governor's flag, steamed into the bay the following morning. A boat approached the shore carrying Captain James Sangster, the Collector of Customs for Vancouver Island. He had been sent ashore by Douglas to find out 'the object of Mr Ebey's visit, it being reported that he intended to seize the sheep and other British property on the island.'

When asked by Sangster what he was doing on San Juan, Ebey replied that he 'was thinking of going to Victoria.' Sangster then pointed to the tent which, by now, Ebey had established as a United States Customs House Post, with the American flag flying. Ebey now stated that he 'was on business.' At this, Sangster sent the boat back to the *Otter* to collect a Union Flag whilst he sought out Griffin. On finding the agent, the customs collector informed him that he had been appointed a magistrate – all the better to deal with trespassing Americans.

On the arrival of the Union Flag, and its hoisting over Belle Vue Farm, Sangster 'returned with Mr Justice Griffin to Mr Ebey's encampment.' There they were introduced to Colonel Henry Webber, who Ebey 'intended to appoint Inspector of Customs on the Island.' At this, Sangster sharply informed Ebey that, if he did, he 'should consider it my duty to arrest him and send him off as this was British Territory.' Ebey quickly pointed out that Webber was 'not yet appointed.' Feeling that he had gone about as far as he could under the circumstances, Sangster invited Ebey to meet Governor Douglas on board the *Otter*. Establishing a pattern that would be seen with interesting frequency in the future, the American refused and, instead, suggested that the governor should come ashore to meet him. Not only would this have been a breach of protocol, it was also seen as a sign of bad manners. In response, Douglas had the *Otter* raise her anchor and return to Victoria. Her Majesty's chief representative in the area had no intention of playing power games with a minor United States functionary.

The following day, Ebey sought out Griffin and handed him a note which read:

> Sir, I wish to ascertain from you the number of sheep, cattle, horses, hogs and other stock now on this island and under your charge. By whom the same were imported, the place from whence imported, the time they were imported, and the name or names of the ship or other vessels in which the same were imported.
>
>   I am dear Sir,
>   Yours Very Truly,
>   Isaac N Ebey
>   Collector of Customs for the District of Puget Sound.

The island magistrate folded the paper and put it in his pocket whilst refusing to respond to any of Ebey's questions. The colonel then produced another paper, this time a formal commission authorising Webber – who was standing by his side – to act as Inspector of Customs for San Juan Island. As Griffin looked on, Ebey publicly gave Webber his instructions with 'the British Union Jack flying at the flagstaff over their heads.' Ebey then returned to his ship and left the island, as Webber set up a tent close by Belle Vue Farm.

On 7 May, Sangster, the British customs collector, paid a call on Webber, the American customs inspector. Sangster asked, 'By Colonel Ebey appointing you as Inspector of this island is it for the purpose of taking possession?'

'It is merely to bring the question to issue.'

'This is a British island and your being so appointed is infringing on my District.'

'I cannot allow that.'

'I now order you to leave the island.'

'I will not go unless taken by superior numbers, and I will resist.'

Sangster decided to test the American's resolve. After a summons had been obtained from Griffin, Constable Holland (almost certainly one of the Hawaiian shepherds specially selected for the duty) tried to deliver the paper to Webber, who refused it. Holland then reappeared with six other men he had recruited to aid him in serving the summons. As they approached, Webber emerged from his tent with a six-barrelled pistol in each hand, two more stuck in his belt and a large knife protruding from his boot. Pointing a pistol at Holland's head, the American stated that if anyone 'put a hand on him, he would fire.' The gallant Constable Holland and his band suddenly found they had better things to do.

Following Webber's determination to face down any effort to remove him forcibly from the island, Sangster went alone to have a word with him. He 'told him of the folly of one man trying to resist six, if I armed them.' Webber replied, 'that he was bound to resist, and would do so to the last, saying at the same time that he had interfered with no one, and did not intend to do so.' The American also pointed to the Union Flag and said that the 'British flag was always up, and if any mischief had been intended, it would have been taken down.'

As it was, no one was terribly excited about anything to do with seizing territory, or demanding taxes. Webber remained on the island for several months and became firm friends with Griffin. Whenever there was a threat from Indian bands, the American always moved in with the magistrate to gain the immunity from attack usually afforded British property. The post of Inspector (or 'Deputy Collector') of Customs, however, remained in being, despite Webber eventually fleeing the island in the face of the persistent Indian threat. The post later went to Oscar Olney who, in turn, was replaced by Paul Hubbs – both of whom sought the shelter of Griffin's farm whenever Indian bands were rampaging through the area.

Sadly, Colonel Ebey did not fare so well. Attacked by Indians at his home on Whidbey Island, he was shot and killed, the natives taking his head home as a souvenir. The Government of Washington Territory, whom Ebey had served well and loyally, forbade retribution out of fear of starting an Indian war.

It was the start of an earlier Indian war that had caused grave concern to Governor Douglas. Whilst on the look-out for bands of Indians menacing Washington Territory, the United States Revenue Cutter *Jefferson Davis* sailed around the islands. Douglas took a dim view of these activities and wrote to the Hudson's Bay Secretary:

> A United States Revenue Cruizer is now stationed around San Juan; she is armed with six guns, and commanded by officers of the United States Navy, they appear resolved to gain forcible possession of the disputed Territory, and I hardly know how to prevent them.

In fact, the activities of the *Jefferson Davis* shortly afterwards in capturing a group of Indian men and women as they headed north, away from Washington Territory, led to the start of the Puget Sound Indian Wars – a distraction welcomed by Douglas.

Not, of course, that either the governor or San Juan Island were allowed to spend the time in quiet contemplation of the situation. Local government reorganisation by the Washington Territory legislature had deemed San Juan Island to be part of Whatcom County, and the Sheriff of the County, Ellis Barnes, with the backing of the County Commissioners, and with the Inspector of Customs off the island in fear of the Indians, was determined that the British should pay the taxes owing to the county. These, in his estimation, amounted to $80.33.

Barnes first landed on San Juan Island in October 1854 and demanded that Griffin pay up. The magistrate, unimpressed by Barnes's bluster, refused to do anything of the sort and escorted the sheriff off the island. Within a few weeks, Barnes was back again with the same demand – and received the same rebuff. He returned again on Christmas Eve, this time armed with notices stating that he intended to hold a sale of British property on the island in order to raise the owed money. Unfortunately for him, no one turned up for the sale, and again he was removed.

In February 1855, Governor Douglas was honoured with a visit by Governor Isaac Stevens of Washington Territory. Stevens, who had served with distinction under General Winfield Scott in the war against Mexico, was an army engineer. It was, in part, this qualification that led to his appointment, as the President (Franklin Pierce) wanted him to use his skills in surveying a route for a railway line from St Paul's, Minnesota, to Puget Sound.

Douglas informed the Hudson's Bay Secretary of the call:

Mr Stevens, Governor of Washington Territory, lately did me the honour of a visit at this place and alluded to the Island of San Juan, merely to remark that the best plan for the settlement of the disputed point of sovereignty would be to leave it to the decision of the supreme Governments, a matter in which I fully agreed with him in opinion.

Douglas further noted:

We have had no further molestation from the American authorities since Christmas Day when the last trial of strength ended in our favour, and I hope it is now entirely decided that the place belongs of right to our Government.

The problem was, no one had told Sheriff Barnes.

5

Unco-operative Sheep and the Mustering of Arms

After almost twenty hours of pulling at the oars, the ten men in two large boats must have been delighted when the shores of southern San Juan Island came into view. They were a surprisingly mixed bunch: the Whatcom County Judge, the Chairman of the County Commissioners, the Coroner, the Whatcom Representative to the Washington Territory Legislature, four lesser mortals, two Indians – and Sheriff Ellis Barnes.

These men were out to settle some unfinished business, and in the way they knew best. Barnes, having failed to obtain the taxes the County Commissioners believed they were owed by British trespassers on American soil, had decided upon a 'Sheriff's Sale,' whereby goods and property of the offending party would be seized and auctioned to the value of the unpaid revenue. Notices had been displayed in the approved official manner, and now the party were about to carry out their duty. If, in the meantime, they could obtain some slight advantage by being the sole bidders for the seized property (sheep being the preferred option), what better reward could there be for all that exhausting rowing?

The keels crunched on the beach at 'Griffin Bay' at about two in the afternoon on 30 May 1855. Stepping ashore, they could see no welcoming party and set off to look for Mr Justice Griffin. They found him, eventually. The magistrate, or one of his shepherds, had seen them coming when still far off. Realising the purpose of their mission, Griffin had driven all the sheep in the immediate vicinity into the woods. The Americans peremptorily demanded the payment of the due taxes. Griffin refused and demanded to see by what authority the demand was being made. The Americans, it seemed, had none. Despite all the grand titles, no one had bothered to provide the party with an official document to authorise their mission. They were, however, armed, and when they demanded to know where the sheep were, Griffin was happy to supply the information. The animals, he told them, were at the northern tip of the island.

The Americans trudged back down to the beach and their boats. It would take a few more hours of hard rowing to reach their destination and, with plenty of daylight hours left, the sooner they got under way, the better. Meanwhile, Griffin, no doubt with a satisfied smile on his face, returned to his duties.

If there had been that smile, it would, equally without doubt, have disappeared as the sun rose the next morning. Alerted by one of his shepherds, Griffin discovered that the Americans, fuming after having been sent on a fool's errand to the sheepless north of the island, had returned to the beach. After roaming around in the early hours of the morning, they had located a sheep-pen about a mile from Belle Vue Farm. Much to their pleasure, the enclosure contained forty-nine fine-quality breeding rams. As the eastern sky began to brighten, Barnes auctioned off the sheep to the gloating bidders at anywhere between 50¢ and $1 each. When he found that he had still failed to reach the sum of $80.33, another two dozen sheep were auctioned off 'unseen.'

The Americans then discovered another flaw in their plan. It was all very well to have purchased the sheep, and it was all very well to have two boats, but unfortunately, sheep and boats are not natural companions. The beach turned into a chaos of running sheep and pursuing men; of sheep and men struggling; of sheep leaving the boats as soon as they were put in them, and, particularly, of wet sheep contending with equally wet, tired and very irritated men.

Griffin, accompanied by the shepherd who had alerted him, raced to the pen to discover that fifteen of the animals were still inside. Setting these free, the two men then headed for the beach. There they found pandemonium still reigning. Most of the sheep had been loaded on to the boats, others were being manhandled over the gunwales, whilst three or four were being held ready. Heading for this latter group, Griffin and the shepherd tried to release the animals, but were roughly fended off. When they renewed their efforts, one of the Americans 'drew from his belt a revolver pistol.' At this, Griffin lost his temper and 'expostulated with them,' shouting that he 'could not possibly contend against such a force as eight armed men against two defenceless persons as myself and my man.'

Fuming at such aggressive and ungentlemanly behaviour, Griffin, 'seeing no other resource … immediately left the spot.'

A canoe was promptly sent over to Victoria to inform Douglas of what was happening. As it was paddled furiously to the west, the two boats, bearing, in addition to the sheep rustlers, an illicit cargo of thirty-four rams, were being frantically rowed in the other direction – only to run aground. Some hours passed before the boats could be got off, hours spent in near panic as they could hear the far-off steam siren of the Hudson's Bay Company steamer *Beaver*. At last, however, they were clear and in home waters as the paddle-steamer arrived on the scene of the outrage.

Governor Douglas was furious – and not just at the Americans. In an immediate communication with the Secretary of the Company, Douglas wrote with pleasing understatement: 'This is an exceedingly annoying affair, and I most heartily regret that our people, though dispersed at their various occupations, and taken by surprise, did not show a more resolute bearing.' Anyone within range who had dared to have pointed a pistol at Douglas stood a very good chance of ending up flat on his back. On the other hand, Douglas was well over six feet tall and heavily built – Griffin was neither. Even the captain of the paddle-steamer did not escape censure – 'The *Beaver* was dispatched to their aid, and was within two hours of catching the fellows in the act, and had she given chace might have overtaken them, and recovered the abstracted property.'

The governor then wrote to Governor Stevens with a demand that a claim for damages be met or charges of criminal acts be brought against the sheep rustlers. He continued:

> I trust your Excellency will take measures to prevent the repetition of such acts of violence on the part of American citizens, which must ultimately lead to dissension and bloodshed, an event which all would have cause to deplore. The Island of San Juan has been in the possession of British Subjects for many years, and is with the other islands in the Archipelago de Arro, declared to be within the Jurisdiction of this Colony, and under the protection of British Laws.

He then issued Stevens with a lightly veiled threat:

> Our united force when exerted in the common cause of humanity is hardly sufficient to restrain the wily savage from deeds of blood, and that influence must in a great measure cease with our friendly relations, and both countries

will suffer from the absence of that wholesome control which now holds
the native Indian Tribes in check.

Stevens was unimpressed. As far as he was concerned Sheriff Barnes
was acting in accordance with his duties; San Juan, after all, was part of
Whatcom County and, therefore, United States property. The Governor
of Washington Territory returned to the old argument:

> The contemporaneous exposition of the Treaty as evinced by the debates in
> the United States Senate shows the Canal de Arro to be the boundary line,
> as understood by the United States at that time.

Referring to a map produced in London in April 1849, Stevens continued,
almost with a touch of sarcasm:

> … the boundary Line is laid down as running through the Canal de Arro.
> This map is compiled from the surveys of Vancouver, Kellett, Simpson and
> others, and would seem to establish, that even as late as some three years ago,
> subsequent to the Treaty, the great English navigators and Hydrographers
> as well as the American Government considered the Canal de Arro, as in
> the terms of the Treaty, the channel which separated the continent from
> Vancouver's Island.

It was, of course, all bluster, meant to distract from the main problem. The
ownership of the islands remained in dispute – a fact recognised even by
the sheep-rustlers. One of them wrote on his escape to Whatcom County,
'we did not wish to be taken prisoners and lie in jail until the boundary
question could be settled by the two governments.'

On Douglas's insistence, the British Government made a claim
against the United States for the sum of £2,990 13s 0d, based on the
loss of thirty-four rams, the recovery of 409 scattered sheep, the hire of
eighteen men for eight days to carry out the recovery, the hire of the
Beaver and incidental expenses. The claim was ignored, possibly after
the United States authorities paid too much attention to the rustlers'
account of the events, which included a tale of being driven to their
boats – not by two unarmed men – but by twenty yelling 'Kanaks'
(Hawaiian shepherds) armed with knives. Such a response, however, on
the part of Stevens and the United States Government, could have led
to the most dire circumstances if the British had decided to respond in
a vindictive manner.

The Indian tribes around Puget Sound had a totally different concept of the meaning of land ownership to that held by the immigrants pouring through the Oregon Trail and other paths to the Pacific West. Despite signing treaties which allowed the incomers on to their land, the Indians believed they still had free access to hunting and fishing grounds regardless of the settlers putting up fences around their newly purchased properties. By the end of 1855 the situation was out of control, as Indians attacked the settlers – often with the most savage cruelty. At the same time, other Indians, to the east of the Cascade Mountains, were driving the United States Army back. To add to Stevens' woes, the northern Indians, looking for easy spoils and the opportunity to join in any attack on the Americans, began to flood southwards in their hundreds.

The American military forces, and the Washington Territory authorities, were caught unprepared for such an event. The supply of weapons and ammunition became a priority, but very little of either was available. When the town of Olympia asked for artillery for their protection, all that could be supplied was two 12-lb cannons, twenty-five cartridges and a total of twenty round and grape shot. For their small arms, the people of Olympia received just 350 rounds of musket cartridges.

With enormous magnanimity, into the breach stepped Governor Douglas. Although Vancouver Island was itself under no threat from the Indians, he ordered the Hudson's Bay Company vessels *Beaver* and *Otter* to patrol the waters through which the northern Indians were passing; he sent a large amount of arms and ammunition directly to the United States authorities; and he arranged for five times that amount to be delivered from the Company forts in the region. It was not until the middle of the following year that the United States Army was able to send two companies of infantry to the north-west to help calm the situation. One went to Port Townsend, at the eastern end of the Straits of Juan de Fuca and the entrance to Admiralty Inlet, whilst the other went to Bellingham Bay, in Whatcom County. In consequence, either by accident or design, Douglas found he had a significant number of professional United States troops close at hand to his south and east. Not that such a development caused the governor to rethink his policy concerning the islands. Instead, he would meet the challenge in like manner.

Across on the other side of the Pacific, an Anglo-French fleet had been sent to attack the Russians at Petropavlovsk on the Kamchatka Peninsula. Not only would victory in such an attack provide a boost to the allies, but there was always the chance that a poor performance by the Russians might lead to territorial opportunities in Russian North America. But, instead of useful gains to British North America, the whole affair descended into a debacle. When, on 30 August 1854, the allied fleet arrived off the peninsula, Rear Admiral David Price carried out a most unusual act for a fleet commander on the eve of battle: he shot himself. Captain Nicholson of the 40-gun *Pique* was left to take charge with the minimum of operational intelligence. Nevertheless, he was helped by a number of Americans who claimed they had deserted from whaling vessels and who knew the layout of the Russian defences. After a desultory bombardment, 700 British and French seamen and marines landed with the Americans as guides – and were promptly led into an ambush. Over 200 men were lost as they fought their way back to the ships. A second attempt between April and June the following year (with the fleet now under the command of Rear Admiral H. W. Bruce, a veteran of Trafalgar) was reduced to a chase after Russian ships, which ended in failure. At this, the allied fleet returned to its base at Hawaii and the war in the east petered out.

Before his pursuit of the Russian fleet, Bruce had asked Douglas to provide hospital facilities on Vancouver Island to provide for possible casualties. Accordingly, three wooden huts were constructed on the shore of Esquimalt Harbour, an inlet just to the west of Fort Victoria. Esquimalt had been noted as a possible harbour for the Royal Navy (despite its name coming from an Indian word meaning 'place of shoaling waters') as far back as 1846, when HMS *Pandora* (part of Kellett's surveying squadron) had carried out an analysis of the area. A number of Royal Navy ships had harboured there since the survey and, in 1852 (probably as a desperate means of getting to the nearest hostelries), seamen from HMS *Thetis* had cut a path through the pine forest to Fort Vancouver. Meanwhile, the main stores and provisioning base of the Pacific fleet remained at Valparaiso, Chile.

In August 1855, Douglas wrote to Lord Russell, the new Colonial Secretary, informing him that the Pacific fleet had paid a visit to Esquimalt. After complimenting the fleet – 'in a state of perfect efficiency' – Douglas assured Russell that Rear Admiral Bruce's views on the question of sovereignty over the disputed islands, 'coincide perfectly with those which the obvious meaning of the first article of the Treaty of July 1846, had led me to embrace.' The governor went on to point out that:

> Since the arrival of the Fleet at this place the Americans have made no attempt to molest the British settlers of San Juan, and I do not apprehend any difficulty with them, as long as we have a military force at hand, to punish their aggressions.

Then came the quiet salesmanship: 'I would take the liberty of proposing to your Lordship that a Naval Store House be erected here, or rather at Port Esquimalt.'

In support came a clearly Douglas-sponsored but, nevertheless, rather luke-warm note from Bruce to the Admiralty:

> My visit here is likely to prove beneficial in settling the difficulties that exist with respect to the territorial possession of the Island of San Juan in the Gulf of Georgia, to which a claim has been attempted to be established by the Americans.

The apparent lack of enthusiasm may have arisen from the fact that – to sailors – the attractions of Esquimalt did not quite match those of exotic Valparaiso. But imperial considerations had to come first, and the Chilean port was finally abandoned for the new base at Esquimalt in 1865.

6

The Boundary Commission

If the sheep raid on San Juan Island had achieved anything at all, it had concentrated the minds of both the British and the American governments onto the boundary problem simmering in the north-west of North America. The British attempt in 1847 to appoint a boundary commission had been all but ignored by the Americans, and a later attempt to resurrect the idea fell before congressional indifference. Now, however, property had been stolen, territory invaded and pistols drawn.

When he heard of the matter, President Franklin Pierce immediately demanded that his Secretary of State, William Marcy, take action to calm things down. On 14 July 1855, Marcy wrote to Governor Stevens:

> He [the President] has instructed me to say to you that the officers of the territory should abstain from all acts, on the disputed grounds, which are calculated to provoke any conflicts, so far as it can be done without implying the concession to the authority of Great Britain of an exclusive right over the premises.
>
> The title ought to be settled before either party should exclude the other by force, or exercise complete and exclusive sovereign rights with the fairly disputed limits. Application will be made to the British government to interpose with the local authorities on the northern borders of our territory to abstain from like acts of exclusive ownership, with the explicit understanding that any forbearance on either side to assert the rights, respectively, shall not be construed into any concession to the adverse party.

By a conciliatory and moderate course on both sides, it is sincerely hoped that all difficulties will be avoided until an adjustment of the boundary line can be made in a manner mutually satisfactory. The government of the United States will do what it can to have the line established at an early period.

To Sir John Crampton, now reinstated as the British Minister to Washington, DC, Marcy wrote:

Sir: I am under some apprehension that collision may take place between our Citizens and British subjects in regard to the occupation of the disputed points along the line between Washington Territory and the British possession on the north of it.

In the hope of avoiding such a difficulty, I have, by the direction of the President, addressed a letter to the governor of that Territory on the subject, and herewith furnish you with an extract from it. I presume the government of her Britannic Majesty will be willing to recommend to her subjects along the boundary in question a similar course until the line can be established. In that way I sincerely hope all collision may be avoided.

Crampton agreed and chose the moment to remind the Secretary of State of the proposal for a joint boundary commission. This time there was no prevarication and the wheels were set in motion.

The principal aim of the boundary commission was to establish once and for all the line on the ground of the 49th Parallel. That would require a physical survey that involved the clearing of trees, climbing mountains, fording rivers and the erection of markers. With both sides of the commission fielding well-qualified surveyors, there should be little reason for wide variation in their findings and, at its completion, it was expected that the boundary question would have been amicably resolved. Except that there was a problem: the route to be taken via a 'channel' from the Gulf of Georgia to the Straits of Juan de Fuca.

To deal with this difficulty the British established two teams of commissioners, one to undertake the land survey, the other to carry out the survey of the water route. The land survey was under the command of Captain (Brevet Major) John Hawkins of the Royal Engineers. When he received his commission, Hawkins led his team to the point on the coast where the 49th Parallel met the Gulf of Georgia. This was at Semiahmoo Bay and 'Camp Semiahmoo' was established a fraction to the north of the parallel. With no sign of the American commission, Hawkins returned to other duties.

For the water survey, the Admiralty chose forty-six-year-old Captain James Prevost. An intelligent man of quiet abilities, Prevost had behind him a worthy, if unremarkable, career. He had served on the north-west coast of America in the early 1850s, arriving in the flagship as a member of the admiral's staff and eventually being given command of his own ship, HMS *Virago*. Along the way, Prevost did his career no harm at all by marrying the admiral's daughter. A deeply committed Christian, whilst protecting British subjects settling in the area, he became aware of the poor conditions of the Indians and decided that the area was ripe for the introduction of some earnest missionary work.

Having brought the *Virago* back to England, Prevost was appointed as 'Her Majesty's First Commissioner for ascertaining and marking out so much of the Boundary under the 1st Article of the Treaty between Great Britain and the United States.' He was further appointed to the command of HMS *Satellite*, a new Devonport dockyard-built screw corvette mounting twenty 8-inch guns and one 68-pounder. In addition to his captain's pay, Prevost was awarded an extra £1 5s 0d per day whilst in the *Satellite* to cover any incidental expenses incurred during his duties. As if that was not enough to bring a glow to his heart, a private note from the Foreign Office Chief Clerk added:

> Lord Clarendon [Secretary of State for Foreign Affairs] … directs me to add that it will probably be very desirable that you should show more than ordinary hospitality to the members of the American Commission and to other American Authorities when you are in contact while engaged in the service of the Commission, and that you may charge in a Continget Account any extra expenses which you may be put to by doing so.

Access to a bottomless Foreign Office contingency account would make any arduous service around the Gulf of Georgia considerably easier to tolerate.

His Foreign Office orders arrived via the Admiralty. After reminding Prevost that the British Government's view was that the boundary line should pass through the Straits of Rosario, Clarendon went on to say:

> It appears to Her Majesty's Government that the line which I have described is so clearly and exactly in accordance with the terms of the Treaty, that it may be hoped you will have no difficulty in inducing the American Commissioner to acquiesce in it.

If, on the other hand, the American commissioner did prove 'difficult,' and only as a last resort, Prevost could propose a compromise channel if one could be found.

The appointment of second commissioner went to Captain George Richards, who was, in a number of ways, a complete contrast to Prevost. Ten years younger than the first commissioner, Richards had been promoted to captain in the same year as Prevost mainly as a result of his courageous dash and enterprise. After being noted for his actions during the First Opium War, he was promoted to commander after gallant leadership in storming the forts on the River Parana during the Anglo-French blockade of Buenos Aires in 1845. Taking part (along with Captain Kellett) in the search for the missing 1845 Franklin Expedition, Richards led a sledge team for hundreds of miles over ice and snow. No sign of the missing explorer was found, but Richards surveyed many miles of undiscovered Arctic coastline and was promoted to captain on his return. For his work with the boundary commission, he was appointed to the 9-gun steam sloop HMS *Plumper* and awarded only the extra pay normally allowed to officers when on survey duty.

Prevost and the *Satellite* (with a missionary for the Indians on board) sailed from Plymouth on 28 December 1856 and arrived at Esquimalt on 13 June 1857. The much slower *Plumper* was expected in the following September.

Eleven days after the *Satellite*'s arrival, the American border commission arrived at Fort Victoria. The commission was headed by Archibald Campbell, a graduate of West Point, a civil engineer and clerk at the War Department. He was assisted by Lieutenant John Parke of the United States Army Topographical Engineers, who acted as the commission's astronomer. Neither commissioner on each side lost time in opening the debate on the question of the 'channel.' Although personal relations between Prevost and Campbell remained cordial throughout, both stuck firmly to their country's view – the Englishman for the Rosario Strait, the American for the Canal de Arro. With no headway being made at face-to-face meetings, Campbell and the American commission left Victoria and made their way to Semiahmoo Bay, taking over the camp left by Hawkins and his Royal Engineers (which was, of course, on British territory). The two sides then continued their debate by correspondence.

Prevost opened the negotiations on 28 October 1857:

> … my entire conviction is that the boundary line should be carried through those waters known as the Gulf of Georgia into the Rosario Strait, to the

Straits of Fuca, and then to the Pacific Ocean. By careful consideration of the wording of the Treaty it would seem distinctly to provide that the channel mentioned should possess three characteristics. 1st. It should separate the continent from Vancouver's Island. 2nd. It should admit of the boundary line being carried through the middle of it in a southerly direction. 3rd. It should be a navigable channel. To these three peculiar conditions the channel known as the Rosario Strait must entirely answer. It is readily admitted that the Canal de Arro is also a navigable channel, and therefore answers to one characteristic of the channel of the Treaty; although I may as well here mention that from the rapidity and variableness of its currents, and from its being destitute of anchorages except at its extreme ends, it is unsuitable for sailing vessels, and would scarcely be used by them so long as the passage through the Rosario Strait remains available, as the currents in that strait being generally regular, and the anchorages convenient and secure, it is by far the most navigable channel of the two. But the Canal de Arro will not meet the remaining characteristics of the channel of the Treaty. It literally and geographically does not separate the continent from Vancouver's Island, that continent having already been separated by another navigable channel, the Rosario Strait; and further, it will be found in tracing the line of the boundary according to the literal wording of the Treaty, which appears to me particularly precise and clear, that the line to reach the Canal de Arro must proceed for some distance in a westerly direction, for which deviation from a southerly direction no provision is made in the Treaty. I am therefore unable to admit that the Canal de Arro is the channel of the Treaty.

The soundness of Prevost's argument made little impact upon Campbell. Concerning the British commissioner's reasoning over the positioning of the treaty's 'channel,' he replied:

While other channels only separate the islands of the group from each other, the Canal de Haro, for a considerable distance north of the Straits of Fuca, and where their waters unite, washes the shores of Vancouver's Island, and is therefore the only one which, according to the language of the Treaty, 'separates the continent from Vancouver's Island.'

As for the suggestion that the American version of the boundary line veered considerably from the 'southerly direction' of the treaty, Campbell was quite dismissive:

It is quite evident, however, that the term 'southerly' is to be understood only in its common and general sense. It is undoubtedly used here in opposition to 'northerly' and simply to show that Vancouver's Island is to be left on the British instead of the American side of the line.

Returning to the definition of the 'channel,' Campbell continued:

> 'Rosario Strait' is a navigable channel, but it does not 'separate the continent from Vancouver's Island.' In no part of its course does it touch upon the shores of either. It separates the islands of Lummi, Sinclairs, Cypress, Guemes and Fidalgo in the east, from Orcas, Blakely, Decatur and Lopez islands in the west, but in no respect does it 'separate the continent from Vancouver's Island.'

As if to suggest that Prevost had not been thorough in his research – or in an effort to block any subsequent attempt at compromise – Campbell pointed out:

> There is another navigable channel between the islands of San Juan, Spieden and Stewart on the west, and Waldren, Orcas, Shaw and Lopez in the east; but, like Rosario Straits, fails to touch the continent or Vancouver's Island.

In answer to Prevost's claim that the Canal de Arro was unsuitable for sailing ships, Campbell, with a true American eye to the future, added:

> The belief is general that eventually steamboats will supersede, in a great measure, the use of sailing vessels.

Finally, Campbell reminded Prevost of the American understanding of the treaty on or about the time of its publication. On 18 May 1846, the Minister to London had written to the Secretary of State, James Buchanan, that the boundary would:

> … divide the territory by the extension of the line on the parallel of 49 to the sea … thence, by the Canal de Haro and the Straits of Fuca, to the ocean.

Furthermore, at the Senate ratification of the treaty, Senator Benton had said in a speech to the house:

[the line] proceeds to the middle of the channel, and thence, turning south, through the Channel de Haro to the Straits of Fuca, then west, through the middle of that strait, to the sea. This is a fair partition of these waters, and gives us everything we want, namely, all the waters of Puget Sound, Hood's Canal, Admiralty Inlet, Bellingham Bay, Birch Bay, and, with them the cluster of islands, probably of no value, between De Haro's Channel and the continent.

On receipt of the letter, Prevost should have leapt upon Campbell's self-imposed trap. If Benton had considered the islands to be '*between* De Haro's Channel *and the continent*,' it had to follow that the islands were not *part* of the continent. Therefore, to meet the wording of the treaty – 'to the middle of the channel *which separates the continent from Vancouver's Island*' – the line *had* to pass through the Rosario Strait. Instead, in reply, Prevost contented himself with pointing out that the wording remained as 'separates the continent from Vancouver's Island,' not the other way around, as would have been the case had the Canal de Arro been intended to be the channel. In addition, he went on to stress the fact that, as the Minister to London's wording had not been used by the treaty-makers, it clearly meant they had not been intended. As for Campbell's use of maps, Prevost had a couple of his own to throw in the ring. Firstly, he informed the American commissioner of a map of Oregon and Upper California published at Washington, DC in 1848:

> … drawn by Charles Preuss, under the order of the Senate of the United States, in which the boundary line between the British possessions and those of the United States, distinctly lithographed and coloured, is carried down the Gulf of Georgia, through the channel now called the Rosario Strait, and thence through the Straits of Fuca to the Pacific Ocean.

As if that was not convincing enough, Prevost then referred to an:

> … attested tracing of 'A diagram of a portion of Oregon Territory,' dated Surveyor-General's Office, Oregon City, October 21, 1852, and signed John B. Preston, Surveyor-General, in which the boundary line between the British possessions and those of the United States is also carried through the channel lying adjacent to the continent or through Rosario Strait. Both these documents being official and published by high authority, afford, I think, strong evidence that the Canal de Haro has not always been contemplated and received in the United States as the channel of the Treaty.

In his reply, Campbell went through his case once again and ended up by saying:

> I can only repeat that my convictions in regard to the channel are so fixed that I cannot admit a doubt on the subject.

Enclosed with the letter was an unofficial note in which Campbell wrote that there was not:

> ... the slightest use in writing or talking any more on the subject so far as concession on my part is concerned.

Deeply annoyed by this inflexible and doctrinaire stance, Prevost sent the *Plumper* (which had arrived in November) to carry out a check on the accuracy of the American positioning of the point where the 49th Parallel met the Gulf of Georgia. Taking passage with Richards, Prevost landed at Camp Semiahmoo to have a meeting with Campbell. There he offered a compromise. The whole archipelago, he suggested, should be considered as one single channel – as if the Gulf of Georgia simply met the Straits of Juan de Fuca without obstruction. Taken thus, the line could continue southwards without deviation. It would mean that some islands would have the line passing through them, but divided islands would not be unique to the north-west of America. It would also mean that the United States would have the bulk of the islands: Guemes, Cypress, Blakely, Decatur, Lopez, half of Shaw and the majority of Orcas, leaving Waldron and San Juan to the British. Campbell rejected the offer out of hand.

On 3 December, with the rejection of each other's 'channel,' and the failure of the British compromise, both commissioners agreed to refer the matter, along with all their correspondence, to their respective governments.

On the 7th, Prevost wrote to the Foreign Secretary, referring to Campbell's last letter, which:

> ... contains so many dogmatic expressions of opinion and is couched in such language as to be hardly courteous. I conceive it, however, to be a fair index of the spirit in which the whole of Mr Campbell's letters have been written ... Personally and privately I have been on the most intimate terms of friendship with Mr Campbell, and our interviews have been of the most harmonious and pleasant description, and it is only in his letters that any unconcilliatory spirit has been manifested.

Finally, Prevost, having at close range observed the scene of dispute, told Lord Clarendon:

> The Rosario Strait appears to me to be, indisputably, the channel through which the boundary line should pass.

He was, however, soon to find himself engaged on very different duties.

7

The Shot is Fired, and the General Responds

In early 1858, Governor Douglas was a busy man. Not only was he running a huge business on behalf of his masters in the Hudson's Bay Company, he was also the senior British representative on Vancouver Island. The Americans were causing him problems over the British-owned San Juan Islands, and a war with the Indians had broken out in Washington Territory, with many of the Indian bands passing through his territory from the north. On their way south, the Indians frequently took the opportunity to attack any Americans they came across. On one occasion, two white men were killed on San Juan Island and, in response, the American revenue cutter *Jefferson Davis* landed troops on the island. The Indians promptly fled and the soldiers returned on board. A little later, the American Inspector of Customs on the island, Paul Hubbs, was lent a platoon of Royal Marines to clear Indians off Orcas Island. These Indian conflicts also meant that Douglas now had professional troops on his borders and United States armed vessels and revenue cutters cruising offshore. Then, just to complicate matters, gold was struck.

The knowledge that there was likely to be gold in the region was hardly new. Gold dust had been obtained from Indians six years earlier, and one prospector was reported to have had 'two pint pickle bottles half full of gold' that he had taken from the Thompson River at Kamloops, New Caledonia, in 1856. In the same year, an entire tribe of Indians began to collect gold from another stretch of the Thompson. Word soon got out and, by mid-1857, Douglas reported to the Company office in London that Americans had started gold-mining on the same river and that, before long, some form of law and order would be needed in the area. Six months later he reported that the prospect of gold:

> … is causing much excitement amongst the population of the United States of Washington and Oregon, and I have no doubt that a great number of people from those territories [will] be attracted thither in spring.

In order to gain some control over the threat of uncontrolled mining, Douglas declared that only the Crown had control over mineral rights throughout New Caledonia – anyone seeking to search for gold would first have to obtain a licence.

The governor then took an action which, in retrospect, he may have had cause to regret. In February 1858, on finding the Company in possession of 50 lbs of gold traded in by Indians, and having no refining facilities on the island, Douglas sent the metal to San Francisco to be processed. Once the purpose of the *Otter's* visit was revealed, the stampede started.

Even compared to the Australian and Californian gold rushes, the effect of the news was astonishing. Dozens of worn-out old ships were brought back into service to transport the would-be miners from California, Oregon and Washington Territory; vessels in Seattle were left unmanned as their crews jumped ship for the goldfields; and soldiers deserted from Forts Bellingham and Townsend. Between April and July, over 16,000 treasure-seekers left San Francisco, with almost 3,000 arriving at Fort Victoria in one day – all this at a time when the population of Vancouver Island was numbered in hundreds. The place was transformed into a tent city, complete with merchants, land agents, gold-brokers and saloons. Many prospectors had arrived at Esquimalt, and, referring to the road cut by the seamen of the Pacific fleet, Lieutenant Richard Mayne of the *Plumper* noted that it had changed beyond recognition:

> Only a few months before, we used to flounder through the mud without meeting a single soul; now it was covered with pedestrians toiling along, with the step and air of men whose minds were occupied with thoughts of business; crowded with well-laden carts and vans, with Wells Fargo's or Freeman's 'Expresses' and with strangers of every tongue and country, in every variety of attire. Day after day they came to Victoria, on their way to the Fraser; the greater part of them with no property but the bundle they carried, and with 'dollars, dollars, dollars!' stamped on every face.

As Mayne remarked, Victoria was not the target of the miners. By sailing ship, steam vessel or canoe, they made their way across the Gulf of Georgia to the mouth of the River Fraser, where they met the first of Douglas's impositions. With the water side of the boundary commission now in abeyance, the governor had requested Prevost to station one of his ships at the entrance to the Fraser in order to demand and issue licences to the miners. Douglas, with his business interests in mind, also endeavoured to see that Fort Victoria would become the supply centre for the miners and their claims.

With the immediate practical issues dealt with, Douglas then had to turn to the wider implications of the mass of Americans turning up on his doorstep. Of greatest urgency was the question of law and order. In addition to the normal skirmishes with civilised behaviour, the Americans had brought with them their crude attitude towards Native Americans. When the natives had shown their resentment at being brushed aside by the miners, the Americans had simply gunned them down and set fire to their villages. This led to a number of massacres of the miners, followed, inevitably, by retaliatory strikes. Even more alarming to the governor was the fact that some of the miners were organising themselves into armed, semi-military combinations. After a visit to the goldfields, Douglas wrote to the Colonial Office to inform the Secretary of State of the attitude he had adopted with the miners:

> I refused to grant them any rights of occupation to the soil and told them distinctly that Her Majesty's Government ignored their very existence in that part of the country, which was not open for the purpose of settlement and they were permitted to remain there merely on sufferance, that no abuses would be tolerated, and the Laws would protect the rights of the Indians no less than those of the white men.

In support of his declaration, and to reinforce his demands, Douglas made the miners – 'a crowd of ruffianly looking men' – give three cheers for the Queen, which they did 'with bad grace.'

To deal with the problem of lawlessness, the Colonial Office arranged for the War Office to send out a 160-strong detachment of Royal Engineers under the command of Colonel Richard Moody. An advance party of the scarlet-coated sappers arrived in November 1858, and were just in time to see the second part of the British Government's answer to the problem of massive American expansion into New Caledonia. On 19 November 1858, at Fort Langley on the Fraser River, an announcement was made in front of a large number of officials. New Caledonia was to become the Crown Colony of British Columbia: a name selected by Queen Victoria herself. No longer was the territory to be in the possession of the Hudson's Bay Company, it now belonged to the Crown, and the colony's first governor was to be James Douglas. He had accepted the appointment, and its handsome salary of £1,800 a year, even though it meant he had to give up his long and deep-rooted Company connections. In compensation he was made a Companion of the Order of the Bath (CB). The capital of the new colony was to be New Westminster – the name, again, chosen by the Queen. The town (later a city) was to be designed and built by the Royal Engineers on the north bank of the Fraser. Even so, it was to be six years before the governor vacated his house at Fort Victoria to move to New Westminster.

Many of the miners went back to California during the winter – some not to return as other goldfields had been discovered in that state. Others gave up their search and drifted southwards, and some, despite Douglas's warning, attempted to settle. Of these, a few reached San Juan Island and, protected by the presence of the American Inspector of Customs, threw up cabins and marked out land for their use. Their intention was to establish a claim on the land, hopefully under the rules of the Washington Territory Donation Land Law, which granted 320 acres of land to each married individual (160 acres to single settlers) who resided on the site for two years. The only problem was that the Donation Land Law had expired in 1855. Nevertheless, within months the American population of the island went from one to twenty-five, with twenty-four of them 'squatters.' The British population remained the same – one Englishman and about fifteen Hawaiian shepherds.

Among the Americans was a man in his late twenties named Lyman Cutler. Faced with the task of clearing a space in the forest, Cutler chose instead to build his cabin and dig up a third of an acre on one of Griffin's most important sheep-runs, used for moving sheep from one pasture to another. As if this was not bad enough, Cutler proved to be an extremely inept builder of fences, so much so that after he had planted a crop of potatoes, one of Griffin's pigs found no barrier to its enjoyment of digging up the newly grown crop and devouring the results of its endeavour. In his later statement, Cutler claimed that the animal had 'been at several times a great annoyance' and yet had, apparently, taken no steps to improve his fencing. Instead, he took a considerably more direct action: he shot the pig.

As neighbourly disputes go, shooting a pig would find a modest place on the scale of possible incidents. Clearly, Cutler did not rate it too highly as he ambled over to Belle Vue Farm to tell Griffin what he had done. Again, according to the American, Griffin reacted badly and became 'very much enraged,' despite Cutler offering to pay a reasonable amount in recompense. The Hudson's Bay Company agent then demanded a payment of $100 for what he, in turn, claimed to have been a prize breeding boar. With hurt feelings at this outrageous British behaviour, and 'astonished both at Mr Griffin's conduct and his proposal,' Cutler turned on his heel and left with the retort (according to the agent) that he would 'as soon shoot [Griffin] as he would a hog if [Griffin] trespassed on his land.'

As if under the direction of some malign deity, that afternoon the Company vessel *Beaver* hove into view at Griffin's Bay and discharged three important people – Alexander Dallas, the local chief factor of the Hudson's Bay Company and Governor of Rupert Land (and son-in-law of Governor James Douglas); Dr William Tolmie of the Puget Sound Agricultural Company (a subsidiary of the Hudson's Bay Company); and Donald Fraser, a member of the Vancouver Island Council. On hearing Griffin's account of the morning's events, he and the three officials, as part of a horse-back inspection of the Company's property on the island, decided to pay a call on Cutler.

Carried along, no doubt, by the sense of their own importance, the four men demanded of the American if it was he who had killed the pig. When he replied in the affirmative, Dallas (according to Cutler) asked 'in a very supercilious manner' how he had dared to do such a thing. Cutler reacted in like manner, telling his visitors that he had offered to pay for the animal, something he would not have had to do if he had kept quiet about it and, furthermore, the pig was 'worthless.' The American claimed that Dallas then declared the island to be a British possession and that if he did not pay the $100 he would be taken to Victoria. To back up this threat, Dallas reminded Cutler that the *Beaver* was anchored offshore and had enough men on board to form a posse, who would come ashore and carry him off. Cutler (by now holding his rifle) then suggested that Dallas must be 'crazy' if he thought that he would get $100 in payment for a pig that 'was not worth ten' – especially as 'this is American soil, not English.' At this the group turned their horses and rode off, one of them (in Cutler's account) shouting over his shoulder something like: 'You will have to answer for this hereafter.'

Such a shout, and all that had gone before, would have been music to the ears of one man stationed far to the south at Fort Vancouver. A cross between pantomime villain and puffed-up pirate, Brigadier-General William Selby Harney was the wrong man in the wrong place at the wrong time. In his own eyes, however, he did have one redeeming factor: he hated the British.

Born in the Southern state of Tennessee, Harney's father and all his uncles on his father's side had fought in the War of Independence. One uncle, Jenethan, had been captured by the British and died after the war of wounds he had received. Another uncle, Selby, achieved the rank of colonel after an active war in which he was defeated several times before being badly wounded and taken prisoner. Harney's father, Thomas, became a major during the war before settling down to marry an Irish woman and becoming a land surveyor. Tragically, he died after being bitten by a rabid dog.

Harney had been intended for the navy, but opted instead for the army in order to follow the path of his neighbour, hero, patron and fellow Tennessean, Andrew Jackson, the general who had such an easy victory over the British at New Orleans. Commissioned immediately – without having to attend West Point – Harney soon earned both a reputation for rashness and a court martial. He escaped the latter as a result of Jackson's intervention. Almost two decades were to pass before Harney was given another chance to show his mettle. Serving in the Indian Wars, he was noted for introducing his men to the new Colt repeating revolver, and for his vigorous, and often reckless, pursuit of his enemy. A rival, nevertheless, agreed that Harney's frequently irresponsible 'stupidity' had 'done more to inject the Indians with a fear of us and the desperate state of their cause, than all the other commanders.'

In 1846, by now a colonel of dragoons, Harney became involved in the war against Mexico in spectacular fashion. Without orders, and against the advice of his own officers, he took his dragoons and volunteers across the Rio Grande and invaded Mexico. The resultant debacle saw the loss of his supply train and gave an important boost to the morale of the Mexicans. One of his senior officers considered the ill-judged action as just another example of Harney's 'extreme imbecility and manifest incapacity,' whilst his direct superior had him removed from his command. Astonishingly, he refused to go and earned yet another court martial, this time at the instigation of the army commander, General Winfield Scott (the same officer who had calmed the Maine situation down by his diplomacy). Reprimanded and forced to apologise, Harney complained to the Secretary of War, William Marcy, who informed President Polk, another of his Tennessean neighbours and a friend of Andrew Jackson. In a blatant act of favouritism, Polk restored Harney to his command and accused Scott of 'personal and political malice.'

Another side of Harney was revealed when, as his forces were passing through Mexico under Scott's command, he came across 150 Mexican troops. Hurling his 500 mounted men at the enemy, he obtained an easy victory, after which he claimed he had attacked and defeated 2,000 men. Nevertheless, at the subsequent Battle of Cerro Gordo, Harney did so well in the main assault that he was recommended for promotion by none other than Scott (although it must be borne in mind that Scott may have hoped to promote him off the campaign).

It was, however, his conduct at the taking of Mexico City that brought Harney to most people's attention. Having captured a number of men from the enemy's 'Legion of St Patrick' (made up of Irishmen who had deserted from the American army), he had the prisoners stand on a wagon with a noose round each of their necks suspended from an overhead gallows. When the Stars and Stripes was run up the flagpole of Chapultepec Palace by infantry Captain George Pickett as a sign of victory, Harney ordered the wagon to be driven away, leaving his victims dangling.

With the end of the war, Harney was transferred to the west, where he took part in campaigns against the Indians. Once again, he was noted for his ferocity when dealing with the natives. One particular example happened as a result of a cow belonging to a wagon train breaking loose and wandering into an Indian camp, where it was received with pleasure and slaughtered for the pot. When the cow's owner reported the details to nearby Fort Laramie, Second Lieutenant John Grattan – a brash young man straight out of West Point – was given permission to track down the offenders, taking with him twenty-nine soldiers, an interpreter and two 12-pounder howitzers. On arrival at the Sioux camp, Grattan demanded the perpetrators of the crime. The Indian chief, Conquering Bear, refused and offered a number of horses in compensation. At this, Grattan ordered his men to open fire and Conquering Bear fell in the first fusillade. Within minutes, Grattan and every one of his men were dead (one young Indian who witnessed the incident went on to become a great warrior chief named Crazy Horse). When news of the event reached Harney, he was in Paris meeting his wife and family, who had set up home there during his field campaigns. Returning immediately, he set off in a series of punishing raids against the Indians, culminating in the Battle of Ash Hollow where his 600 dragoons fell upon a 250-strong Sioux village and killed eighty-five warriors and an unknown number of women and children, taking seventy women and children prisoner. As a result of his depredations, Harney earned the name among the Sioux of 'The Butcher.'

In 1858, Harney, by now a brigadier-general, was appointed to the military command of the Department of Oregon and set up his headquarters at Fort Vancouver. It was not long before he made his presence felt, not least among his own staff. A completely legal request for the reimbursement of expenses by an officer was rejected by Harney. When the officer requested an explanation, he was charged with being 'subversive of good order and discipline,' court-martialled for 'contempt and disrespect to his superior officer' and found guilty. On another occasion, Harney decided to build new accommodation for himself outside the fort. The only problem with the idea was that he intended to use his officers and men as the workforce. One officer resigned rather than be employed as his carpenter; another was court-martialled for expressing the view that such employment might be wrong. In September 1859, during the course of an argument, one officer became so enraged that he drew a pistol and aimed it at Harney before fleeing from the fort.

None of Harney's activities in relation to his subordinate officers was, however, as absurd as his arrest of one of his lieutenants for heading a report 'Fort Vancouver. W.T.' instead of 'Headquarters, Department of Oregon.' When news of this reached General Winfield Scott – now the most senior officer in the army – he called the incident 'an act of stupid outrage' and ordered the officer's release. Anonymous letters, purportedly from Harney's officers, referred to him as being 'all matter and no mind,' 'one of the weakest officers and most arrogant humbugs in the army,' and 'a laughing stock.'

Harney may have been irresponsible, irrational and impulsive, but he was also quite capable of being highly devious. Contemporary American events were beginning to take on a shape that cast a lengthening shadow across the country, important events that would provide a key role for the brigadier-general.

In 1857, one of America's major financial institutions collapsed through widespread fraud, an occurrence that led to the bulk of British investment in the United States being withdrawn. This event, coupled with a massive drop in the price of grain thanks to Russia's return to world markets after the Crimean War, and the loss of almost thirteen and a half tons of gold bullion at sea during a hurricane, rocked the American economy. The effect was particularly felt in the Northern states, but less so in the South, where the slavery-based cotton industry weathered the storm. This, in turn, led to an increasing demand from the North that slavery be abolished. It was not long before Northern pressure, and Southern resistance, began to reveal a widening crack in the Union. The Northern states emphasised hard work, enterprise and commercialism as the foundations of society. The South argued that slavery exposed the slaves to the benefits of Christianity and security, whilst the slave owners – freed from labour – could pursue interests in the arts, sciences and politics to the benefit of society in general.

Harney was, if nothing else, a southerner. Raised in a slave state, he would have been sensitive to the movements of the time that ranged from anti-slavery activities to burgeoning secessionist groups. His hero, Andrew Jackson, and his supporting neighbour, President Polk, were both slave-owners. In response, Harney decided to play the great game. His opportunity in the north-west was unique. If he could trigger a war with Great Britain, the North would be greatly weakened, and the resulting turmoil would allow the Southern states to break away from the Union. If, on the other hand, the Southern states decided to support the North, Harney could oversee the invasion and capture of all the British territory west of the Rocky Mountains as far north as the border with Russian North America. Even more, as was gleaned from intelligence received by Captain Prevost, Harney would gain the glory needed for a future nomination for President. Whichever fate dictated, secession, 'Manifest Destiny' or a tilt at the presidency, Harney would win and Britain lose. All he needed was a war.

8

The South Arises in the West

It would seem to have been an act verging on the reckless to have declared an unnecessary war with Great Britain in mid-1859. The British Army was probably in better condition than it had been even at the end of the Napoleonic Wars. The Crimea had exposed the weaknesses of its leadership, and the generals who had lost touch with the realities of modern warfare had been quietly retired to be replaced by officers of proven competence. The Indian Mutiny of 1857 had seen the demise of the East India Company, and the transfer of its military force had seen the army increased by nine experienced infantry regiments, three cavalry regiments and several troops and batteries of artillery. The same conflict had seen the raising of an entire regiment of volunteers from British North America: the 100th Foot. They had not seen action, but had, nevertheless, demonstrated a willingness to defend the Crown. More experience of warfare had been gained by the Opium Wars, along with a Pacific base at Hong Kong. Army officers' commissions could still be purchased, but the practice was already on its last legs, competence being seen as more of a premium than wealth.

The Royal Navy stood alone in its experience and tradition. From the Baltic to South America, from India to the North Pacific, and from fleet actions to anti-slavery patrols, the Royal Navy considered the oceans of the world to be its own backyard. The press-gangs of old were no more than a memory, professional training and engagements of service had changed the ship's companies into career seamen and officers no longer needed the foothold of 'influence' to succeed. The variety of responses the Royal Navy had frequently demonstrated had become renowned. In India, the Crimea, New Zealand and China, Royal Marines and naval brigades made up of seamen showed that the Royal Navy was as effective ashore as it was at sea. The tradition of victory begun in the eighteenth century had become the core of its philosophy.

The United States of America, on the other hand, had only a small professional army of about 15,000 men. None would deny their courage, but most of their experience of combat had been against the ill-armed Native Americans. Some were veterans of the Mexican War, but few had faced the force and firepower of a modern army. In addition, there was a large militia numbering close to 2.5 million men who – a contemporary noted – had acquired 'a certain knowledge of military exercises, but submit very little to subordination.'

The United States Navy, basing itself upon the Royal Navy (the army was inclining more to the Prussian model), was small but active. With a dozen ships of the line, the same number of frigates and over forty sloops, brigs, steamers and store-ships, the entire firepower of the American navy was about 2,000 guns. Its officers and men were competent and on two occasions during the Opium Wars had actually gone to the Royal Navy's rescue. In one of these incidents, although a neutral in the conflict, American seamen had manned a British warship's gun during a battle, declaring that 'Blood is thicker than water.'

Ignoring the suspect abilities of the state militias, the United States of America, with its Northern and Southern states profoundly divided on the question of slavery, with its Atlantic and Pacific coasts vulnerable and easily blockaded and with its southern border liable to attack by a still-vengeful – and European-supported – Mexico, would have found itself surrounded, out-gunned and without allies. Or would it?

On Britain's doorstep and behind her back if she turned her eyes towards the United States, France stood ready to take revenge for the humiliations heaped on her half a century earlier. With the ghosts of Waterloo exorcised by the campaigns during the Crimean War, and with victories against the Austrians at Montebello, Palestro and Magenta, the French Army (and the French Navy, with its heavy armament of shell-firing guns) could prove a formidable foe. The Emperor, Napoleon III, had nurtured a personal dislike of Britain from the time it was learned that the bombs used in an assassination attempt against him the previous year had been manufactured in England. An Irish newspaper was almost beside itself with excitement at the possibility of a French invasion:

… it is difficult to conceive how any man can say that the Emperor of the French is not preparing for a war with England. It will be the most popular act of his life.

The *New York Journal of Commerce*, unaware of the possibilities being created far to the north-west of its own country, did not agree:

We do not deny the Emperor of the French may be induced by ambition, and what he may consider to be 'impelling circumstances,' to attempt to invade England … But should it ever be made, it will prove a signal and disastrous failure.

The French *Univers*, on the other hand, felt that by throwing 'three hundred thousand men upon the British shores,' the invasion leader:

… would have no difficulty in freeing Ireland, India, Canada, and the colonies from the British yoke. He would destroy all the arsenals and ports on the British shores, and England, humiliated, and reduced to the rank of a third-rate Power, might be left to make the best of her new position.

Iron-plated steam frigates were being built at Cherbourg, and the keels of transports capable of carrying 300 men and horses were being laid down at the same port. The French Government had just purchased two steam transports for the specific purpose of towing twenty-four iron gun-boats – ostensibly to China.

In response to this threat, the British were strengthening their coastal defences and building warships to the extent that Chatham dockyard had been forced to increase its workforce – and even award them a novel payment known as 'overtime.'

If the United States remained united, Great Britain would have found her to be a difficult, but not impossible, opponent. There was, however, a good chance that the states would fall apart, those to the south recognising the huge importance of Britain as a market for their cotton, those to the north unwilling to accept the threat to their economy and burgeoning industries without the support of the South. In either case, if the French became involved – and there seemed every possibility that they would, especially as their army and navy were already on a war footing – Britain would, at the very least, risk the loss of her North American colonies.

It is doubtful if any such wide international considerations went through the mind of the American Inspector of Customs, Paul Hubbs, as he paddled his canoe from San Juan to a meeting with his immediate superior with a letter of complaint about the actions of the Hudson's Bay Company. Although not specifically about the threat of legal action against the trigger-happy Cutler (the letter had been written some days before the challenge by Dallas and his friends), Hubbs urgently stressed that he and the other Americans on the island should be provided with some form of military protection against the 'odious' and 'intolerable' representatives of the Company.

Having made his point with the customs collector, Hubbs then made his way to the nearby Fort Bellingham to meet an old friend, Captain George Pickett – the same man who had hoisted the flag at Chapultepec Palace during the Mexican War. Like Hubbs (who was from Tennessee) and General Harney, Pickett was a southerner. In addition to his experiences in the war against the Mexicans, Pickett had fought – alongside Hubbs – against the Indians in the White River War, a conflict brought about through Governor Stevens' treaty-making attempts three years earlier. However, by the middle of 1859, conflict with the Indians had been reduced to little more than the occasional forays by bands of braves in search of slaves or loot. By now aged thirty-four, twice made a widower and in command of Company 'D' of the 9th US Infantry, Pickett could see little opportunity to further his career. Even the news brought by Hubbs of the local difficulties on San Juan Island would have seemed little more than a neighbourhood squabble that would, in time, fizzle out.

On his return to the island, Hubbs brought with him a large American flag. Determined to show solidarity in the face of British aggression, the Americans on San Juan had decided that they would celebrate Independence Day. On this occasion, the events of 4 July marked the start of a charade as calculated as any farce presented on stage.

The day itself went well, with the newly obtained Stars and Stripes being hoisted up a particularly tall flagpole erected behind Belle Vue Farm. The flag rose to a fusillade of celebratory rifle-firing and suffered the indignity of being pierced by one of its own citizen's bullets. As the celebrations continued, Charles Griffin raised the Union Flag in quiet response.

For the next six days the American flag flew boldly and unchallenged from its lofty flagpole. A blaze of red, white and blue, the flag stood out like a bright signal against the sky above the islands, a signal that was answered in the early afternoon of 9 July as the United States Propeller *Massachusetts* steamed into Griffin Bay. Shortly afterwards, a boat was rowed ashore, from which stepped none other than the military commander of the Department of Oregon, General William Selby Harney.

Harney had conveniently decided on a tour of inspection of his northern area. His first port of call was at Fort Steilacoom on Puget Sound. The fort's commander, and the commander of the Puget Sound District under Harney, was Lieutenant Colonel Silas Casey. The colonel had fought alongside General Winfield Scott during the Mexican War and had so distinguished himself that he had earned promotion from captain to his current rank. Although he did not hesitate to defend settlers from Indian attack in his district, he was, nevertheless, no supporter of Governor Stevens when Stevens demanded that any Indian attack should be met by savage retribution. He also refused to allow the governor to extend his control of the militia to the regular troops under Casey's command. Although described as 'a reserved, unassuming gentleman,' Rhode Island-born Casey was not easily moved on the point of principle.

From Fort Steilacoom Harney moved on to Fort Bellingham, where he was accommodated at the house of the fort's leading citizen, former judge Edmund Fitzhugh, a southerner and a member of Sheriff Barnes's sheep-rustling expedition. It was not long before they were joined by Captain Pickett.

It would not take a great deal of thought to consider what the chief subject of conversation would have been. An aggressive brigadier-general eager to rock the boat of Anglo-US relations, an ageing captain keen to grab the chance of further advancement and a civic dignitary who had been sent scuttling from San Juan Island in a canoe full of stolen rams. Added to which, all were southerners who could not fail to have been aware of the growing divide between the states. Major Granville Haller, commanding Company 'I' of the 4th US Infantry, at that time based at Fort Townsend and cruising the islands in search of Indian raiding parties, later wrote:

> … my candid impression has been that on the night spent at Bellingham Bay the matter was orally agreed upon – the hog incident to be seized upon as the pretext, and the exclusion of British law and British troops from San Juan Island to become the *casus belli*.

At Harney's next destination, the secret came out. Calling upon Archibald Campbell and the boundary survey at Semiahmoo, the general said nothing to the commissioner, but his staff let it slip to Campbell's secretary, Warren, that one way or another, Harney intended to land Pickett and his company on San Juan Island.

After his meeting with the boundary commissioner, the *Massachusetts* took Harney and his staff to Victoria to meet Governor James Douglas. It was only to be a brief call, the main purposes of which was to obtain fuel and water and to thank Douglas for the help he had given in fending off Indian attacks. There was no mention over dinner of any difficulty concerning any island in the archipelago just across the Canal de Arro to the east.

The following morning, 9 July, observers on board the ship could see the large Stars and Stripes waving boldly over clear ground just to the north of the pine-clad southern tip of San Juan Island. What, then, could be more natural than for the military commander of the area to pay a call upon his fellow citizens?

The general had not been ashore long before he was deluged with ready-made complaints about the conduct of the British. Such behaviour was not to be tolerated under any circumstances, and the defenceless Americans demanded the protection of the army. But could it really be that simple – the threat of a visit by a magistrate over the death of a pig? Could that alone really be the excuse to land an entire company of American soldiers? Harney knew that such an action, in such a cause, would not convince even the most callow of outside observers. There was, however, always the unfailing terror of the threat from the northern Indians, and even the possibility that the British, unprincipled as well as being arrogant bullies, would actually encourage the Indians in their descent upon the settlers. There it was, an excellent basis on which to provide protection to innocent citizens. All Harney had to do was to wait for a letter of complaint or a petition from the American islanders. Once it arrived, he would be able to take the appropriate – and decisive – action. After a final conference with Hubbs on board the ship, at which the programme of events was finally agreed, Harney left to begin his return to Fort Vancouver.

9

The Order is Given

On 11 July 1859, the United States Inspector of Customs on San Juan Island, Paul Hubbs, gathered together as many of the American residents as he could (along with at least one or two who just happened to be passing through) and asked them to sign a petition he had written. The letter opened by describing an assault by Indians on the inspector himself, and was followed by details of more deaths on the island through native attacks. It then went on:

> According to the treaty concluded June 16, 1846, between the United States and Great Britain, (the provisions of which are plain, obvious, and pointed to us all here,) this and all the islands east of the Canal de Haro belong to us; we therefore claim American protection in our present exposed and defenceless position.
>
> With a view of these facts, and for the essential advantage of having this and the surrounding islands immediately settled, we most earnestly pray that you will have stationed on this island a sufficient military force to protect us from the above-mentioned dangers until we become sufficiently strong to protect ourselves.

The petition was signed by twenty-two Americans, three of whom had the surname Hubbs, and one named Lyman Cutler. No one mentioned a pig.

Unfortunately, and no doubt to Harney's great annoyance, a week after the petition had been signed, it still had not arrived at Fort Vancouver. The general, now back at his headquarters, knew that time was not something of which he had an excess. It was already mid-July and the prospect of declining weather conditions north of Puget Sound would have an effect upon military operations in the area. Furthermore, the political and social problems in the east of the country were already at simmering point and could easily boil over at any time. Taking a huge gamble, Harney decided to set in motion the main thrust of his scheme.

On 18 July, Captain Alfred Pleasonton, Harney's Assistant Adjutant-General, wrote to Pickett at Fort Bellingham:

Captain: By Special Orders No. 72 ... you are directed to establish your company on Bellvue or San Juan Island, in some suitable position near the harbour at the southeast extremity. The general commanding instructs me to say the object to be attained in placing you thus is two-fold, viz: First. To protect the inhabitants of the island from the incursions of the northern Indians of British Columbia and the Russian possessions. You will not permit any force of these Indians to visit San Juan island or the water ways of Puget Sound in that vicinity over which the United States have any jurisdiction. Should these Indians appear peaceful you will warn them in a quiet but firm manner to return to their own country, and not visit in future the territory of the United States; and in the event of any opposition being offered to your demands, you will use the most decisive measures to enforce them; to which end the commander of the troops stationed on the steamer *Massachusetts* will be instructed to render every assistance and co-operation that will be necessary to enable your command to fulfil the tenor of these instructions.

Second. Another serious and important duty will devolve upon you in the occupation of San Juan island, arising from the conflicting interests of the American citizens and the Hudson's Bay Company establishment at that point. This duty is to afford adequate protection to the American citizens in their rights as such, and to resist all attempts by the British authorities residing on Vancouver's Island, by intimidation or force, in the controversies of the above-mentioned parties.

This protection has been called for in consequence of the chief factor of the Hudson's Bay Company, Mr. Dallas, having recently visited San Juan Island with a British sloop-of-war, and threatened to take an American citizen by force to Victoria for trial by British laws. It is hoped a second attempt of this kind will not be made, but to insure the safety of our citizens the general commanding directs you to meet the authorities from Victoria at once, on a second arrival, and inform them they cannot be permitted to interfere with our citizens in any way. Any grievances they may allege as requiring redress can only be examined under our own laws, to which they must submit their claims in proper form.

Not only was Pickett offered no advice concerning the matter of the unresolved boundary question, but the ageing, 35-horsepower Hudson's Bay Company steamer *Beaver* had been replaced by a well-armed Royal Navy 'sloop-of-war.' The threat of force from an armed American had been transferred to Dallas, the son-in-law of the Governor of British Columbia. After some lines on the logistics of the 'occupation,' the letter continued:

> The general commanding is fully satisfied, from the varied experience and judgement displayed by you in your present command, that your selection to the duties with which you are now charged will advance the interests of the service, and that your disposition of the subjects coming within your supervision and action will enhance your reputation as a commander.
>
> In your selection of a position, take into consideration that future contingencies may require an establishment of from four to six companies retaining the command of the San Juan harbor.

The last paragraph strongly indicates that Harney was of the opinion that the British would not simply allow the occupation to go unchallenged – just the reaction he was looking for.

Special Order No. 72 also carried the instructions that, in addition to closing down Fort Bellingham, Major Haller's base at Fort Townsend was also to be abandoned and the troops transferred to Fort Steilacoom; not that Lieutenant Colonel Casey would profit operationally from such a rearrangement. In fact, quite the opposite.

On the same day that the order was dispatched to Pickett, Captain Pleasonton also wrote to Casey who, so far, was completely in the dark about what was going on. On receipt of the letter, Casey would not have failed to notice that, with the closure of Forts Bellingham and Townsend, his command of the Puget Sound District had also disappeared. The letter was simply addressed to him as 'Commanding Fort Steilacoom.'

At first, Casey was informed that the *Massachusetts* (not a naval vessel, belonging instead to the Army's Quartermaster's Department) was placed under his orders 'for the better protection and supervision of the waters of Puget's Sound.' However, after some detail concerning the closure of Fort Townsend and a brief mention of Indian incursions, Harney promptly removed his authority over the *Massachusetts*:

> The ordinary rendezvous of the steamer *Massachusetts*, for wood and water,
> will be San Juan island; and should the commander of that island desire
> the assistance of any force from the ship for purposes connected with the
> defence of the island, the officer in command of the ship will be instructed to
> furnish the force and co-operate with the troops in all measures requiring its
> safety and protection. At the end of every two months the ship will visit Fort
> Steilacoom to obtain supplies, and for the muster and inspection required by
> the regulations. The command on the steamer *Massachusetts* will be borne on
> the post return of Fort Steilacoom, as a component part of the garrison.

In other words, Casey was responsible for the ship's administration and its
crew (made up of the former Fort Townsend 'I' Company of the 4th US
Infantry), but both he and Major Haller had to accord to the wishes of
Pickett, a junior officer. Later in the letter, Casey was casually informed of
another development:

> As the ship is mounted with eight thirty-two pounders, and the proper
> ammunition has been provided, the crew will be instructed under the
> direction of the master of the vessel in their use, to obtain the most efficient
> action from all parties in cases requiring it.

As the use of such powerful guns was pointless against Indian raiding
parties, the only purpose of such an instruction would have been to
prepare the vessel for action against other ships, or for shore bombardment.
The ship's master, Captain Fauntleroy, was, like Harney, Pickett, Fitzhugh
and Hubbs, a southerner.

The day after dispatching the letters to Pickett and Casey, Harney
(probably now in possession of the islanders' petition) wrote to General
Winfield Scott at the Army Headquarters, New York City, to inform him
that San Juan Island was:

> ... the most commanding position we possess on the water; overlooking
> the Straits of Haro, the Straits of Fuca, and the Rosario Strait, it is the most
> suitable point from which to observe and prevent the northern Indians from
> visiting our settlements to the south of it. At the southeastern extremity
> one of the finest harbours on this coast is to be found, completely sheltered,
> offering the best location for a naval station on the Pacific coast.

The words 'we possess' may have fallen with some surprise on the ears
of the General Scott, but they were as nothing compared with what was

to follow. After the strategic introduction, Harney went on to tell how he was petitioned by the Americans on the island to protect them from the Indians:

> … as well as the oppressive interference of the authorities of the Hudson's Bay Company at Victoria, with their rights as American citizens. Mr Hubbs informed me that a short time before my arrival the chief factor of the company at Victoria, Mr Dallas, son-in-law of Governor Douglas, came to the island in the British sloop-of-war *Satellite*, and threatened to take one of the Americans by force to Victoria for shooting a pig of the company. The American seized his rifle and told Mr Dallas if any such attempt was made he would kill him on the spot. The affair then ended. The American offered to pay to the company twice the value of the pig, which was refused.
>
> To prevent a repetition of this outrage, I have ordered the company at Fort Bellingham to be established on San Juan island for the protection of our citizens, and the steamer *Massachusetts* is directed to rendezvous at that place with a second company to protect our interests in all parts of the sound.

From the obvious falsehoods contained in the letter, Harney was taking a considerable risk, depending, no doubt, on the several weeks that would elapse before it arrived in New York. Not only had he, once again, transformed the *Beaver* into the *Satellite*, but had also declared that the American islanders had requested his aid against the 'oppressive interference' of the Hudson's Bay Company. In reality, the only mention of the Company in the petition had been praise for its 'timely aid' in defending them against the Indians.

Now there was nothing further to do. Pickett, Casey and Haller would receive their orders and act upon them; with luck the British would react violently to the invasion on what they considered to be their territory; and by the time the national legislature at Washington, DC learned what had happened, they would find themselves already at war. If all went well, within a very short time a new country would be created from the Southern states as they broke away from the weakened Union. On the other hand, if the plan failed, Harney would be seen as no more nor less than an honest defender of his country and his countrymen – and had not previous generals of such metal, including his hero Andrew Jackson, found themselves in the White House?

10

The Americans Land and
the Royal Navy Sails

With many Americans thronging the streets of Victoria, and with numerous cross-border contacts in existence, it was not long before word reached Governor Douglas that something was afoot. Fort Bellingham was being closed down and Fort Townsend reduced to a sergeant and a couple of men to look after the fort's garden. By now well in the majority, the Americans on San Juan were beginning to take on an attitude which suggested they knew something of importance that was unknown to the British. Hoping to take a grip on the problem before it got out of hand, Douglas decided to replace Griffin as the island's magistrate. A tall, one-eyed Irishman, Major John De Courcy, was appointed to the post with instructions to remove American squatters from the Hudson's Bay Company properties and, where necessary, obtain bail money from any who objected in order to ensure they would later appear in court in Victoria. If needed, he could request assistance from the Royal Navy and the Royal Engineers stationed in British Columbia. Nevertheless, De Courcy was enjoined 'to avoid giving any occasion that might lead to acts of violence.' To underline his authority, the Royal Navy had been requested to transport the new magistrate to the island in a warship.

The senior naval officer in the area was Captain Michael De Courcy – a relative of the newly appointed magistrate. He was a man of strong opinion and direct action who, seventeen years earlier, had almost single-handedly introduced the concept of 'gunboat diplomacy.' As a lieutenant in command of the brig HMS *Charybdis* he was ordered to pursue Columbian pirates who had captured two British merchant ships.

Entering the port of Cartagena, and receiving no satisfactory reply to his demand that the perpetrators be handed over, De Courcy, despite being armed only with a single cannon and two carronades, took on the entire Cartagenan fleet. After he had captured a corvette and followed it up by sinking a brig, the entire fleet surrendered.

HMS *Satellite*, still under the command of Captain Prevost, the senior water boundary commissioner, sailed from Esquimalt on 27 July. By the early afternoon she had rounded the southern point of San Juan Island and was about to enter Griffin Bay, when Prevost and Major De Courcy saw a sight that made their eyes gape with surprise. There, in the bay, was the *Massachusetts*, with her boats being pulled to and fro from the Hudson's Bay Company wharf. Ashore, on the far side of a round lagoon, tents and the smoke from campfires could be seen just where the trees thinned out at the edge of a thickly wooded slope. Blue-uniformed soldiers toiled along the stony, flotsam-strewn beach carrying stores from the wharf to the camp. Close inshore, the side-wheeled steamer *Shubrick* lay at anchor, with the senior American boundary commissioner, Archibald Campbell, on board.

Pickett and the *Massachusetts* had arrived on the previous evening. Hubbs had been sent for and had the situation explained to him. The arrival of Company 'D' was not a casual visit, but the start of a permanent establishment on the island. Not, of course, that Hubbs was in any way surprised; he was more than delighted that the American islanders' petition had resulted in such a positive action.

The following day, the sixty-six American troops, dragging three brass howitzers, disembarked and set up their camp. Oddly enough, for a professional soldier, the site chosen by Pickett was poor in the extreme. Poorly equipped with barely enough tents, Pickett had decided to set up his camp beneath an east-facing slope directly fronting the sea. It left his tents totally unprotected against the guns of a ship that could easily be brought alongside with her broadside aimed from a very short range. No naval gunner could have wished for an easier target.

As the tents were being erected, Pickett had a poster displayed close to the wharf. It read:

> Military Post, San Juan Island.
> Washington Territory, July 27, 1859.

> I   In compliance with orders and instructions from the general commanding, a military post will be established on this island, on whatever site the commanding officer may select.

II   All the inhabitants of the island are required to report at once to the commanding officer in case of any incursion of the northern Indians, so that he may take such steps as are necessary to prevent the future occurrence of same.

III   This being United States territory, no laws, other than those of the United States, nor courts, except such as are held by virtue of said laws, will be recognised or allowed on this island.

Griffin, still unaware that he had been replaced as magistrate, and dumbfounded by the unwelcome activity taking place within yards of his farm, again quietly raised the Union Flag.

That afternoon, Major De Courcy landed and set off to seek out whoever was in charge. On finding Pickett, De Courcy introduced himself and demanded to know what was going on. In his subsequent report to Douglas, the magistrate wrote:

I asked him, 'By what right or for what reason he had landed and occupied this island.' To which he answered that he did not consider that I, or any other person, had the right to ask such a question; but as it was generally known to everyone about, he had no objection to state that he occupied and landed on the island by order of his Government. I then informed him that his acts were illegal; that he was trespassing, and that it was my duty to warn him off the premises and island.

With no further progress on the point possible, De Courcy set off to tour the area on foot in company with two of the *Satellite*'s officers. They had not gone far when they ran into Hubbs accompanying the trigger-happy Lyman Cutler. When it was known that the British were landing a magistrate, Pickett had dispatched Hubbs to place Cutler under arrest in an attempt to forestall any British plans to do the same. De Courcy, probably unaware who the two Americans were, simply walked past Hubbs and Cutler without acknowledgement. When the two arrived at the American camp, Pickett, now less sure of his ground, decided that Cutler should hide in the woods rather than be detained in the camp.

As this was going on, the *Massachusetts* left Griffin Bay to return to Bellingham Bay. She was shortly followed out of the harbour by the *Satellite*, leaving De Courcy ashore. Prevost (after having paid a courtesy call upon Campbell on board the *Shubrick*, where both avoided talking about the very events that were happening around them) had to get back to Esquimalt to inform Captain De Courcy and, in due course,

Douglas, about the activities taking place on the south-east tip of San Juan Island.

When he heard the news, Douglas was furious. The Americans had stolen a march on him by deceit. There was, he concluded, only one possible response: the American troops had to be removed from the island, and if force had to be employed, then so be it. The most obvious means of ejecting the Americans was the Royal Navy and Douglas had a number of naval vessels immediately to hand.

In his position as governor, Douglas carried the extra title of 'Vice-Admiral.' It was not a naval rank, nor did it carry any authority over the Royal Navy and its officers. A hang-over from a statute dating back to 1389, the title gave Douglas, under the 'Admiralty Offences (Colonial) Act' of 1849, the authority to appoint commissioners to enquire into acts of piracy or other sea-borne offences, and the allocation of 'prizes.' The local senior officers of the Royal Navy, on the other hand, were bound to listen to requests from governors and act upon them when it appeared to be in the interests of Great Britain to do so. Accordingly, Captain De Courcy approved Douglas's request that a ship be sent to Griffin Bay, although he may have had some reservations over the governor's instructions to the ship's captain.

HMS *Tribune* was a screw-driven wooden steam corvette launched in 1853. She mounted one 10-inch gun (ideal for shore bombardment) and thirty 32-pounders. Her captain was Geoffrey Phipps Hornby, the son of an admiral and the brother-in-law of the Earl of Derby. He had entered the Royal Navy at the age of twelve and later served as flag-lieutenant to his father on the Pacific station, returning with the rank of commander. In the nature of things at the time, it did Hornby's career no harm when, in 1852, his brother-in-law became Prime Minister and his father was appointed a lord of the Admiralty. Unfortunately, after just eleven months, the Chancellor of the Exchequer's budget was rejected by the House of Commons and Derby was forced to resign; not, however, before Hornby managed to achieve promotion to captain. After six years on half pay, during which time he toured India and ran the family estate, Derby regained office and Hornby was appointed to the *Tribune* on the China station. There he was ordered to transfer a detachment of Royal Marines to Vancouver Island. Now he had Douglas's instructions before him. He was to go straight to Griffin Bay, ensure that no more American troops were landed and see that no entrenchments were dug by the occupation force. He was authorised to use force in support of the magistrate if necessary, but, absurdly, not to give cause for a 'collision.'

Why Douglas believed the Americans would suffer being bundled into their boats and pushed off the island without vigorous protest is unclear, but Hornby's instructions left him with a dilemma. How could he use 'force,' yet not cause a 'collision'?

As the *Tribune*'s boilers were being fired up and her gunners checked their weapons, events on San Juan had moved forward. Charles Griffin, in his role as the Hudson's Bay Company agent, had at last stirred and sent a note to Pickett:

> Sir: I have the honour to inform you that the island of San Juan, on which your camp is pitched, is the property and in the occupation of the Hudson's Bay Company, and to request that you and the whole of the party who have landed from the American vessels will immediately cease to occupy the same. Should you be unwilling to comply with my request, I feel bound to apply to the civil authorities. Awaiting your reply,
>
> I have the honour to be, sir, your obedient servant.
> Chas. Jno. Griffin,
> Agent Hudson's Bay Company.

Within the hour he had his response:

> Sir: Your communication of this instant has been received. I have to state in reply that I do not acknowledge the right of the Hudson's Bay Company to dictate my course of action. I am here by virtue of an order from my government, and shall remain till recalled by the same authority.
>
> I am, sir, very respectfully, your obedient servant.
> George E. Pickett,
> Captain 9th U.S. Infantry, Commanding.

Pickett knew full well that the words 'I am here by virtue of an order from my government' was nothing more than a bluff. The order was from his commanding general – and even generals are responsible *to* government, not *for* government.

Shortly after this exchange, the black-hulled *Tribune* hauled into view and, joining the *Satellite* (now returned from Esquimalt), dropped her anchor opposite the American camp. Suddenly, Pickett began to see things a little differently. Faced with a battery of heavy firepower, the American captain swiftly put pen to paper on the afternoon of 30 July and dashed off a note to Colonel Casey:

My Dear Colonel: ... From the threatening attitude of affairs at present, I deem it my duty to request that the *Massachusetts* be sent at once to this point. I do not know that any actual collision will take place, but it is not comfortable to be lying within range of a couple of war steamers. The *Tribune*, a 30-gun frigate, is lying broadside to our camp, and from present indications everything leads me to suppose that they will attempt to prevent me carrying out my instructions.

Just to complete his day, Pickett was then served with a summons to appear before Major De Courcy in his capacity as the island's magistrate. In fact, Pickett had by now obtained his own magistrate, Henry Crosbie, from Bellingham via the *Massachusetts*. Crosbie was the Whatcom County coroner and had been on nearby Orcas Island to set up an inquest after a murder. The two opposing magistrates had met, gone through the formalities of telling each other that they were the actual and sole legal representative on the island, and then settled down in an amicable, and working, relationship.

Pickett had also found himself faced with another difficulty. 31 July was a Sunday, and nothing was going to stop the holiday crowds from flooding over to San Juan to see what the fuss was all about. Pickett claimed that 'some five hundred people have visited us.' The *San Francisco Times* journalist at Victoria recorded that:

Vessels for the conveyance of passengers to the seat of war were in demand. Small boats were chartered for the trip, and several steamboats departed with visitors, Both English and American, to the island of San Juan, a distance of fifteen or twenty miles from this place ... Most of those who went to the island did so, perhaps, through curiosity; but others no doubt, went determined to lend a hand to their respective countries.

Most of these 'sovereigns' (as Pickett referred to the visitors) remained good humoured and merely stared at the dark-blue-coated soldiers with their newly issued Hardee, or 'Jeff Davies' hats, cocked up on one side, decorated with a Jaeger hunting horn on the front and plumed with ostrich feathers (two for officers, one for other ranks). Some, however, after indulging themselves in the alcohol they had brought with them, began to display certain hostility towards the Americans. Pickett was forced to 'use a great deal of my peace-making disposition' in order to calm things down.

Hornby and the *Tribune* had arrived on the evening of the 29th, when Major De Courcy went on board to discuss matters with the captain.

In the captain's cabin, the magistrate also found Alexander Dallas, the governor's son-in-law (who had been present during the early days of the current situation) and the Vancouver Island attorney-general, George Cary. They agreed that, keeping to their instructions, De Courcy would serve Pickett with a summons whilst Hornby would ensure that no further troops were landed. Should the summons have no effect (and, probably, none present believed that it would), the *Tribune* would land seamen and Royal Marines to arrest Pickett and his men. At that point, if the Americans refused to agree to the British demands, Hornby was at liberty to use his overwhelming firepower.

Dallas and Cary, bearing a note from Hornby to Captain De Courcy, returned to Victoria the following day in the *Beaver*. The note informed De Courcy that:

> ... the Americans have formed a camp about 200 yards from the beach, in which they have two howitzers; the ground rises considerably behind the camp, and on either side, at a distance of 300 yards, it is flanked by woods.

Almost certainly using intelligence brought by Major De Courcy, the note continued:

> I am assured that the force at the disposal of the American captain consists of 50 soldiers, with the two howitzers above mentioned, and about the same number of armed civilians; and if they take to the bush, the Magistrate does not see how they could be arrested, at the same time they might be expected to commit serious depredations on the cattle of the Hudson's Bay Company.

The latter comment was probably included at the request of Dallas, whose chief, and most immediate, concern was the Company's property on the island. The Company chief factor also reported to Douglas, insisting that the number of ships and men facing the Americans should be increased. The governor agreed, and sent a demand to Captain De Courcy that he should take his own ship, HMS *Pylades*, with her twenty 8-inch guns and her single 68-pounder carronade. On receipt of his instructions, De Courcy decided the time had come to have a word with the governor. Not only was Douglas assuming powers to which he had no right, but the *Pylades* was standing by to take the newly promoted Lieutenant-Colonel John Hawkins of the Royal Engineers (and the boundary commission) to San Francisco to catch the Panama packet. The colony's Legislative

Council was to meet on 1 August, and would authorise the colonel's dash to London to make sure the British Government knew what was going on. Furthermore, De Courcy, experienced in action and with a commendable service in the Royal Navy to his credit, doubted that a show of strength such as was demanded by Douglas would be at all helpful. Neither he, nor his fellow captains, Prevost, Richards and Hornby, would have retired tamely from the scene had they been in Pickett's position. And, if the Americans were to be overwhelmed at great cost, war would have been the only outcome. De Courcy decided that he would not be the cause of a war that might be avoided by simply holding fire.

Taking Captain Richards with him, De Courcy set off immediately to confront Douglas at his home. By protesting their case strongly, the naval officers found that the governor was willing to listen to their argument. To have placed himself in a position where his attempts to direct the operations of the Royal Navy were publicly snubbed would have been a serious embarrassment. He needed De Courcy and his ships, but they did not need him. At the end of the meeting it was decided that the delivery of the summons to Pickett would be delayed or, if it had already been served, there would be no follow-up action. Hornby would not prevent more American troops from landing nor oppose the building of any fortifications. In the meantime, Prevost would be sent over to Semiahmoo to see if the American boundary commissioner, Campbell, could shed any light on the situation. Richards would go over to the mainland to collect more Royal Marines and the *Pylades* would take Colonel Hawkins to San Francisco. At the subsequent Legislative Council, the members agreed with De Courcy's proposals (which had already been acted upon), and went further by dropping a demand to land troops and agreeing to withdraw the now redundant magistrate, Major De Courcy.

On San Juan Island, Hornby had attempted to arrange to meet Pickett ashore on the 31st, but the American was away from the camp. As it turned out, the delay was fortunate, for later that day Hornby received his new instructions. As he wrote to his wife:

> I have received fresh orders to take no steps against these men at present, or prevent others from landing. The object now seems to be to avoid a collision at all hazards until we hear from the American authorities … The Governor told me it would be as well if I called on the commanding officer and told him what my orders were. When I called he was away, and before he returned my visit I had received my counter-orders, so I have not the disgust of having blustered and then been obliged to haul in my horns.

On his return call, Pickett impressed Hornby as a typical American, who 'seems to have just the notion they all have of getting a name by some audacious act.' The Englishman further noted that the infantry officer sounded more like a 'Devonshire man than a Yankee.' He also observed that Pickett had intimated that General Harney 'had hopes of winning the presidency.'

Whatever Hornby had picked up from the American's visit, Pickett had certainly noticed that, from the *Tribune*'s deck, his camp was absurdly exposed to the ship's guns. As soon as he was ashore, he gave orders that the camp was to be struck and relocated. It was to be moved over the saddleback ridge and re-established overlooking the beach to the south. Pickett's insistence on remaining on the neck of a ridged peninsula, and in an area of open ground flanked by dense forests is, at best, eccentric. It would have taken Hornby very little time to round the point and bring his broadside to bear on the new American camp. He chose, however, to remain where he was in order to avoid demonstrating any ill-intent.

The following day, Pickett suffered even more discomfiture. The *Massachusetts* arrived, bringing reinforcements under Major Haller. They had been dispatched by Colonel Casey in response to Pickett's letter of the 30th. Casey had reported the request and the action he had taken to Harney, adding the sour note: 'Not having been informed of the tenor of Captain Pickett's instructions, I could not of course advise him with regard to them.'

Haller, still annoyed at being passed over in favour of a junior officer, landed and located Pickett. The major was not impressed by the way things had been handled. He was especially angered by Pickett's insistence that he would open fire on any attempt by the British to remove him from the island. Not only did Haller believe that this attitude would inevitably result in the swift annihilation of the American troops, but it would also guarantee war against Great Britain. The whole thing, he felt, was a mess. As a result of Pickett's removal from Fort Bellingham, an Indian attack had been launched that had resulted in several deaths. Only Haller's fortunate appearance on the scene had prevented matters from getting out of hand. The major then gave Pickett two proposals: firstly, that he and the reinforcements he had brought on the *Massachusetts* should go ashore; and secondly, that the British be allowed to land an equal number of troops without opposition. The captain could not possibly agree. To have complied with the former suggestion would have handed over command to Haller. That, in turn, would have led to the automatic adoption of the second proposal, and the neutralising effect of the presence of British troops on the island, by agreement with the Americans, would have destroyed Harney's grand plan of bringing about a war.

Haller left Pickett in disgust and returned to the *Massachusetts*. Waiting for him on board he found Captain Richards of the *Plumper*, who had just arrived on the scene with more Royal Marines and Royal Engineers. They had met during one of the *Plumper*'s visits to Fort Townsend and had become friends. Richards introduced Haller to Lieutenant-Colonel Hawkins, who had crossed to the island to find out the latest situation before leaving for San Francisco in the *Pylades*. During their conversation, Haller gave the British officers the latest news from Europe. On 24 June, the French had defeated the Austrians at the Battle of Solferino. The balance of power in Europe had changed dramatically and the French were now casting a vengeful glance towards Britain.

The effect on international relations aside, Richards and Hawkins suddenly realised something else. It appeared, from the news given by Haller, that mail from Britain was taking about three weeks longer than that of the Americans. That being the case, could there be news of a settlement over the boundary dispute that the Americans knew about, but had yet to reach the British?

11

Opening Negotiations

The morning of 3 August found three British ships at anchor in Griffin's Bay. Prevost and the *Satellite* had hauled in after a failed attempt to find Campbell at Semiahmoo. Hornby, now armed with an official protest by Douglas, but disconcerted by the news of Solferino and the possible delay in the mail, decided to continue as if nothing had happened. He sent his most junior (and, therefore, most dispensable) lieutenant, Hamilton Dunlop, ashore with a note for Pickett. He wrote:

> Sir: Having received instructions from his excellency Governor Douglas to communicate with you in reference to the landing of the United States troops under your command on the island of San Juan, I have the honour to propose a meeting should take place between yourself and any other officers of the United States military forces on the one part, and captains of her Britannic Majesty's ships on the other, (on board her Majesty's ship *Tribune*,) at any hour that may be convenient to you, that we may, if possible, conclude such arrangements as will tend to preserve harmony between the subjects of the States in this island.

The reply was not long in coming. Pickett chose to make a point. He had, after all, visited Hornby on board the *Tribune*. Furthermore, he was obliged to send all copies of any correspondence between him and the British to Harney at Fort Vancouver, and he was keen to make an impression. His reply read:

Sir: Your communication of this instant, favored by Lieutenant Dunlop, has been received. I have the honor to say, in reply, that I shall most cheerfully meet you, and whatever officers of her Majesty's service that you may select, in my camp at whatever hour you may choose to designate. Be assured that my wish corresponds with yours to preserve harmony between our respective governments.

Hornby's eyebrows may have raised a fraction at this impertinence, but, taking the view that there would be nothing to be gained by standing on ceremony, replied:

Sir: In reply to your letter of this morning, I have to inform you that I shall do myself the honour of calling on you at 2p.m., in company with the captains of Her Britannic Majesty's ships.

Pickett must have known that in both rank and general capability, he was heavily out-gunned by three Royal Naval captains. To start with, his army rank of captain was only equivalent to the United States Navy and the Royal Navy's lieutenant. He was faced with three men of equivalent rank to an army colonel. Not, of course, that rank had any bearing when considering different nationalities, but the inherent respect for rank that attaches itself to such organisations can be inhibiting. Even more, he was aligned against the well-connected Hornby with his natural, almost aristocratic, casual elegance; Prevost with his keen, analytical mind; and Richards, the tough fighter and polar explorer. Pickett, on the other hand, had come bottom of his class at West Point, where he was described as 'a jolly good fellow with fine natural gifts sadly neglected.' In true American style, out-numbered, out-gunned and surrounded, the infantry captain decided his best option was to dig in and refuse to budge.

As the meeting opened, Hornby presented Pickett with a copy of the letter to Governor Stevens by the Secretary of State, William Marcy, in 1855. The letter had constrained the Washington Territory officers to 'abstain from all acts on the disputed grounds which are calculated to provoke any conflicts ...' Was such a constraint part of the 'tenor' of Captain Pickett's instructions? Or was the captain aware of any change in the 'friendly footing' of the two nations? Pickett replied by pointing to the date of Marcy's letter. It was at least four years old.

Hornby then asked Pickett for 'the terms on which you occupied the island of San Juan.' The American replied that he had done so by order of the 'general commanding' who, he believed, had acted under the orders of the United States Government.

With the raising of the stakes, Hornby produced an official note of protest from Governor Douglas. It read:

> By James Douglas, C.B., governor and commander-in-chief in and over the colony of Vancouver's Island and its dependencies, vice-admiral of the same, &c.
>
> The sovereignty of San Juan, and the whole of the Haro archipelago, has always been undeviatingly claimed to be in the crown of Great Britain. Therefore, I, James Douglas, do hereby, formally and solemnly, protest against the occupation of the said island, or any part of the said archipelago, by any person whatsoever, for or on behalf of any other power, hereby protesting and declaring that the sovereignty thereof by right now is, and always has been, in her Majesty Queen Victoria and her predecessors, Kings of Great Britain.
>
> Given under my hand and seal, at Victoria, Vancouver's Island, on this second day of August, one thousand eight hundred and fifty-nine, and in the twenty-third year of her Majesty's reign.
>
> James Douglas

As Pickett put the governor's note to one side, Hornby continued by suggesting to the American 'that the fact of occupying a disputed island by a military force necessitated a similar action on our part,' which, of course, 'involved the imminent risk of a collision between the forces,' especially as there was 'a magistrate of each nation now acting on the island, either of whom might call on those of their country for aid.' Far better, in Hornby's opinion, if the magistrates were withdrawn and any problems from the different nationalities be dealt with by the respective commanding officers. Pickett, however, was adamant:

> I, being here under orders from my government, cannot allow any joint occupation until so ordered by my commanding general, and that any attempt to make such occupation as you propose, before I can communicate with General Harney, will bring on a collision which can be avoided by awaiting this issue. I do not for one moment imagine that there will any difficulty occur on this island which will render a military interference

necessary; and I therefore deem it proper to state that I think no discredit can reflect upon us, or our respective flags, by remaining in our present positions until we have an opportunity of hearing from those in higher authority.

This was then underlined by Pickett with the most outrageous negotiating somersault:

Should you see fit to act otherwise, you will then be the person who will bring on a most disastrous difficulty, and not the United States officials.

Hornby responded to this nonsense by pointing out the obvious, that:

… as officers of the United States government had committed an act of aggression by landing an armed force on this island pending the settlement of our respective claims to its sovereignty, without warning to us, and [hinting at Pickett's junior rank] without giving you a discretionary power of making any necessary arrangements, that the United States and its officers alone must be responsible for any consequences that might result, either immediate or future … The responsibility of any such catastrophe does not, I feel, rest on me or her Majesty's representative at Vancouver's Island.

There the situation stood. The sixty-six Americans under Pickett were clinging to a fragile tissue of reasoning beneath which lurked Harney's grand plan for the breakaway of the Southern States. Against them, the British awaited the imminent arrival of the flagship, HMS *Ganges*, at Esquimalt, mounting a total of 167 guns and crewed by almost 2,000 men. Although only a small number were Royal Marines and soldiers from the Royal Engineers, experience in the Crimean War, in India during the mutiny and in China, had shown the value of the Royal Navy's seamen in land engagements, and all ship's companies, including stokers and signallers, were trained to form effective 'naval brigades.' Even the relatively small *Plumper* carried at least one field-gun manned by naval gunners.

Not unreasonably, Pickett was alarmed at the prospect of facing such odds. After the meeting with Hornby, Prevost and Richards he dashed off a 'hasty' letter to Harney:

I have had to deal with three captains, and I thought it better to take the brunt of it. They have a force so much superior to mine that it will be merely a mouthful to them; still I have informed them that I am here by order of my commanding general, and will maintain my position if possible.

They wish to have a conjoint occupation of the island: I decline anything of that kind. They can, if they choose, land at almost any point on the island, and I cannot prevent them.

In a revealing, and possibly dangerous, comment, Pickett continued:

I have endeavoured to impress them with the idea that my authority comes directly through you from Washington.

Enclosed with the letter, Pickett sent the formal protest from Governor Douglas handed to him by Hornby. In his reply to Douglas, Harney elevated Hornby's suggestion of landing British troops to help in the legal administration of the island into 'threatening a joint occupation ...' He then continued:

As the military commander of the department of Oregon assigned to that command by the orders of the President of the United States, I have the honor to state, for your information, that by such authority invested in me I placed a military command upon the island of San Juan to protect the American citizens residing on that island from the insults and indignities which the British authorities of Vancouver's Island and the establishment of the Hudson's Bay Company recently offered them by sending a British ship-of-war from Vancouver's Island to convey the chief factor of the Hudson's Bay Company to San Juan for the purpose of seizing an American citizen and forcibly transporting him to Vancouver's Island to be tried by British laws.

I have reported this attempted outrage to my government, and they will doubtless seek the proper redress from the British government. In the meantime, I have the honor to inform your excellency I shall not permit a repetition of that insult, and shall retain a command on San Juan island to protect its citizens, in the name of the United States, until I receive further orders from my government.

The letter was a perfect example of bluster and exaggeration. The Company's transport *Beaver* had yet again been transformed into a 'ship-of-war,' and the liberal sprinkling of words such as 'insults,' 'indignities' and 'outrage' served to convey the impression of justified anger. Of incursions by bands of northern Indians – the original purpose of the American petition from San Juan Island – there was not a mention.

There was, however, in view of the British response, a chance to raise the temperature still further. Pickett was informed that:

> The general approves the course you have pursued, and further directs that no joint occupation or any civil jurisdiction will be permitted on San Juan island by the British authorities under any circumstances.
>
> Lieutenant Colonel Casey is ordered to reinforce you with his command as soon as possible.

In addition, and in an attempt to widen the issue, Harney wrote to Brigadier-General Newman Clarke, commanding the Department of California, requesting that he forward a letter to the 'Senior Officer of the United States Navy Commanding Squadron on the Pacific Coast.' In justification, Harney told Clarke:

> I will thank you, general, to cause this communication to be transmitted to the proper officer of the navy at your earliest opportunity, as speedy action on his part will do much to allay the excitement which is fast spreading among our people at the overbearing conduct of the British authorities.

To the senior naval officer, Harney wrote:

> … at this time I have a company of United States troops in possession of San Juan island, to prevent any repetition of the insults that have been offered to our citizens by the British authorities of Vancouver's Island. This company I have ordered to be strongly reinforced which the British authorities have threatened not to permit, but also to remove the present force from the island. This I do not believe they will attempt, but I shall make every effort to meet and frustrate any design to place such an indignity upon our flag; and as we have no national vessel belonging to our navy in the waters of Puget's Sound to observe the three British vessels of war that have been placed in a threatening attitude over the harbour of San Juan island, I have the honor to request you, as the commander of the United States naval forces on the Pacific, to order to Puget Sound such force as you can render available to assist in the protection of American interests in that quarter, and to enable us to meet successfully any issue that may be attempted to be made out of the present impending difficulties.

Despite Harney's plea, nothing happened, either because the senior naval officer, with only six sloops to patrol the entire western seaboard, had better things for his ships to do, or because the Connecticut-born northerner, Brigadier-General Newman Clarke, had an eye to his Southern colleague's intrigues.

At this stage, Harney was aware that his initial plan had misfired. It had been intended that the British would have promptly attacked Pickett, causing losses among the American troops. Not, of course, that the brigadier-general would have been too concerned over casualties. Most of Pickett's men were recently arrived Irishmen, whose loyalty had yet to be confirmed (he would not have forgotten the Irish deserters of the 'Legion of St Patrick' during the Mexican War). With such a 'collision,' Harney would have been justified in sending reinforcements to the island, the fighting would have spread – possibly to the United States' mainland territories – and a declaration of war between Britain and America would have been only a formality. Now, thanks to the forbearance and pragmatic approach of the Royal Navy, the situation had calmed down. There remained the possibility that the arrival of Colonel Casey with reinforcements might cause matters to flare up. The only other thing that could be done would be to make sure the United States Government and the army high command were given the right information, especially as the newly promoted Lieutenant-Colonel Hawkins was racing back to England with news of the occupation.

Enclosing the correspondence that had so far been exchanged, Harney once again stressed to the Adjutant-General – based at Washington, DC – that he had sent Pickett, and was in the course of sending Casey, solely because of the 'insults and indignities' the British were offering the American residents 'on every occasion.' Hubbs, apparently, had made 'an official complaint' of 'the outrages perpetrated' on the United States citizens. The death of the pig was raised once again, with Cutler being treated 'with contempt' by Griffin, the Hudson's Bay Company chief factor arriving in a 'ship-of-war' and threatening to take the American to Victoria 'by force.' Even worse, the British had threatened to send the northern Indians to fall in force upon the Americans: 'I felt it my duty therefore to give these citizens the protection they sought with such just and pressing claims.' Skulduggery was clearly present, as was shown by the fact that:

Governor Douglas is the father-in-law of Mr Dallas and, having the local rank of vice-admiral, he commands the British navy in the Sound. This accounts in some measure for the use of the British ship-of-war in the supervision of the interests of the Hudson's Bay Company.

Consequently, as Harney would have it seen:

> To attempt to take, by armed force, an American citizen from our soil, to be tried by British laws, is an insult to our flag and an outrage upon the rights of our people, that has roused them to a high state of indignation.

In his final paragraph, Harney summed the situation up after protesting his own desire for a peaceful outcome:

> I desire to assure the department that while there is no one more desirous than myself for an amicable settlement of the difficulties raised by the British authorities of Vancouver's Island at this time, I shall use all the means at my command to maintain the position I have assumed in regard to San Juan island; being fully convinced that whatever respect and consideration might have been yielded to the statements of a doubtful claim advanced in due form, have been forfeited by the overbearing, insulting, and aggressive conduct her Majesty's executive officers have displayed not only towards our citizens but to the officer commanding our troops at San Juan.

Having sent the letter, Harney still fretted over the fact that he may not have given the Adjutant-General (and, therefore, the army high command and Congress) enough ammunition, not only to lend support to his actions, but also to demand swift retribution. The following day, 8 August, he sent another note, claiming that the British residents on San Juan Island had paid taxes through the American inspector of taxes (thus indicating recognition of United States sovereignty) and had 'never attempted to exercise any authority on the island, except clandestinely.' However, on Pickett's arrival, Douglas had promptly appointed 'a justice of the peace and other civil authorities.' Harney then continued:

> I believe I have now fully and fairly explained all the facts which have any bearing upon the occupation of San Juan island, which was made an imperious necessity by the wanton and insulting conduct of the British authorities of Vancouver's Island towards our citizens.

In his having 'fully and fairly explained all the facts,' Harney did not fail to include a wealth of wild exaggeration, distortion and downright lies.

12

Reinforcements

If General Harney's initial plan had misfired, Governor Douglas's idea of a proper response to the American occupation of San Juan Island had fallen equally flat. In common with the local press and many members of the colony's legislature, Douglas was at first dumbfounded and then outraged at the Royal Navy's failure to sweep the American troops into the sea. How could such an overwhelming British force still be sat in Griffin Bay while the invaders remained sat by their campfires? Even worse, as the seamen on the ships watched, the Americans began the erection of wooden buildings brought over from Fort Bellingham. The occupation was beginning to take on a permanent air, yet still the Royal Navy did nothing. To top it all, under the benign presence of the warships, such civil authority as remained on the island had begun to co-operate.

Just days after the arrival of the American troops, sellers of dubious alcoholic products appeared on the scene. The troops ashore, no doubt, welcomed the arrival of such a popular initiative, but the officers would have been considerably less accommodating. Justice Crosbie demanded that no alcohol be sold on the island without a licence issued by him and, in the 'prevailing state of affairs,' he would not be issuing any licences. The grog-sellers then had the temerity to apply to Major De Courcy, still on the island despite the proposal to remove him. De Courcy supported Crosbie and refused to issue a British licence – a refusal backed up by the threat to arrest anyone found selling alcohol. This was not quite the same as recognising Crosbie's authority, but clearly, where it was in the interest of both sides, De Courcy was not going to ignore, or run counter to, the American's actions.

In the meantime, Hornby had written to Douglas explaining his reasons for not ejecting the Americans. Firstly, his force far outweighed that of Pickett, an obvious fact that could be seen by everyone. Therefore, by not landing and attacking the Americans he would be seen as demonstrating both restraint and consideration for the lives of all concerned. Such a path of moderation would never bring the Union Flag into disrepute. Secondly, he had mobility of action, whereas Pickett's men would be either bound to their camp or scattered throughout the forest. Thirdly, if the British were protesting about the landing of soldiers on the island, it would hardly secure their case if they did the same. Finally, just because the Americans had behaved badly, there was no reason why the British should do likewise.

In addition, Hornby suggested to the governor that, after the French victory at Solferino, the situation in Europe was such that the British Government would not welcome an outbreak of hostilities with the United States over a small island at the southern end of the Gulf of Georgia – and that would surely happen if he landed a force to oppose Pickett.

Much to Douglas's discomfiture, Hornby had supporters ashore. Leading members of the Hudson's Bay Company had written to the governor expressing the view that, as the boundary commissioner Campbell was present at the landings, the orders must have come from the American Government, just as Pickett had informed Hornby. Also, with many Americans already established on Vancouver Island, there was the very real danger that an insurrection would break out if the troops on San Juan Island were attacked.

In an effort to play to the gallery, Douglas addressed the Legislative Council with the first formal announcement of the landings. In a curious mix of bombastic phrases and conciliatory wheedling, the governor attempted to keep the pot boiling. He was, he claimed:

> … forced to believe that the late unwarrantable and discourteous act, so contrary to the usages of civilised nations, has originated in error, and has been undertaken without the authority of that government.

After confirming the right of the British to the possession of San Juan Island, the consequent dispatch of the Royal Navy and the apparent disagreement between Pickett's orders and the presidential opinion expressed in Macy's letter of 1855, Douglas continued:

We may presume from that circumstance that the notice in question was framed in ignorance of the intentions of the United States government, and that the pretensions set forth will not be maintained. Entertaining such opinions, I have not failed to impress on her Majesty's naval officers now stationed at San Juan the desire of her Majesty's government to avoid every course which may unnecessarily involve the suspension of the amicable relations subsisting between Great Britain and the United States. At the same time, those officers have been instructed and are prepared to assert the rights and to maintain the honor and dignity of our sovereign and her dominions.

Hornby, torn between 'amicable relations' and asserting British 'rights' had followed neither path. Instead, he had concentrated on avoiding a violent clash and remained, with his far superior forces, in control of the situation.

Douglas remained unimpressed. He had a card up his sleeve that he would be able to play in a day or so. The governor's card, however, would prove to be from a different pack.

As the *Pylades* made her way south to deliver Lieutenant-Colonel Hawkins to San Francisco, she ran into strong south-easterlies that not only kept her offshore, but also delayed her passage to such an extent that it was decided that Hawkins would be better off taking a merchant steamer going directly to Panama. Consequently, Captain De Courcy turned his ship about and made, once again, for Esquimalt. As he did so, his lookouts sighted the magnificent, if outdated, 84-gun HMS *Ganges*, the flagship of the Pacific squadron bearing Rear Admiral Robert Baynes, a Scotsman who had seen action during the Napoleonic Wars, and had been on board the flagship at the Battle of Navarino in 1827. Knowing nothing of the situation on San Juan Island, his first reaction on being told by De Courcy was, 'Tut, tut! No, no; the damned fools!'

The *Ganges* arrived at Esquimalt on 5 August and Baynes repaired immediately to the governor's house. There he found Douglas ready to bring Hornby's lack of action to the admiral's attention. But, much to the governor's anger, Baynes stood resolutely by his captain. Hornby had behaved both correctly and honourably. By his conduct, the captain of the *Tribune* had – so far – prevented a war from breaking out, and Baynes intended to see that policy pursued as far as possible without injury to Britain's cause. Where Hornby, under the direction of Captain De Courcy, had taken hold of the situation in defiance of Douglas's instructions, Baynes was now to take charge in the name of the Admiralty. That was where his orders came from – not from Governor James Douglas.

The governor fumed at this turn of events, so different from what he had expected. In a letter he promptly penned to the Colonial Secretary, he complained that:

> … Hornby did not deem it advisable to carry out my instructions … the absence of movement of this kind has not only increased the confidence of the occupying party; and it places me in a difficult position, for so much time having elapsed the carrying out of the movement of this period, deprives it of most of its force.

In turn, Baynes informed the Secretary to the Admiralty that Douglas had actually allowed the American squatters to remain on San Juan Island, and had allowed Colonel Ebey to place revenue officials there. If the Americans had followed this up by landing troops, they could hardly be expected to do otherwise in the face of such lack of judgement and downright negligence from the governor.

However, with the admiral having taken the pressure off by his arrival, the Americans promptly brought it back on again.

Shortly after Baynes' arrival at Esquimalt, Lieutenant-Colonel Casey received General Harney's letter ordering him to reinforce Pickett. The colonel lost no time in responding to his new orders and set sail in the side-wheeler *Julia* from Fort Steilacoom, intending to land on San Juan Island in the early hours of Wednesday 10 August.

He had not long sailed when he fell in with the survey-vessel *Active*, under the command of Captain James Alden. Sent by Pickett with a message for Casey, Alden told the colonel it was likely that if he tried to land troops at Griffin Bay, he would come under the fire of the guns on board the *Tribune*. Casey noted the information, but decided to press on regardless (no doubt with the image of a glowering Harney firmly stamped on his mind).

En route to the island, Casey called in at Fort Townsend, where he found commissioner Campbell in retreat from a stinging exchange of letters with Captain Prevost. The captain, trying to discover if Campbell had prior knowledge of the occupation, had described the Americans landing as:

> … an act so unprecedented in the history of civilized and enlightened nations, and so contrary to that natural courtesy which is due from one great nation to another, cannot be productive of good …

Prevost continued to express his fervent hope that the commissioners between them could act to 'avert pending evil.'

Campbell, with little idea of what was going on, decided that a frontal attack was the only way to mask his ignorance. He replied:

> … there pervades in your whole communication a vein of assumption and an attempt at intimidation by exciting apprehensions of evil, not well calculated to produce the effect you profess so ardently to desire …

After further exchanges of letters in the same tenor, Prevost decided that to continue would be a waste of time and paper.

Now, after joining Casey on his voyage to San Juan Island, Campbell was, at last, made fully aware of the state of things right in the middle of his own area of responsibility – and he was not happy.

As the *Julia* approached San Juan Island in the early hours of the morning, Casey realised there was a possibility of coming under fire from the British, compounded by a heavy pall of fog lying over the island's southern end. The ship's captain was reluctant to enter Griffin Bay in such conditions, especially as the tide would then be at its lowest. Instead, the ship headed for the beach on the south-west of the peninsula, on the opposite side of the ridge from the bay. Dawn's arrival gave enough light to land the reinforcements and light howitzers they had brought. With his men safely ashore, Casey then took the *Julia* around the point and entered Griffin Bay to moor alongside the Hudson's Bay Company wharf. Sure enough, there was the *Tribune* with her guns run out. Undeterred, Casey started the unloading of the stores and ammunition, all of which was completed without being 'interfered' with by the British. Just as the task was about to be finished, Casey received an urgent note from Pickett requesting his presence at the American camp.

On having made his way to join Pickett, Casey was concerned to see that the *Satellite*, originally on her way from Esquimalt to join Hornby at Griffin Bay, had seen the activity ashore on the south-west beach and had positioned herself offshore to see what was going on. In Pickett's mind, Prevost was readying himself for an attack, as the ship was brought broadside-on to the beach. The Americans were certainly in a weak position. If the *Satellite* had opened fire from such close range, all that the troops could have done would be to have fled over the ridge behind them. This, of course, would have brought them under the guns of the *Tribune*. When asked by Casey what his plans were, Pickett could only come up with his original idea of spiking his guns and taking to the forest for shelter.

The colonel agreed, 'Not having time to form any well considered plan of my own, with regard to the state of affairs.' Yet another consequence of Harney's giving command of the operation to a junior officer.

Now, however, Casey was in charge and he sent an officer to the *Tribune* with a request that Captain Hornby would meet him at the camp 'for the purposes of a conference.' At first, Hornby declined, saying that he 'was much engaged' (a sure sign that he did not want to be seen jumping with indecent eagerness to the command of an American officer). Nevertheless, later in the day, Hornby arrived at the American camp in company with Captain Prevost and commissioner Campbell. After explaining why he had landed troops on the south beach, Casey then told Hornby that '... he regretted that Captain Pickett had been so much harassed and threatened in the position he had occupied.' When Hornby refused to comment, Casey went on to enquire who the senior officer was, and where he could be located. He was told that Admiral Baynes was in command and that he could be found at Esquimalt. At this, Casey announced that he 'wished to have a conference with the admiral' and that he 'would go down to Esquimalt the next day for the purpose of the interview.'

The following day, 11 August, the *Shubrick* steamed into Esquimalt harbour bearing Casey and Pickett in their dress uniforms along with commissioner Campbell. On mooring up, the colonel sent Pickett across to the *Ganges* with a note for Baynes. Forgetting where he was, Casey had headed the note 'United States Steamer *Shubrick*, Esquimalt Harbor, W.T.' It is unlikely that Baynes, or the governor (whom Pickett had also found in the admiral's cabin), would have been impressed with the colonel's apparent belief that he was still in Washington Territory (W.T.). The note read:

> Lieutenant Colonel Casey, United States army, commanding the forces on San Juan island , presents his compliments to Admiral Baynes, commanding her Britannic Majesty's naval forces on the Pacific Coast, and would be happy to meet the admiral in conference on board the United States steamer *Shubrick*, in the harbor, at his earliest convenience.

The gap between the rank of a rear admiral and a lieutenant colonel is just slightly wider than that between a naval and an army captain, but, whereas for the sake of progress Hornby had been prepared to visit Pickett in his camp, it would have been unthinkable for a flag officer – of any nation – to be rowed from his flagship to a lighthouse tender at the behest of a junior officer – *of any nation*. Especially under the stern, unbending eye of a critical governor. Baynes sent Pickett back with a reply:

Rear-Admiral Baynes presents his compliments to Lieutenant Colonel Casey, and regrets that circumstances prevent him from doing himself the honour of meeting Lieutenant Colonel Casey on board the *Shubrick*. But Rear-Admiral Baynes will have great pleasure in receiving Lieutenant Colonel Casey, or any one who may wish to accompany him on board the *Ganges*.

At this, Casey, imagining an insult, replied:

Lieutenant Colonel Casey regrets that circumstances prevent Rear-Admiral Baynes from accepting his invitation to meet him on board the *Shubrick* according to his request.

He then steamed from the harbour in high dudgeon, commenting that he:

was of the opinion that I had carried etiquette far enough in going 25 miles to see a gentleman who was disinclined to come 100 yards to see me.

So ended an intelligent initiative begun with good intent, but ending up on the rocks of protocol (or stubbornness – Casey had, after all, actually gone twenty-five miles, only to be 'disinclined' to go an extra 100 yards). To make matters worse, when Harney learned of Casey's visit to Esquimalt, he had his Adjutant-General inform the colonel that:

The general regrets, under all circumstances, your visit to Esquimalt harbor to see the British admiral, but is satisfied of your generous intention towards them. He instructs you for the future to refer all official communication desired by the British authorities to these headquarters, informing them at the same time that such are your orders.

The last thing that Harney wanted was a colonel using his initiative in a search for a peaceful outcome. He was, however, trying to arrange a promotion for Pickett.

The following day, the *Massachusetts* arrived at Griffin Bay bearing further reinforcements in the shape of Major Haller's troops. Once they had landed, the *Massachusetts*' eight 32-pounder cannons were unshipped and sent ashore, where, with their small-wheeled truck carriages, intended for use on the wooden decks of a ship, they were found to be 'rather difficult to manage.'

In addition to the eight cannon and a small number of howitzers, the Americans could muster fifteen officers and 424 men. Against them (including the *Ganges*) were ranged five warships mounting 167 guns, manned by 1,940 seamen and soldiers. Casey's reinforcements had reduced the odds to about four and a half to one, with close to two and a half Americans for every British heavy gun. Furthermore, Harney had managed to bottle up his entire northern command on a small island that could be very easily blockaded by the British.

13

The Chief Antagonists Correspond

As the *Massachusetts* was landing her guns, the Vancouver Island House of Assembly began putting forward its reply to Governor Douglas's address sent to it just over a week earlier. The members did so in a manner that showed them to be no different to politicians the world over who are safe from the dangers of the front line. The Speaker of the House opened by declaring that an opportunity had been missed. Instead of agreeing to the boundary commission, the British Government should have realised that the Americans 'worship' the dollar and simply purchased San Juan Island. Now, however:

A general on his own authority had invaded our territory. His grounds for doing so were based on falsehood and carried out clandestinely. What more could be expected of a man who has spent a lifetime in warring with Indians?

Even worse was the response:

His excellency sends troops and ships. Why all this expense and show if for parade? Why were not the troops landed? Instead of fighting, her Majesty's captains take to diplomacy. It shames me to think that the *Satellite* was running around after Commissioner Campbell. I am ashamed to think that post captains were holding a pow-wow with a subaltern of the American army. They should have landed their troops and avoided all degrading negotiations. But more troops have landed in spite of post captains and admirals. Yes, a militia must be raised. We must defend ourselves, for the position we occupy today would make the iron monument of Wellington weep, and the stony statue of Nelson bend his brow.

After some discussion on the merits or otherwise of not landing troops, the final address to the governor was approved. It read:

> The House acknowledges the receipt of your Excellency's communication of the 3rd instant relating to the clandestine invasion of San Juan island by United States troops, and the steps to be adopted in relation thereto.
>
> Since that communication it is well know that additional forces have been landed. The house would therefore inquire why the British forces were not landed to assert our just right to the island in question, and to uphold the honour of our country and our Queen.
>
> The House would most urgently impress upon your Excellency to enforce upon her Majesty's government the necessity of demanding from the government of the United States not only immediate withdrawal of those troops, but also strenuously and at all risks to maintain her right to the island in question, and also to all other islands in the same archipelago, now so clandestinely, dishonourably, and dishonestly invaded.
>
> It is not for our country to be wantonly and insolently insulted, but redress must be demanded.

The address ended with a demand that more colonists must be persuaded to come from Britain and that 'liberal grants of land' should be made as an inducement.

If the Governor was pleased to receive such support from the legislature, his pleasure would have been further boosted by the attitude taken by the local newspaper, the *British Colonist*. Beneath a banner headline that demanded 'Why were not Troops Landed at San Juan?,' the leading article built upon '… the severe strictures passed on our naval officers by the speaker.' It was almost beyond belief that 'the naval authorities had refused to land' and that such 'conduct is justly reprehensible.' The article continued:

> An error has been committed by somebody. Either the administration should have been satisfied with a pacific policy, manifested by serving the United States authorities with a formal protest or an assertion of our sovereignty in the first place and then allowed the matter to rest until

dispatches were received from the imperial government, or it should at once have landed troops on the island, without making such a display of force or asking permission.

Instead, the writer complained, 'we have made a grand and useless parade, and done nothing but render ourselves ridiculous.'

He would, no doubt, have had more to complain about had he seen the activities on San Juan Island. Casey had decided that Pickett's second camp was just as exposed to cannon fire as had been his first. Consequently, he chose a new site further to the west along the ridge and on ground sloping to the north. Although still exposed to gunfire from the sea, it had the advantage of rising ground to the east, which was soon in the process of being turned into a redoubt for the *Massachusetts'* cannon. This work was undertaken by the troops from the Corps of Engineers under the direction of Lieutenant Henry Robert, a young man of high ability which would see him eventually rise to the command of the entire corps.

Despite all the preparations for war, and to the outrage of the customs inspector, Hubbs, the two sides rubbed along well with each other. Colonel Casey would attend Sunday church services on board the *Satellite* alongside Captain Prevost and, as the Americans rowed their stores ashore, the ship's band played 'Yankee Doodle Dandy.' Hubbs had tried to cause a problem at one stage by refusing Major De Courcy permission to return to the island unless he paid revenue on his personal property. Casey, however, had Pickett warn Hubbs off and the matter was dropped.

On another occasion, the alarming sound of gunfire could be heard from the American camp. But those in the know could rest easy as the succession of sharp reports rolled out across the waters. The firing was a salute to Governor Richard Gholson, who had taken over Washington Territory from Isaac Stevens (Stevens himself, now the Representative to Congress for the Territory, had visited earlier, but only in a private capacity). When Harney had appealed to the governor for support in his occupation of San Juan Island, Gholson had nearly fallen over himself to be seen as loyal to the general's actions:

… should the contemplated emergency arise, your just expectation of the course to be pursued by myself shall *not* be disappointed, and that in such an event I have an abiding faith that the citizens of the Territory will with enthusiastic alacrity respond to any call necessary for the defense of individual rights, the rights of their country, or their county's honour.

Nevertheless, after carrying out a formal inspection of Casey's troops, he was pleased to be welcomed on board the *Satellite* to take tea and witness gunnery evolutions.

At this stage Douglas decided to write, once again, to Harney. After thanking the general for his 'frank and straightforward manner,' the governor pinned down one of Harney's major falsehoods:

> I am glad to find that you have done so [landed troops] under your military instructions from the President of the United States as military commander of the department of Oregon, and not by direct authority from the cabinet at Washington.

Of course, Harney had neither instructions from the President, nor the Washington Territory legislature. Douglas continued by assuring the general that Hudson's Bay Company officials had no more power than 'any of the other inhabitants of Vancouver's Island' and that no warships had been used during the chief factor's visit to San Juan Island. Harney's attention was then drawn to Marcy's letter of July 1855, with the almost sarcastic comment, 'a copy of which I herewith inclose for your information, as I presume that the document cannot be in your possession.' The governor then pointed out how he felt 'deep regret' that Harney had not communicated with him first to learn of the actual facts behind the pig-shooting incident, and that he had not taken advantage of the opportunity to raise the matter during their meeting at Victoria the previous month. Finally, having given '… a distinct and emphatic denial of the circumstances, which you allege induced you to occupy the island …,' Douglas ended with:

> I must call upon you, sir, if not as a matter of right at least as a matter of justice and humanity, to withdraw the troops now quartered upon the island of San Juan, for those troops are not required for the protection of American citizens against British authorities, and the continuance of those troops upon an island, the sovereignty of which is in dispute, not only is a marked discourtesy to a friendly government, but complicates to an undue degree the settlement in an amicable manner the question of sovereignty, and is also calculated to provoke a collision between the military forces of two friendly nations in a distant part of the world.

In his reply, Harney mentioned his pleasure at the 'prompt disavowal' of any intention to 'commit any aggression upon the rights of American citizens' and declared that he could not have raised the question of the pig incident with Douglas during his visit to Victoria as 'I was without knowledge that any occurrence had taken place on San Juan island to outrage the feelings of its inhabitants.' This was, to say the least, extremely unlikely, as Hubbs had met Pickett and Pickett had met Harney days before the general arrived to meet the governor. Nevertheless, in a weak attempt to underline the notion that he had authority to land troops on the island, the general ended by telling Douglas that he did 'not feel myself qualified to withdraw the present command from San Juan island, until the pleasure of the President of the United States has been made known on the subject.'

Expecting a reply from his superiors in the very near future, Harney dispatched another letter to the Adjutant-General at Washington, DC, on 29 August. Intended to confirm the righteousness of his actions, it was not long, once again, before he plunged into wild exaggerations and complete falsehoods:

> From the time of my assuming the command of this department until the occupation of San Juan island I was most careful neither to increase nor change the position of the force on Puget's sound, that there might be no misconceptions of my acts, on the part of the British, of the good faith which animated me in the observance of treaty stipulations. Time and again our light-houses were attacked, and the wives and children of our citizens on that coast were brutally murdered by British Indians.

The attacks on lighthouses came from nowhere but Harney's imagination. Nor, of course, did he mention that by moving Pickett from his post at Fort Bellingham, he had himself encouraged attacks on American citizens. Following a lurid description of the Hudson's Bay Company's alleged alliance with aggressive Indians (which included, bizarrely, the introduction of the far distant – and no longer existing – East India Company's 'barbarities and atrocities'), Harney reeled back in shocked disbelief:

> Judge, then, of my astonishment and mortification in my late visit to San Juan to find an unworthy advantage had been taken of my forbearance to outrage our people in the most insulting manner.

Yet again, the humble *Beaver* was transformed into a 'British ship-of-war,' the chief factor 'abuses one of our citizens in the harshest manner,' and Douglas's 'attempted denial' is nothing more than a 'quibble.' Finally, almost as an afterthought, yet another justification for the landing of troops was brought forward:

> From all the events which have occurred before and since the occupation of San Juan island, I am convinced the British Government have instituted a series of acts aiming at the eventual sovereignty of San Juan island, in consequence of its paramount importance as a military and naval station.

Not in itself a convincing reason for the invasion of a disputed territory, but a considerably better one than the death of a pig.

14

The President Becomes Involved

President James Buchanan was one of the must unusual men to hold that great office. Mild-mannered, unassuming and eager to please, he ended up pleasing no one. Born in Pennsylvania, Buchanan began his adult life as a lawyer and was, for a while, engaged to be married. Unfortunately, the agreement came to an abrupt end as the result of an unknown 'misunderstanding,' which led to the death of his former fiancée from 'hysteria' – or possible suicide. Never marrying, Buchanan became the only bachelor President, sharing accommodation with a former Vice-President (who was the only bachelor to hold that position). Although a northerner, he supported the principle of slaves being held as property, and gave his backing to the pro-slavery faction in Kansas Territory. A believer in 'Manifest Destiny,' he once declared that it was the will of God for his 'race to spread themselves over the continent of North America.' Consequently, as Secretary of State under President Polk, he had supported the 'Fifty-four Forty, or Fight!' policy until, alarmed at burgeoning British opposition, he proposed the 49th Parallel as the border, eventually becoming a signatory to the resultant treaty. At a time of peace and calm, Buchanan would have displayed all the qualities required of a great president. Sadly, however, his administration was weighed down with problems rising from the question of Southern slavery. The North was adamantly opposed to any compromise, his own party was on the verge of a fatal division between northerners and southerners, and Buchanan himself was seen to be withdrawing in the face of an overwhelming storm.

For Harney and his fellow-conspirators far away to the west, there could be no better time to rock a boat already on the verge of capsizing. In fact, they could look to the President himself for their inspiration. During his inaugural address, Buchanan had raised the problem of defending the Pacific states and had come up with the proposal to build a 'military road' to the west. The reason a road was needed was because:

> In the event of a war with a naval power much stronger than our own we should then have no other available access to the Pacific Coast, because such a power would instantly close the route across the isthmus of Central America.

Such words could easily have haunted Buchanan after his Secretary of State, Lewis Cass, urgently sought a meeting clutching in his hand Harney's 19 July letter to General Winfield Scott. The last thing the President wanted, with the very nation itself crumbling and cracking around him, was a war against Great Britain. And, who knows, such a war could have already broken out: the letter itself had been dispatched six weeks earlier. Even worse, the affair appeared to be the result of someone 'shooting a pig.'

At almost exactly the same time, the British Minister to Washington, DC, Richard Bickerton Pemmel Lyons, 2nd Baron Lyons of Christchurch, heard the news of the occupation. Lyons was the son of a Royal Navy officer and had himself served as a midshipman before entering the Diplomatic Service. He was fully aware of the American difficulties, and of the possibility of a deliberately engineered distraction, especially against the British. Now, from the newspapers, originating with a report in the *New York Herald*, Lyons found he was faced with the possibility that fighting had broken out in the far north-west. At a hastily arranged meeting with Cass, Lyons was handed a copy of a letter sent in reply to Harney. The letter was sent on 3 September by William Drinkard, the chief clerk at the War Department and the acting Secretary of War in the absence of the Secretary, John Floyd, and read:

> The President was not prepared to learn that you had ordered military possession to be taken of the island of San Juan or Bellevue. Although he believes the Straits of Haro to be the true boundary between Great Britain and the United States, under the treaty of June 15, 1846, and that, consequently, this island belongs to us, yet he had not anticipated that so decided a step would have been resorted to without instructions.

After a rather patronising definition of what was meant by the term 'dispute,' the letter then resorted to the usual Buchanan failure to grasp the problem:

> The President will not, for the present, form any decided opinion upon your course on the statement of facts presented in your dispatch. He will await further details, which he expects to receive from you by the next steamer. He is especially anxious to ascertain whether, before you proceeded to act, you had communicated with Commissioner Campbell, who could not then have been distant from you, and who was intrusted by this government, in conjunction with the British commissioner, to decide this very boundary question.
>
> In the meantime care ought to be taken to appraise the British authorities that possession has thus been taken solely with the view of protecting the rights of our citizens on the island, and preventing the incursions of the northern Indians into our territory, and not with any view of prejudging the question in dispute or retaining the island should the question be finally decided against the United States.

Lyons sent a telegram to the Foreign Secretary, Lord John Russell, explaining the situation and assuring Russell that the American Government had no knowledge of what was going on, nor did they give their support. He followed this up with a letter enclosing a copy of Drinkard's communication of the 3rd to Harney. Russell was not impressed. In reply he reminded Lyons that:

> It is of the nature of US citizens to push themselves where they had no right to go, and it is of the nature of the US government not to venture to disavow acts which they cannot have the face to approve.

The situation was not improved when Colonel Hawkins arrived at Washington, DC, with an eyewitness account of the events on San Juan Island and with dispatches from Douglas. Harney's role, its implications and its design became much clearer. Again Lyons demanded clarification from Cass: did the American Government know what was going on? Refusing to be intimidated, the Secretary of State tried to deflect the question by returning to the matter of the boundary. Almost as if in anticipation of what had happened, Lyons and Russell had corresponded a few weeks earlier on this very subject and the Foreign Secretary had come to the conclusion that approval of the middle channel should be sought. If agreed, Russell's proposal would guarantee San Juan Island to the British, a situation from which he would not budge:

> Her Majesty's government must, therefore, under any circumstances, maintain the rights of the British Crown to the island of San Juan. The interests at stake in connection with the retention of that island are too important to admit of compromise, and your lordship will consequently bear in mind that whatever arrangement as to the boundary line is finally arrived at, no settlement of the question will be accepted by Her Majesty's government which does not provide for the island of San Juan being reserved to the British Crown.

When Lyons brought this to Cass's attention, the Secretary of State thought otherwise, arguing that the British had been given Vancouver Island in its entirety despite the fact that its southern end lay south of the 49th Parallel. Refusing to accede to Russell's stand over San Juan Island, Cass replied:

> If this declaration is to be insisted upon, it must terminate the negotiations at its very threshold; because this government can permit itself to enter into no discussion with that of Great Britain, or any other power, except upon terms of perfect equality.

In Britain, the press had now got hold of journalistic versions of the story and were not getting too excited about it. According to the *Illustrated Times* of 4 September:

> The belligerent parties have both means at hand for aggressive measures, four vessels of war representing the Government of the United States, and three that of Great Britain … There was a doubtful rumour that the British steamer *Satellite* had attacked the island and killed thirty Americans. Upon the whole there is no fear of a rupture.

The editorial of the same day, under the headline 'The Last Little American Difficulty,' noted:

> Our Yankee cousins have a small bit of political tactics which rather ought to excite the mirth than the anger of the British people. It consists in getting up, every now and then, a little 'difficulty' with this country, which for a while blazes away in the newspapers and at public meetings, and finally

disappears, in smoke, without serious results … One might be apt to think that, if quarrelling with Britain is popular, Britain must be hated by the American populace. But that would be a mistake. It is not hatred of Britain, but conceit in themselves, that is the attraction of these little disputes to the Yankees … They like excitement – talk; in fact, the pleasure of seeming to be going to war, yet with a secret assurance that they won't, which adds to the piquancy. And Britain is the only Power of which the States can be jealous, for all other Powers are exposed to their contempt, as not being free or not being 'Anglo-Saxon.' The fact that we are infinitely stronger than they – for they have as good as no standing Navy – would calm a less knowing and lively race.

In fact, the Americans, through General Harney, had done no more than commit 'a breach of international courtesy.'

What the editor did not know at that stage, was that Harney's letter announcing that he had landed heavy guns and reinforcements on San Juan Island had arrived in Washington, DC, and even Buchanan had woken up to the threat. No longer could the President, Secretary of State and the Secretary of War sit back in the hope that the matter might blow over. Something had to be done – and they knew who would have to do it.

15

Scott Arrives on the Scene

In the early hours of 21 October, General Harney was fast asleep in his quarters at Fort Vancouver. He had dealt with Drinkard's letter as best he could under the circumstances. Replying to the Secretary of War, John Floyd (a pro-slavery southerner who was under investigation for sending government contracts and guns to the South), Harney had dismissed the suggestion that he had not consulted commissioner Campbell on the grounds that 'no exigency had arisen requiring it.' To the Commissioner himself, Harney had used the excuse that 'I was informed that you were en route to Washington.' To Floyd, the general continued with a farrago of falsehoods:

> I would respectfully call the attention of the President to the unqualified denial of Governor Douglas, in his dispatch of the 13th August, that any attempt had ever been made to arrest an American citizen and convey him to Victoria to be tried by British laws. At the very moment this denial was being penned, three British ships of war were in that harbor, by the orders of Governor Douglas, to support a British stipendiary magistrate sent by Douglas to arrest the same American citizen (Cutler,) of San Juan, who would have been arrested but for the positive interference of Captain Pickett; indeed, so pressing and urgent were the British to possess themselves of Cutler, that Captain Pickett did not hesitate to report his capture could only be averted by occupying the island in force.

So, quite clearly, everything was the fault of the British. Douglas had sent three warships and a magistrate to arrest Cutler, in consequence of which

Pickett landed gallantly to protect a fellow American. The fact that he was, in effect, actually writing to the President of the United States did not prevent Harney from completely inverting the entire story. Still, the letter had been sent only eleven days before, and there was plenty of time for events to topple out of control before any call for clarification could come from Washington, DC.

It could only have come as a surprise, therefore, that at two o'clock in the morning a sharp knock on his bedroom door announced that Lieutenant-Colonel George Lay wished to speak to him. To Harney's sleepy brain it must have seemed like a nightmare, as Lay announced that the General-in-Chief of the Army, General Winfield Scott, was on board the steamer *Northerner* – at that moment moored off Fort Vancouver.

At this staggering news, Harney began to rouse himself, but Lay informed him that General Scott was asleep, and would not require the brigadier-general until eight o'clock that morning. It is, however, unlikely that Harney returned to a peaceful slumber throughout the small hours.

Although General Scott was aged seventy-two, considerably overweight, suffering from gout and was recovering from a riding accident, Buchanan, Cass and Drinkard knew there was no other man who could be depended upon to handle the situation on San Juan Island, whatever it was. Even though he was not noted for his vindictiveness, for Scott there was also the inevitable pleasure of being able to bring to heel the maverick Harney, the same man who, through his connections, had thwarted him during the Mexican War. Accepting the commission without delay, Scott received a letter from Drinkard:

> The President has been much gratified at the alacrity with which you responded to his wish that you would proceed to Washington Territory to assume the immediate command, if necessary, of the United States forces on the Pacific coast.

After explaining the background to the problem arising from the 1846 treaty (and confirming the American view that the Canal de Arro was the channel intended by the treaty), the letter drew his attention to an enclosed copy of the response by Marcy in 1855. From there, Drinkard explained further, 'General Harney deemed it proper' to put Captain Pickett and his company on the island. An action, and the subsequent events, which 'present a condition of affairs demanding the serious attention of this government.' The letter continued:

It is impossible at this distance from the scene, and in ignorance of what may have already transpired on the spot, to give you positive instructions as to your course of action. Much, very much, must be left to your own discretion, and the President is happy to believe that discretion could not be intrusted to more competent hands. His main object is to preserve the peace and prevent collision between the British and American authorities on the island until the question of title can be adjusted by the two governments. Following out of the spirit of Mr Marcy's instructions to Governor Stevens, it would be desirable to provide, during the intervening period, for a joint occupation of the island, under such guards as will secure the tranquillity without interfering with our rights. The President perceives no objection to the plan proposed by Captain Hornby, of her Majesty's ship *Tribune*, to Captain Pickett …

If Scott found that a 'collision' had already taken place, such an incident 'would vastly complicate the case, especially if blood shall have been shed:'

It would be a shocking event if the two nations should be precipitated into a war respecting the possession of a small island, and that only for the brief period during which the two governments may be peacefully employed in settling the question to which of them the island belongs.

If, on the other hand, the British had attempted to seize the island by force, the President felt justified that Scott would not 'suffer the national honor to be tarnished.'

Yet, while Buchanan's justification of Scott's appointment may have been based on the sound facts of the general's experience, there may have been a darker side to his choice. The political arena was full of parties, groups and even states actively and loudly lining up against each other. But his was more than a political matter. Already there was talk of states seceding from the Union, and that could only mean open conflict. The President (although a northerner) had shown not the slightest leanings towards the cause of abolitionism, the Secretary of State had lost his own attempt at the presidency thanks to opposition from an anti-slavery faction and the Secretary of War was a southerner. Virginia-born Scott was also a southerner, but one who could be guaranteed to support the Union cause. What better move could be made than to send the General-in-Chief of the Army to the farthest, most remote place in the country?

The news of Scott's appointment soon reached the British press. The *Illustrated Times* reported:

General Scott has been ordered to go to the Pacific with a view of dealing with the [San Juan] question on the part of the Government at Washington. General Scott is a very aged individual, of great diplomatic experience; and it is to be hoped that his instructions are that nothing offensive to England is to be permitted.

This rather mild reporting was supported by a far more bombastic editorial:

In the great Western World, things look more peaceful again. The President has superseded the blustering rover who attacked the British Empire with seventy men and was extinguished by quiet contempt. As even America can hardly produce two Generals of such foolish audacity, we may trust that all danger from the San Juan difficulty is over. But we can promise Harney and his tribe that unlimited concession will not be made, and that if, after calm inquiry, our rights prove indisputable, they will be maintained as such. We can hardly fancy anything more contemptible, than an audacity which does not even rest on strength – which, like the calculated insolence of a low fellow to his betters, is safe from the very superiority of the party assailed. 'England is very strong, very reasonable, and very peaceful; she would not like to shed kindred blood: let us have a blow at her!' This is the reasoning of the Harneys, who squirt out insolence as they do tobacco juice. Luckily, the better class of Americans are wiser and more honourable men; and the outrage, being atoned for, will in due time be forgotten, along with Harney himself.

Scott had left his headquarters at New York in the side-wheel steamer *Star of the West*, taking with him as his aide-de-camp Lieutenant-Colonel Lay. He also took his assistant adjutant, Colonel Lorenzo Thomas, and Dr Charles Crane. The party crossed the Panama isthmus and boarded the mail steamer *Northerner*, whose captain had knocked two staterooms into one to give the general more room.

At eight o'clock on the morning of the 21st, Harney reported to Scott, who told the brigadier-general that he was on his way to Portland for a few ceremonial events. As the *Northerner* clattered up the Columbia River, Scott looked at a number of letters and dispatches that Harney had brought with him, but made no comment regarding his orders from the President. After having spent much of the day kicking his heels as bands played and salutes were exchanged, Harney was, at last, called into Scott's stateroom. Seizing the opportunity, the brigadier-general began forcibly to state his case. Scott cut him short, and told him that, whether he liked it or not, the British were to be offered joint occupation of the island.

Aghast at what he was being told, and ignoring the possibility that a joint occupation could also lead to a 'collision,' Harney loudly protested. Again Scott silenced him, snapping, 'We've both got our superiors!'

The situation did not improve for Harney. Scott rescinded the punishments the brigadier-general had applied to his recalcitrant junior officers, and then proceeded heavily to suggest that Harney should leave his current post and take up an appointment at St Louis, Missouri. Such a move, with its greater responsibility, would, in effect, amount to a promotion. What was important, however, was that Harney be removed from the scene of the potential conflict. Scott urged Harney to consider seriously the move and to give him an answer as soon as possible.

At Fort Vancouver Scott found that, by sheer chance, Captain Pickett had arrived at the headquarters that day to sit as the judge-advocate of a court martial. Interviewed in a none too gentle manner by the General-in-Chief, the shaken Pickett was able to state that all was quiet on San Juan Island and that only one British vessel – the *Satellite* – remained in Griffin Bay.

The *Northerner* sailed the next day and Scott managed to annoy Governor Gholson by not calling upon him during his passage to Fort Townsend. Immediately on his arrival, Scott wrote to Governor Douglas, sending Colonel Lay over to Victoria with the letter. In it Scott made a solid proposal:

> Without prejudice to the claim of either nation, to the sovereignty of the entire island of San Juan, now in dispute, it is proposed that each shall occupy a separate portion of the same by a detachment of infantry, riflemen, or marines, not exceeding one hundred men, with their appropriate arms only, for the equal protection of their respective countrymen in their person and property, and to repel any descent on the part of hostile Indians.

Although Scott had made a firm proposition, he had no intention of imposing his proposal without discussion:

> In modification of this basis any suggestion his excellency may think necessary, or any addition he may propose, will be respectfully considered by the undersigned.

While waiting for a reply, Scott decided to have a look at the contested island himself, taking the *Massachusetts* as his means of transport. As he crossed over the Straits of Juan de Fuca, the *Northerner* hove into view carrying an acknowledgement of his letter from Douglas. It was an unfortunate meeting. As the mail packet came alongside, she collided with the *Massachusetts*, carrying away the army vessel's jib-boom and losing her own ensign staff, the ensign itself falling into the cold waters and bobbing up and down like a doleful omen.

As a result, the troops on San Juan and the seamen on board the *Satellite* were treated to the sight of a battered headquarters ship steaming slowly passed the southern end of the island. Scott had decided he did not need to land, and pressed on instead to Bellingham Bay. It was a mistake. On his return to Fort Townsend to see if a reply had arrived from Douglas, the *Massachusetts* grounded herself firmly on to a sandbank less than 100 yards from the Smith Island lighthouse. In consequence of Scott's presence, for the next twenty-four hours the headquarters of the entire United States Army was a battered steam vessel aground on a sand bar.

Douglas had taken three days before drafting his reply. After expressing his 'warm congratulations' on Scott's arrival, the governor turned the proposal down. Whereas Scott had been 'specially accredited' by his government, Douglas was 'not in possession of the views of her Majesty's government' and was, therefore, 'not at liberty to anticipate the course they may think fit to pursue.'

Instead of dividing the island between the troops of the two nations, Douglas made a different proposal:

> I would submit, therefore, for your consideration, that for the protection of the small British and American population settled on the island there should be a joint civil occupation, composed of the present resident stipendiary magistrates, with such assistants as may be necessary, and that the military and naval forces, on both sides, be wholly withdrawn.
>
> Should it, however, hereafter appear that a military force is indispensable for protection, I can see no objection to such a force being landed upon San Juan, with such understanding as the British and American authorities may mutually determine upon.

Scott (by now anchored in Padilla Bay, on the mainland) was disappointed, but not downhearted:

> It is with regret I learn that the basis for the settlement of the immediate San Juan difficulty I had the honor to submit has not received your acceptance, and that sentiment is deepened at finding myself unable to accept your proposed substitute. We ought not, however, to despair

of finding the means of maintaining the peace of the frontier till the good sense and good feelings of our governments shall have had time to supervene and directly to dispose of the whole subject of the disputed island forever.

The insistence that the American troops be removed from the island was surely unnecessary. Such a demand had not been made by Lord Lyons, Her Majesty's Minister to Washington, DC, and therefore the British Government's representative to the United States. Once again, Scott laid out his proposal, in a formal '*Projet of a Temporary Settlement, Etc.*' for a joint occupation (a *Projet* being a plan or draft document, usually for a treaty). Camps would be established at a different part of the island for 100 soldiers, and with each commanding officer given the power to arrest and punish any civilian troublemakers from their own nation.

Douglas replied immediately. Yet again, he could not 'assent to, or carry into effect' Scott's proposal. He was, after all, only 'authorised to maintain treaties as they exist.' The governor then reminded the general that the British were the innocent party in the events that had happened:

> You must permit me, sir, further to add, that her Majesty's authorities in this colony have, with respect to the United States, committed no violation of existing treaty stipulations, nor have been guilty of any act of discourtesy whatsoever towards the government of that nation, but have on all occasions during the late exciting events exhibited a degree of forbearance which will, I trust, be accepted as a guarantee that by no future act will we seem to impair the pacific relations existing between Great Britain and the United States.

Then, after consulting Admiral Baynes, Douglas reiterated their position regarding the disposition of armed forces on or about the island:

> Should you, sir, after the explanations I have herein given in reference to my official powers and position, proceed to carry out your pacific mission, and divest the large military force now on San Juan of its menacing attitude by removing it from the island, we will instantly withdraw the British naval force now maintained there.

In his own eyes, the governor's proposal could have only meant one thing: that *all* the American troops should be removed from the island. Instead, Scott chose to read the words quite differently. The '*large* military force' could be taken to mean 'as opposed to the *small* military force.' Seeing light where none actually existed, the general replied:

> I do not hesitate at once to order the number of United States troops on that island to be reduced to the small detachment (Captain Pickett's company of infantry) originally sent hither in July ... A copy of my orders in the case I inclose herewith for the information of your excellency. They will be fully executed as soon as practicable by the employment of the propeller *Massachusetts*, the only craft suited to the purpose in these waters.

After having dispatched the reply, Scott, realising that he may have made a mistake, had Colonel Thomas follow it up with an addendum. Instead of Pickett's company, another company, under the command of Captain Lewis Cass Hunt (a relative of the Secretary of State), would remain. This last-minute change of commander fell in by chance with British ideas. Vancouver Island's Colonial Secretary, William Young, had written to Scott that, 'Captain Pickett is of somewhat hasty temperament and somewhat punctilious and exacting.' Far better that the Americans should leave someone in command who would oversee 'a continuation of perfect harmony and tranquillity, until the unfortunate question of title may be forever set at rest.'

Over-riding a recent command from General Harney that Forts Bellingham and Townsend were to be closed down, Scott's final order read:

> As soon as practicable Lieutenant Colonel Casey or other commanding officer on the island of San Juan will proceed to send therefrom all the companies under his orders, except Captain Hunts, to the posts at which they previously belonged, vis: Company I of the 4th infantry to Fort Townsend; company A of the 4th and H of the 9th infantry to Fort Steilacoom; company D of the 9th infantry to Fort Bellingham; and last, the companies of the 3rd artillery to Fort Vancouver.
>
> Captain Hunt and his company and Assistant Surgeon Craig will remain on the island till further orders for the protection of the American settlers.
>
> Lieutenant Colonel Casey will cause the heavy guns on the island to be replaced aboard of this propeller, and will send the light battery to Forts Townsend, Bellingham, and Steilacoom.

Whether he liked it or not, Douglas had been outmanoeuvred by the general. The Americans' speedy response to what they had seen as an opportunity to reduce the pressure had left him floundering. He could hardly object to the reduction in forces, nor could he keep the warships standing by in Griffin Bay, as he had assured Scott that 'by no future act will we seek to impair the pacific relations existing between Great Britain and the United States.' Only by the removal of the ships could he demonstrate his continued goodwill and preserve his honour. He certainly could no longer seek the ejection of the remaining infantry company from the island. It was, nevertheless, a marked improvement over the situation created by Harney. Not, of course, that the brigadier-general had given up his grand plan: Scott's design for peace could still be brought down.

1. The Great Seal of the United States, 1782. (*All images are author's collection*)

2. Captain David Porter, of the USS *Essex*

3. President James Monroe (1817–25)

4. *Above:* Captain James Hillyar of the HMS *Phoebe*

5. *Right:* Governor James Douglas

6. *Below:* The United States Military Commission to the Russians during the Crimean War

7. *Above left:* Colonel Isaac Ebey, the United States Customs Collector for Washington Territory, who was shot and beheaded by Indians in 1857

8. *Above right:* James Prevost as a rear admiral. He commanded HMS *Satellite* and was commissioned to survey the water boundary

9. *Above:* Charles Griffin, agent for the Hudson Bay Company, whose pig was the cause of all the trouble

10. The Hudson Bay Company's ship *Beaver*

11. *Above:* The British Land Boundary Commission. Captain John Hawkins is seated in the centre

12. *Left:* HMS *Satellite*

13. *Above:* President Polk (1845–9)

14. *Right:* Captain George Pickett

15. Fort Vancouver, headquarters of the Hudson Bay Company, later to be the headquarters of General Harney

16. HMS *Tribune* with her guns run out

17. HMS *Ganges* flying the flag of a rear admiral at the foretop

18. General Winfield Scott, General-in-Chief of the United States Army

19. Colonel Silas Casey, commander of Fort Steilacoom on Puget Sound

20. Captain Geoffrey Phipps Hornby of the HMS *Tribune*

21. United States troops at their first camp on San Juan Island

22. *Left:* General William Selby Harney, who was appointed to the military command of the Department of Oregon in 1858

23. *Below:* The British camp with its blockhouse at the water's edge and Young Hill to the rear

24. *Bottom:* An early photograph of the British camp. Accommodation is still beneath canvas and the fenced-in vegetable garden is under construction

25. *Above left:* Captain Lewis Cass Hunt, who replaced Captain Pickett on San Juan Island

26. *Above right:* Colonel George Wright, who replaced General Harney as commander of the Department of Oregon

27. *Left:* Captain George Bazalgette, the first commander of the British detachment on San Juan Island

28. *Top:* British reinforcements leave for Canada

29. *Above:* The American camp

30. *Left:* HMS *Forward*

31. *Left:* Major-General Isaac Stevens, Governor of Washington Territory

32. *Above:* Major-General Irvin McDowell, Commander of the Pacific Department

33. *Below:* Captain William Delacombe with his family on the steps of their quarters at the British camp

34. Map of San Juan Island showing the British and American camps

35. The land border cutting a swathe through the pine forests marking the border of the 49th Parallel

36. Royal Marines on parade at the British camp

37. The *Alabama* Claims Commission in session

38. Wilhelm I, Emperor of Germany, who eventually made the decision on the San Juan water boundary

39. The Royal Marines garrison on parade at the British Camp

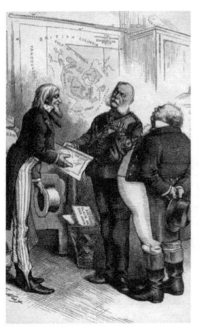

40. *Above left:* The Emperor of Germany awards the San Juan Islands to the United States in front of a wall map of the island. Great Britain's case is in the waste paper bin

41. *Above right:* Admiral James Prevost

42. The Royal Marines pose for a last photograph before leaving San Juan Island

43. In an American cartoon, Nova Scotia sets sail for the United States under a flag bearing the words 'We Want to Annex'. Awaiting them is another flag with the word 'Welcome'. Meanwhile, a Newfoundland dog looks on with interest

44. Americans fighting alongside the Boers at Ladysmith. Webster Davis, who tried to drum up support for the Boers in America, stands in the centre with his hands behind his back

A Different War Looms

As Casey began to plan for the partial evacuation of San Juan Island, two dark clouds appeared on the horizon. Of least concern was the complaint of an Irish-born entrepreneur named William Moore, who, claiming American citizenship, peddled rum and other liquor to the American troops. Such activities, however, were illegal, and Moore ended up in front of Magistrate Crosbie. Found guilty, he was put to work the next day alongside military prisoners digging trenches, until a constable named Cutler (almost certainly the pig-killing squatter who had started all the trouble) took him before Crosbie once again. This time the magistrate ordered Moore to pay $75 before discharging him. At this stage, the outraged Irishman suddenly remembered that he was, in fact, British. Taking his canoe across to Victoria he lodged a complaint with Douglas, who had no option but to raise the matter with the Americans. Scott, believing that Moore had 'grossly mis-stated or exaggerated his case,' passed the affair on to Casey. In the end, the matter simply fizzled out if for no better reason than nobody could really be bothered with it.

A second problem was considerably more important, as it bore the stamp of Harney's further efforts to stir up difficulties. As noted earlier, on 11 August, Colonel Casey had sailed across to Esquimalt in the hope of meeting Admiral Baynes, only to find that the admiral would not meet him on board the *Shubrick*, offering instead to meet Casey on board the flagship. At this the colonel had left the harbour, noting that he:

… was of the opinion that I had carried etiquette far enough in going 25 miles
to see a gentleman who was disinclined to come 100 yards to see me.

Even worse, as far as Casey was concerned, was that he earned Harney's rebuke
for his efforts. Now, ten weeks after his visit to Esquimalt, Casey wrote again to
Harney telling him that, in his letter to the general about the visit, he did not:

> … state the principle reason which governed me in not proceeding to the
> flag ship *Ganges*, for the purpose of having an interview with the admiral
> on board that ship, in the harbor of Esquimault. I have thought it due to
> myself, that the reason should be made known to the general commanding
> the department, and I should respectfully that the following be considered a
> part of my communication of the 12th of August, 1859.

After he had landed with reinforcements, Casey had met Captains
Hornby and Prevost, along with Commissioner Campbell, on 10 August.
During the meeting he had asked Hornby the whereabouts of the senior
naval officer. The captain had replied that Baynes was at Esquimalt. At this,
Casey informed Hornby that he wished to have an interview with the
admiral and would be going over to the harbour to do so. However,
according to Casey's new letter to Harney:

> Soon after my conference with Captain Hornby, I was informed by
> Mr Campbell, the United States Commissioner, that Rear-Admiral Baynes
> was actually on board the British steamship *Tribune*, in the harbor of San
> Juan island, at the very time I was informed by Captain Hornby in the
> presence of the British and American commissioners, that the admiral was
> at Esquimault harbor, twenty-five miles distance.
>
> I was somewhat astonished at this, and considered that I had not been
> dealt by with that openness and candor which the object to be brought
> about seemed to demand.
>
> I resolved notwithstanding this, to comply with my promise to meet
> the admiral at Esquimault harbor; but knowing what I did, thought it not
> incumbent on me to repair on board the *Ganges*, for the purpose of the
> contemplated interview.

This was an extraordinary suggestion. Casey appears to have been saying
that, after being told by Campbell that Admiral Baynes was on board
the *Tribune* in Griffin Bay at the time of the meeting with Hornby and
Prevost, he still took the *Shubrick* across to Esquimalt, only to return

deliberately without seeing the admiral. He then informed the general of his actions (missing out the part about Campbell's information), invented the '100 yards' story, was censored by Harney for his troubles and then, two and a half months later, rewrote the events as an example of British villainy. Why Baynes would have been skulking on board the *Tribune* is not revealed, nor why (in an unheard-of deviation from hallowed practice) Baynes did not have his flag flying from the *Tribune's* mizzen top. The only answer, of course, was that Baynes was never on board in the first place.

Not that such a consideration would have stopped Harney from taking full advantage of such an apparent indignity (nor bar the general from being a possible source of the suggestion). In full Harneyesque flow, the general informed Scott that he was so outraged at the show of:

> … duplicity and bad faith exercised towards us by both the colonial and naval authorities of Great Britain in reference to San Juan island, that I desire to place it on record.
>
> This statement exposes three high officials of her Britannic Majesty's service, viz: the British commissioner, the admiral, and the senior captain of the navy in these waters to the imputation of having deliberately imposed a wilful falsehood upon the authorities of a friendly nation to advance the sinister designs of the British government in obtaining territory that rightfully belongs to the United States.
>
> Is it too much to suppose they would be found guilty of like conduct should they be permitted to assume a position in which it would aid their purposes?

Scott, not about to be taken in by the synthetic ranting and manufactured outrage of Harney, and eager to lose none of the advantage he had gained, ignored the letter's doubtful premise. He was, however, reminded of something much more important. There had been no response to his suggestion that Harney accept a transfer to St Louis, Missouri. Clearly it was time to press the point home.

As the *Massachusetts*, damaged after her grounding, limped towards San Francisco, she came across the *Northerner* and Scott transferred himself and his staff on to the mail steamer for a more speedy voyage. It was probably a mistake for, shortly after the transfer, the ship suffered boiler damage and had to go inshore. Scott took the opportunity to write to Harney:

> I have no doubts that one of the preliminary demands which will be made by the British government upon ours, in connection with your occupation of the island of San Juan, will be your removal from your present command.

In such an event it might be a great relief to the President to find you, by your own act, no longer in command.

I make the suggestion from public considerations solely, and have not received the slightest hint to that effect from Washington.

To take effect in conformity with your own wishes, I inclose herewith a conditional order to repair to St. Louis, Missouri, and assume the command of the department of the west.

If you decline the order, and I give you leave to decline it, please throw it into the fire; or, otherwise, before setting out for the east, call your next in rank to you, and charge him with the command of the department of Oregon.

Even though the letter contained a clear implication that Scott wanted Harney out of the area, Colonel Thomas was instructed to enclose an actual order to that effect:

Brigadier General Harney will repair to St. Louis, Missouri, and assume command of the department of the west. Colonel Wright, 9th infantry, or the next senior present, will be charged, until further orders, with the command of the department of Oregon, and will be instructed to repair to Fort Vancouver.

By command of Lieutenant General Scott.

There was now no mistaking the General-in-Chief's intentions. It was clear to all that Harney was to transfer immediately to the east. Clear to all, that is, except Harney. Events in the east, perhaps even unknown to Scott, had shaken the nation.

On 16 October, the Federal Armoury at Harper's Ferry had been attacked by twenty-two men under the command of a leading abolitionist named John Brown. It was believed by Brown and his followers that the capture of the armoury would trigger a slave uprising throughout the South. In fact, not a single slave rose in support. Consequently, Brown was captured and hanged. News of the alarming incident would have been flashed to Fort Leavenworth, Kansas, by telegraph and then taken overland to Fort Vancouver. It was no time for Harney to buckle under Scott's demands, not whilst there was still time to trigger a distracting international incident in the far north-west.

As a result, on receipt of the General-in-Chief's letter, the brigadier-general replied, informing his superior officer:

I am not disposed to comply with such an order. I do not believe the President of the United States will be embarrassed by any action of the British government in reference to San Juan island; nor can I suppose the President would be pleased to see me relinquish this command in any manner that does not plainly indicate his intentions towards the public service.

I am, sir, very respectfully, your obedient servant.

Furthermore, through Governor Gholson – no friend of Scott's after the General-in-Chief had advocated civil authority on San Juan to be subordinated to the military – Harney had the Washington Territory legislature pass a resolution commending his actions. This appealed to the President 'to continue the present able, experienced, and prudent officer in command.'

This was countered by Scott on his return to Washington, DC, writing to the Secretary of War, underlining his view of Harney:

The highest obligation of my station compels me to suggest a doubt whether it be safe in respect to our foreign relations, or just to the gallant officers and men of the Oregon Department, to leave them longer, at so great a distance, subject to the ignorance, passion, and caprice, of the present headquarters of that Department.

The British press only managed to get half the story:

General Scott has arrived in the island of San Juan, and has superseded Harney, who is said to have left the place in much disgust.

The Fort Victoria press, however, managed to find a lighter side to the problems. Under the headline 'San Juan Question Settled,' the *Victoria Gazette* went on to explain:

A joint occupation of the Island of San Juan has been agreed upon. Paul K Hubbs, Esq., U.S. Revenue collector for the Island of San Juan, on the part of the United States, and Miss Flora Ross, a true and loyal subject of Her Majesty, Queen Victoria, resident of Bellevue, on the part of Great Britain, have agreed to enter into a matrimonial connection, and jointly occupy the Island.

It is to be assumed that the future Mrs Hubbs might have had a thing or two to say about her husband's involvement in an attempt to engage their respective countries in a war. He certainly played no more part in the unfolding events.

17

The Royal Marines Arrive

Captain Lewis Hunt was a man of fixed opinion. He had little time for 'popular' (i.e. democratic) government and was outraged at the Washington Territory legislature's resolution backing Harney. It was, he felt:

> … the legitimate result of popular government. It was to please the dear people that Harney made his coup, and he did please the people, silly, blind, fools that they are.

As for the brigadier-general himself, Hunt was of the opinion that he was 'our silly stupid commander' and 'a reckless, stupid, old goose' who was a 'dull animal.' Hunt also had little time for Pickett. When Scott's Assistant Adjutant-General, Colonel Thomas, had written to him with his instructions, they had contained the words:

> These papers will show the spirit in which it is expected you will execute the delicate and important trust confided in you, the general having full confidence in your intelligence, discretion, and (in what is of equal importance in this case) your courtesies.

Hunt took this to be a list of qualities found lacking in Pickett, along with his own impression that his predecessor had shown 'poor judgement.' He was particularly annoyed at that part of his instructions which read:

Captain Pickett will, of course, be at liberty to take back to Fort Bellingham the property carried over to the island, such as doors, window-sash, etc, as also his company property, but it is hoped that some part of the excellent shelter he erected may be transferred to you.

Captain Hunt managed to persuade Pickett to leave the buildings intact, only to find himself presented with an invoice for $300. The situation between the two men was not improved when Hunt piled all of Pickett's company stores remaining on the island into a schooner, which was promptly driven onto rocks and wrecked with the loss of most of the stores. Ironically, the vessel was named *General Harney*.

To add to his woes, Hunt was faced with increasing problems with the clutch of wooden huts that had grown up around the Hudson's Bay Company wharf on Griffin Bay. The establishment of the camp had led to an increasing influx of whisky-sellers, gamblers and prostitutes, who gleefully preyed upon the (not altogether unwilling) soldiers. In an attempt to combat this menace, Hunt had the magistrate (a man named Newsome, who had replaced Crosbie) set up a court to try the whisky-dealers. Not only did he find that no jury would convict the miscreants, and that the magistrate resigned in disgust, but that Harney wrote to him demanding he:

… make a full and complete report to these Headquarters of all your actions affecting citizens up to this time, and hereafter you will take no steps regarding them without reporting the same immediately to this office.

Exasperated and annoyed by this response, Hunt sent a 'salty' reply back, along with a petition from the 'actual settlers upon the island, and tillers of the soil' who demanded '… that a stop should be put to the unlicensed and uncontrolled liquor dealing carried on upon the island,' and that 'military power may be brought to bear promptly for the suppression of this great nuisance in our midst.' With realistic pessimism, Hunt noted: 'With Harney all things are possible, and I should not be very much surprised if he gave his wrath full swing and removed me.'

Reports of his difficulties had even reached the British press:

The squatters on San Juan are shooting one another in disputes about 'town lots,' under the guns of the 'army of occupation.' This is the normal state of such enterprises – the robbers quarrelling over their booty.

All in all, Hunt preferred to be taking tea with his new friend, Captain Prevost, on board the *Satellite*.

There was no such harmonious relationship between Rear Admiral Baynes and Governor Douglas. Baynes had never been in favour of the agreement reached between the governor and General Scott. Instead, he would have held out for the complete removal of the American soldiers, on the grounds that such a move would return the situation to the 'status' it had previously enjoyed. In addition, he could see little to be gained from locking up 100 Royal Marines (a scarce and valuable resource) on the island. Douglas, by now, had changed his mind, and was no longer convinced that the American occupation should be countered by the landing of British troops – probably as a result of the Colonial Office remarking that the British Government felt:

> … it to be cause of satisfaction that your original intention of sending British troops to the island for the purpose of a joint occupation was not carried out. Such a measure might have led, at the moment in question, to further disagreements, or even a collision.

Baynes had also written to the Admiralty in explanation of why he had supported Captain Hornby's refusal to land troops on the island:

> Throughout this untoward affair we have been perfectly passive, exercising a degree of forbearance which their Lordships may not, perhaps, altogether approve, but called for, in my opinion, by the almost certainty of a collision at this distant point causing a rupture between the two nations; and I felt that as long as the dignity and honour of the British flag was in no way compromised, I should be best carrying out the views of Her Majesty's Government, and in the interests of these colonies, by avoiding the risk.

The whole affair, Baynes felt, was nothing more than 'an irritating matter.'

The admiral was supported by none other than the American commander of the forces on San Juan Island, Captain Hunt, who considered Baynes, that 'noble old fellow,' had:

> … saved us from a war, a war in which the commercial interests of 50 million souls, of the same race, would have been destroyed, not to speak of the horrible consequences in other respects.

Now, however, in response to Scott's visit and in recognition of his '*Projet of a Temporary Settlement, Etc.*,' the British Government, in the shape of the

Duke of Newcastle, the Colonial Secretary, had decided to approve the idea of a joint occupation of the island. When notice of this decision reached Douglas in January 1860, the governor told Baynes to land troops on the island. But the admiral, knowing well Douglas's earlier eagerness to do just that at a highly critical moment, asked to see the orders. The governor then dug his heels in and refused to do so, on the grounds that, as the senior representative of Her Majesty in the colony, he was not at liberty, or inclination, to show his orders to anyone. At this, Baynes, in the undeviating belief that his orders should come from the Admiralty, and not from a civilian administrator, sent off to England for a set of his own orders. They arrived in February, confirming that he should '... furnish 100 Marines, with a captain of Marines, to occupy the island on our side.' The troops were to carry 'appropriate arms,' which did not include 'the employment of cannon.'

Now, with the backing of a solid authorisation, Baynes set into motion his Admiralty instructions. There was no difficulty in supplying the Marines, as over 100 had been brought across from China by Hornby in the *Tribune* in response to American unrest and political agitation in the goldfields. Retaining the senior Marine officer, Major Thomas Magin, on board the flagship, Hornby appointed Captain George Bazalgette of the Royal Marine Light Infantry to command the detachment. He was to be supported by Lieutenant Henry Cooper and Second Lieutenant Edward Sparshott. They would command eighty-three other ranks, including Colour Sergeant John Prettyjohn, who had won the Victoria Cross at the Battle of Inkerman during the Crimean War.

Bazalgette had been born in Nova Scotia, where his father was the Adjutant-General. First commissioned in May 1847, he had seen service in China during the taking of Canton, before volunteering to transfer to British Columbia, where he and his fellow Marines served alongside the Royal Engineers. Bazalgette's brother, Evelyn, had served with distinction in the Crimean War, only to lose his life during the Indian Mutiny. His cousin, Joseph, earned enduring fame and a knighthood as the engineer who designed and built the London sewerage system, thus rescuing the capital from the dreadful 'big stink.'

Bazalgette's orders from Baynes read:

The object of placing you there is for the protection of British interests, and to form a joint occupation with the troops of the United States. As the sovereignty of the island is still in dispute between the two governments, you will on no account whatsoever interfere with the citizens of the United States, but should any offence be committed by such citizens which you think it advisable to notice you will send a report of it immediately to Captain Hunt, or officer commanding the US troops. American citizens have equal rights with British subjects on the island. Should the officer commanding the US troops bring to your notice offences committed by British subjects you will use your best judgement in dealing with the case, and I authorise you, if you deem it necessary, to send them off the island by the first opportunity. If any doubts arise as to the nationality of an offender you will not decide in the case before you have consulted with the US commanding officer, and not even then unless your opinions co-incide. You will place yourself in frank and free communication with the commanding officer of the US troops, bearing in mind how essential it is for the public service that the most perfect and cordial understanding should exist between you, which I have every reason to feel assured you will at all times find Captain Hunt ready and anxious to maintain.

Importantly, it can be seen that Bazalgette was empowered to act as his own magistrate without the civilian interference suffered by Hunt.

Originally, there had been five possible sites allocated for the British base on San Juan Island. One of these was a fine harbour on the east of the island, favoured by Captain Prevost, but Baynes preferred a base on the western shore if possible. Consequently, a site originally surveyed by Lieutenant Richard Roche of HMS *Satellite* was selected.

Situated on the north-west corner of the island, 'Garrison Bay' (as it soon became known) was both idyllic in its surroundings and ideal from a defence point of view. The foreshore was protected by two embracing peninsulas, admitting only a narrow, easily defended entrance, which was itself guarded by an offshore island. To the rear of the base rose a hill 700 feet high, offering protection from the landward side. Fresh water and fuel were easily available. On a large, level area by the water's edge (originally an Indian camp site), all that needed to be done was to complete the tree clearance started by the natives to provide a parade ground and space for accommodation. It was on this land, strewn with countless clam shells left by the Indians, that Bazalgette and his red-coated Marines, armed with Enfield rifled muskets, put up their tents on 23 March 1860, under the gaze of harbour seals and blue herons.

On her way to Garrison Bay, the *Satellite* called in at Griffin Bay, where a letter was sent ashore for the attention of Captain Hunt, informing the American commander that the Royal Marines were about to be landed north of his position. The courtesy Scott had demanded of Hunt towards the British was readily reciprocated.

18

Replaced by a Northerner

As the Royal Marines set about establishing their camp at Garrison Bay, Captain Hunt, snug in his newly built quarters at the American camp, opened his official mail to find that all the problems with the whisky-sellers and pimps at San Juan Town had vanished at a stroke. No longer would he have to squabble with civilians over whom he had no authority or control. No longer would he have to deal with drunken soldiers, Indians and squatters. The lack of a magistrate would no longer be his concern. 'Special Order Number 41,' signed by Captain Pleasonton on behalf of General Harney, informed him that he was to take his soldiers to Fort Steilacoom. He was to be relieved by none other than Captain George Pickett. Hunt lost no time in sending a letter off to a friend who would ensure that the news reached General Scott.

It was seven months since Brown's failed raid at Harpers Ferry, and President Buchanan had failed to come to grips with the problem of slavery that was threatening to tear the country apart. In his State of the Union message, Buchanan told his people:

> As sovereign States, they [the slave-owning states], and they alone, are responsible before God and the world for slavery existing among them. For this the people of the North are not more responsible and have no more right to interfere than with similar institutions in Russia or Brazil.

At this, the opposition Republican Party saw a great opportunity and piled on the pressure as Buchanan's own party, the Democrats, began to tear itself apart. As the news of a crumbling administration reached across to distant Washington Territory, General Harney knew that his options were falling away. This was no time to follow Scott's suggestion that he move to St Louis, Missouri, nor was it the time to have San Juan under the command of a bored, complaining officer such as Hunt.

Pickett returned to the island on 30 April, relieving Hunt, who went off to marry Colonel Casey's daughter, Abbey. This, however, was a changed Pickett. Despite Harney's instructions to him that the islands were part of Washington Territory and that the 'General Commanding is satisfied that any attempt to ignore this right of the Territory will be followed by deplorable results, out of his power to prevent or control,' the former bombastic infantry captain had now seemingly modified his attitude and appeared to seek a life of peace and harmony amongst the forests and meadows of San Juan Island.

There was little such tranquillity far to the south at Fort Vancouver. When word of Harney's latest action reached eastwards and found Scott, the old general exploded with rage. In a furious letter to John Floyd, the Secretary of War, Scott pointedly observed:

> If this does not lead to a collision of arms, it will again be due to the forbearance of the British authorities; for I found both Brigadier General Harney and Captain Pickett proud of their conquest of the Island, and quite jealous of any interference therewith on the part of higher authority.

He then went on to remind the Secretary of War that he had:

> intimated a doubt to the War Department whether Brigadier General Harney could carry out my pacific arrangement, respecting the occupation of the island, with good faith, or even with courtesy, and hence one of my reasons for wishing to relieve him from his command.

Almost a month later, word of the events on San Juan Island reached the ear of Lord Lyons, the British Minister at Washington, DC. He immediately wrote to Lewis Cass, the Secretary of State, pointing out that:

> … the recent orders of General Harney are inconsistent with the arrange-ments made by General Scott, approved by the President, and accepted by Her Majesty's government … I am confident that the government of the United States will lose not a moment in taking measures to arrest the deplorable consequences, which would, indeed, be only too likely to

follow and disturbance on the settlement so justly and wisely effected by General Scott.

Cass appeared to have been caught unaware of what had been going on. Although the Secretary of War had known for weeks, he had not passed the information on to the Secretary of State. But, then again, Floyd, like Harney, was a southerner with little interest in supporting harmonious relations with Great Britain at a time when a 'collision' could prove to be a crucial distraction as the Southern states broke from the Union. When the President was informed, Cass was able to report to Lyons that Buchanan had reacted with 'both surprise and regret.' Almost within hours of the news reaching the White House, 'Special Order Number 115' was on its way to Fort Vancouver:

> Brigadier General William S. Harney, United States Army, will on the receipt hereof, turn over command of the Department of Oregon to the officer next in rank in that department, and repair without delay to Washington city, and report in person to the Secretary of War.

On 14 July 1860, a humiliated, but nonetheless fuming, Harney passed through Fort Victoria on his way to Washington, DC, via San Francisco. Neither Governor Douglas nor Admiral Baynes turned out to show the respect normally accorded someone of the rank of General Commanding Washington Territory. Baynes noted that he had:

> … received no communication from him and consequently did not feel myself called on to show him any attention after the coarse and unwarrantable language he had made use of in his letter to the Adjutant General of October 29th, 1859, with regard to myself, Captain Prevost and Hornby, as well as her Majesty's Government.

The Olympia newspaper *Pioneer & Democrat* had spread the rumour that 'the gallant General' had been invited to Washington, DC to discuss a campaign against the Shoshoni Indians. Fort Victoria's *Colonist*, however, did not believe a word of it and declared: 'We cannot look upon it as a reason for his recall, other than as a public excuse, whilst the real reason is San Juan.' Lieutenant Charles Wilson, serving with the Royal Engineers in British Columbia, was quite firm in his conviction that 'General Harney (the San Juan filibuster) has been recalled for his disobedience of orders or something of that kind, so that we may not after all go to war with our cousins.'

On his arrival at Washington, DC, Harney set about producing a vigorous defence of his actions, but he need not have bothered. With the support of the President, Floyd, the slavery-supporting southerner, had no intention of losing the qualities shown by Harney in his attempt to stir up difficulties with the British. He may not have succeeded, but he had come very close. Consequently, the Secretary of War appointed Harney as Commander of the Department of the West, based at St Louis, Missouri – the very position Scott had offered him, and the one he had refused. Missouri, although supportive of the Southern states, had assumed a much too neutral stance and needed a Southern-supporting general in a Union uniform to steer it in the right direction. No one fitted the role better than William Selby Harney.

With Harney gone, the command of the Department of Oregon fell on the shoulders of Colonel George Wright, a veteran of the Mexican War and a friend of Pickett. Wright was a northerner and either knew nothing of, or cared nothing for, Harney's failed schemes. An Indian-fighter of long experience, he had earned a tough reputation in his campaigns. On one occasion, after inflicting a number of defeats against the Indians, he over-saw the slaughter of almost 800 of the enemy's horses to make a point. At another time, when the Indians asked for peace, Wright replied by saying:

> I did not come into this country to ask you to make peace; I came here to fight. Now, when you are tired of war, and ask for peace, I will tell you what you must do; you must come to me with your arms, with your women and children, and everything that you have, and lay them at my feet; you must put your faith in me and trust in my mercy. If you do this, I shall then dictate the terms upon [which] I will grant you the peace. If you do not do this, war will be made on you this year and next, and until your nation shall be exterminated.

Clearly, Wright was not a man to be swayed by sentiment. He was an experienced commander who felt he had better things to do than get deeply embroiled with the British over a small island in the far north of his territory. He confirmed Pickett's appointment as commanding officer on San Juan but stressed that Harney's last orders were to be ignored and those of General Scott to be reinstated. It was not to be long before Pickett persuaded Wright of the advantage held by the British commander on the island in having complete authority over his own nationals on the island. Wright gave orders that Pickett should be placed in the same position.

This was the point at which the situation on San Juan stabilised. The key element proved not to be the superior officers at Fort Vancouver or Esquimalt, nor the national governments posturing thousands of miles away, but the officers on the ground. Both Pickett and Bazalgette, the infantryman and the Royal Marine, were from middle-class backgrounds, were career professionals and both knew nothing would be gained from blatant posturing or attempts at securing advantage over the other. It was not long before Pickett was able to write to the British commander to talk of '... the perfect understanding which has existed between us, both officially and personally since my arrival on the island.'

The desire for co-operation rather than confrontation was not limited to the officers. The Royal Marines, many of whom were West Countrymen, but also included men from Ireland and Scotland, rubbed along easily with the men of Pickett's command. The 'enlisted men' of Company D, US 4th Infantry, included forty-one Irishmen, fourteen Germans, three Englishmen, two Scotsmen and two Canadians. Only ten came from the United States, unless the two young children of the camp laundress were included – their mother came from Ireland.

On 24 May, Queen Victoria's birthday, a celebration was held at the British camp to which the Americans were invited. In return, Bazalgette, his fellow officers and his men were cordially invited to attend the 4 July celebrations at 'Camp Pickett,' an invitation which (bearing in mind the date) was gladly accepted in the spirit in which it was intended. In between these dates, a race meeting was held near the American camp, at which the Sweep Stake was won by the Hudson's Bay Agent Charles Griffin on his black mare, Bessie. Captain Pickett's horse, Port Townsend, misbehaved and 'bolted for the springs.' Another race, the Farmer's Purse, saw a win for the American second-in-command, Lieutenant Forsyth, as this time it was Griffin's horse's turn to bolt.

One marked difference between the British and the American camps was the logistical support each received. Bazalgette had arrived with bell tents and marquees, a 27-foot whaler, building materials and two cooking stoves. It was not long before he was demanding '84 tin pannikins, 36 tin plates, 3 dishes, 10 camp kettles, 18 lanterns, 1 measures set, and a small quantity of stationery.' Requests were also made for paint, tools, fishing lines, furniture, scrubbing brushes, meat hooks and belt pegs. Admiral Baynes saw to the provision of an extra clothing allowance for the Marines. Barracks (originally referred to on the plans as 'Privates' Mess,' but quickly becoming known as the more usual Royal Marine 'Barracks') were erected for the men and NCOs, whilst accommodation was provided for the officers at the southern end of the camp by the water's edge. The majority of these buildings were erected by civilian contractors from Fort Victoria. A small vegetable garden was soon dug and the camp's victualling provided for by Augustus 'Gus' Hoffmeister, a civilian who farmed cattle close to the site. At a central point on the water's edge, a guard or block-house was erected to serve both as a point of defence and as a prison. An unusual structure, its upper story was turned 45° to its lower story, thus allowing no approach to be undefended by fire from its rows of loop-holes.

The block-house at the British camp was, almost certainly, a copy of the one already in existence at the American camp. Situated on the exposed slopes of the saddle ridge overlooking Griffin's Bay, and built or erected entirely by the soldiers, Camp Pickett was soon in dire need of restoration, a need matched only by the continued reluctance of the Oregon Command storekeepers to supply it. Even worse, San Juan Town (still the haunt of drunks and pimps) lay almost on its doorstep.

Nevertheless, the shortage of paint and nails and the occasional leaky roof was more than made up for by the absence of war-like Indians, the disappearance of General Harney and the burgeoning social whirl. Made up, that is, until far, far to the south-east, the rumble of cannon-fire rolled around the waters of Charleston Harbour.

19

A Remarkable Incident

Buchanan's presidency was limping to an undistinguished end when Abraham Lincoln was elected as his successor on 6 November 1860. His reaction to the secession of South Carolina the following months was to do nothing. When, two months later, Georgia, Florida, Alabama, Mississippi, Louisiana and Texas also broke away, Buchanan had no other interest than handing the problem over to Lincoln.

Having lost the will to fight against the break-up of his country, Buchanan certainly had no time for Lord Lyons' proposal in December 1860, that the question of San Juan's ownership should be put out to arbitration. The British suggested that the matter be submitted to either the King of the Netherlands, the King of Sweden & Norway or the President of the Swiss Federal Council. Unfortunately, the matter was complicated by the additional proposal that the United States pay $500,000 to the Hudson's Bay Company and its commercial offshoot, the Puget Sound Agricultural Company, for the loss of property caused by the Oregon Treaty. The proposal eventually reached the Senate, but became lost in the frenzy of emotions caused by the seceding states.

The frenzy was not helped when, on 9 January 1861, the paddle-steamer *Star of the West* (the same vessel that had taken General Scott south from Washington fourteen months earlier) was sent to supply Fort Sumpter, guarding the entrance to the harbour at Charleston, South Carolina. As the vessel crossed the bar, she came under cannon-fire from the shore and was forced to turn back. Still Buchanan failed to act decisively.

The Confederate States of America was organised in February under the presidency of Jefferson Davis, a former senator with a distinguished military record, especially in the war against Mexico. He had been given the command of the Mississippi forces but, after just a few weeks, was elected to the presidency.

Lincoln, by now sporting a beard on the recommendation of an eleven-year-old girl, was inaugurated as president on 4 March. At this, the Confederacy mounted its first action against the North. Fort Sumpter, having refused to surrender to the surrounding Southern forces, came under a fierce bombardment. On 12 April, over 3,000 missiles were hurled at, and over, its walls. Two days later, with its magazines at risk of exploding (although only four barrels of gunpowder remained), the fort surrendered. Despite the intensity of the attack, the fort's defenders had suffered no injuries. However, deciding to abandon the fort to a 100-gun salute as the Stars and Stripes was lowered, two soldiers were killed when their gun blew up.

Lincoln immediately demanded the handing of all forts and armouries to US forces and the raising of 75,000 men to put down the insurrection. The first response to this was the instant secession of Virginia, North Carolina, Tennessee and Arkansas. This left the slave-owning states of Kentucky, Missouri, Delaware and Maryland opting for neutrality, a fragile condition that was soon under threat from internal factionalism.

After a number of small, opening skirmishes, the first real shock of battle took place on 21 July at Manassas in Virginia (known as 'Bull Run' by Northern historians). Sixty thousand men fought that day. In the end, the Union troops left in a disorderly rout, with the Confederate soldiers too exhausted to pursue them. As the sound of musketry and cannonading died away, far to the north-west, Captain George Pickett, a loyal son of Virginia, was still wearing the blue uniform of the Union Army.

On 11 June, an order from Colonel Wright demanded that the American camp on San Juan Island be closed down and the troops be sent to San Francisco in preparation to be moved to the east. Pickett informed Bazalgette of the development, telling him:

> I cannot take my leave without expressing to you both in my own name and that of my officers, the gratification we have experienced from our very pleasant intercourse with you during the passed year, and our sincere regrets at having to break up these associations.

Bazalgette also had cause to regret the removal of Pickett. They had become such firm friends, that it was not at all unusual for them to be seen together enjoying the social life of Fort Victoria. The Royal Marine captain replied:

> It is with great regret that I learn of your departure, but rest assured that the acquaintance formed during our sojourn on this island will ever be remembered with very pleasant reminiscences both by myself and officers.

Ten days later, Wright's order was cancelled, as rumours of impending Indian attacks around Puget Sound had reached Fort Vancouver. Now, rather than risk being sent to the east as part of the Union Army, Pickett grasped the nettle and submitted his resignation on 25 June. With the administration required for such a matter often taking some time, the Pacific commander, General 'Bull Head' Sumner (another Mexican War veteran), gave Pickett 'leave of absence,' a courteous act that allowed him to leave his command at the first opportunity without the disgrace of being seen as a deserter. Pickett repaid the kindness by remaining at his San Juan post until 25 July when both he and his company were replaced by Company H, 9th US Infantry, under the command of Captain Thomas English.

The delay in leaving the island allowed Picket to enjoy a final 4 July celebration, at which Bazalgette won the Sweep Stake on his horse, Jerry.

After calling at Fort Steilacoom finally to hand over his company property, Pickett headed south to San Francisco. On his way he called at Olympia to arrange for the care of his four-year-old son, James ('Jimmie'), a result of his marriage to an Indian woman he had met at Semiahmoo Bay. Like his first wife, his Indian bride had died shortly after childbirth, but the child had survived.

After crossing the Panama isthmus, Pickett arrived in New York before heading north to Canada. This unexpected direction was probably in order to avoid having to pass through the front lines to reach Virginia. With the Union blockade not yet fully in place, Canada would be a likely source of a vessel that could take him south. In any event, Pickett arrived at Richmond, Virginia, on 13 September, where he was appointed a captain of infantry in the Confederate Army. Ten days later, he was ordered to Fredericksburg with the rank of colonel.

Where all had gone well for Pickett, at St Louis, Missouri, things began to unravel even before the outbreak of war. General Harney, now Commander of the Department of the West and based at St Louis, continued his work of covert support for the secessionist states.

With Missouri in the hands of a secessionist governor, a Republican congressman from the state, Francis Blair, decided that he would

organise Unionist supporters into a militia. Harney showed no interest
in Blair's efforts, so the congressman, using his political connections (his
brother was Postmaster-General at Washington, DC) arranged to have
Captain Nathaniel Lyon transferred to St Louis from his duties at Fort
Riley, Kansas. Lyon was a fiery abolitionist who had been sent to Kansas
by Harney in pursuit of other abolitionists who were not only ignoring
the requirements of the Fugitive Slave Law (i.e. returning slaves to their
owners), but actively assisting slaves to escape to Canada. Instead of
hunting down the law-breakers, Lyon had been helping them.

On his return to St Louis, Lyon immediately demanded that he be
allowed to take over the St Louis armoury with Blair's volunteers – a move
that would have given the volunteers access to the weapons contained
therein. Harney refused. Lyon and Blair were outraged and letters were
sent to Washington, DC. On 13 March 'Special Order Number 74,' arrived
at Harney's headquarters. It was signed on behalf of the Secretary of War
by the newly appointed Adjutant-General, Colonel Lorenzo Thomas, the
same officer who had been Scott's assistant adjutant when the General-
in-Chief was sent to sort out the San Juan problem. The order read:

> Captain N Lyon, Second Infantry, the senior officer of the line present and
> on duty at the Saint Louis Arsenal, Mo., is assigned to the command of the
> troops and defenses at that post.

If Lyon and Blair thought they had ruined Harney's schemes, however,
they were swiftly disabused. The general informed the captain:

> It is not supposed that in issuing that order the Secretary of War deigned
> you should exercise any control over the operations of the Ordnance
> Department, and you will not, therefore, regard the officers and men of
> that branch of the service stationed at the arsenal as forming a portion of
> your command.

Lyon was banned from access to the weapons. Once again, Blair
pulled strings.

Unfortunately for the Unionists, communications with Washington,
DC, had broken down, so Blair sent telegraphs in every possible
direction. For days there was no reply whilst, at the same time, secessionist
militiamen were clearly beginning to organise themselves throughout
Missouri. Then Blair had a stroke of luck. Colonel Fitz-John Porter, a
member of Scott's staff, had just been sent by the General-in-Chief to act

as Assistant Adjutant-General in Pennsylvania. On 21 April, Porter was sitting near to the Capitol's telegraph office when the governor walked in with a telegraph which he was asked to read. Addressed to the governor, it had come from Blair and read:

> An officer of the Army here has received an order to muster in Missouri regiments. General Harney refuses to let them remain in the arsenal grounds or permit them to be armed. I wish these facts to be communicated to the secretary of War by special messenger and instructions immediately sent to Harney to receive the troops at the arsenal and arm them. Our friends distrust Harney very much. He should be superseded immediately by putting another commander in the district. The object of the secessionists is to seize the arsenal with its 70,000 stand of arms, and he refuses the means of defending it. We have plenty of men but no arms.

Porter lost no time, and immediately telegraphed to Harney:

> Captain Nathaniel Lyon, Second Infantry, is detailed to muster in the troops at Saint Louis, and to use them for the protection of public property. You will see that they are properly armed and equipped.

To underline the order, and to add weight to his colonel's rank, Porter signed the telegraph off with 'By order of Lieutenant-General Scott.' Such stiffening of the order proved, however, to be unnecessary. The following day, Harney received another telegraph, this time from Washington, DC, signed by the Adjutant-General, Colonel Thomas:

> GENERAL: I am directed by the Secretary of War to say that you are hereby relieved from command of the Department of the West, which will devolve upon the senior officer in the department, and you will repair to this city and report to the General-in-Chief.

Unlamented, at least amongst the Missouri Unionists, Harney stepped on board the overnight mail train to Washington, DC on the evening of 24 April. What happened next would have stretched the imagination of the most gifted story-teller – and even then would be dismissed out of hand as much too improbable.

Harper's Ferry, the scene of the John Brown raid eighteen months earlier, had been in the hands of the Confederates for a week. At one o'clock on the morning of 25 April, the sentries heard the three warning shots in succession that announced the arrival of a train bearing Union soldiers. Immediately, heavy guns were aimed down the track, their crews ready to open fire the moment the train appeared. Colonel William Baylor saw the train go past, but could see no troops. Galloping up to the engine, he ordered the train to be stopped, which it did, just out of range of the guns. When he found the train's conductor, Baylor asked him if there were any soldiers on board. There was, apparently, just 'One old fellow in uniform asleep on the mail-bags in the first car.' Baylor took a few soldiers with him and found himself in possession of only the third prisoner to be taken in Virginia: and his prisoner was a brigadier-general named William Harney.

Harney reacted to his capture 'with a pleasant remark,' and spent the rest of the night at the local general's lodgings. Later that morning he was put on his own parole and made his way by train to the Confederate capital at Richmond. There he met General Robert E. Lee, the commander of the Confederate Army; General Joseph Johnston; the Confederate 'special agent,' D.G. Duncan; and Commander Maury of the Confederate Navy, a famous hydrographic surveyor whose father was a Confederate general and whose older brother had been in the USS *Essex* when she was captured by Hillyar in 1813. There they had, safe in their hands, one of only four generals serving in the United States Army at the outbreak of the war, an officer of vast experience, known to be a tough fighter and a demanding leader. Their response, however, was to let him go. Within hours, he was back on a train bound for Washington, DC.

After the meeting, Duncan wrote to L.P. Walker, the Confederate Secretary of War, informing him that Harney had been arrested:

> … on his way from Saint Louis to Washington under orders. He came willingly on parole. Governor and council released him. Advised General Robert E Lee and Commander Maury, hoping to win him over. Harney expressing Southern sentiments …

According to a rumour spreading amongst the Confederate troops, Harney had been on his way to Washington, DC, to resign his commission. Apparently, he then intended to leave for Europe rather than fight against his fellow countrymen.

Now, having been actually ordered to Washington, DC on what amounted to disciplinary charges, and having been captured by the enemy and released, the Secretary of War astonished everyone by revoking Harney's dismissal and sending him back to St Louis, reinstated as Commander of the Department of the West.

Harney returned on 11 May to a scene of chaos. Captain Lyon, unencumbered by senior officers, had stamped down hard on any secessionist sympathies. As Harney was meeting his Confederate friends, Lyon had taken over the armoury and shipped 20,000 muskets and 110,000 cartridges to Illinois, before arming his Unionist volunteers. He then surrounded a camp of Southern militia and forced their surrender without a shot being fired. Marching his prisoners through St Louis, the Unionists came under a barrage of stones and insults from crowds lining the streets. Their response was to open fire into the crowd, killing many men, women and children. One of the men watching the scene, who was forced to throw himself to the ground to protect his young son, was the President of the 5th Street Railway Company. His name was William Tecumseh Sherman, who, three years later, led his troops in a famous march through Georgia.

The following day, the day of Harney's return, St Louis was a scene of rioting and destruction. The situation was perfect for a loyal, resolute Unionist general to demand that the governor declare martial law for the protection of his citizens. With men like Lyon under his command, and under such circumstances, the general could have routed any secessionists and ensured that Missouri entered and remained within the Unionist camp. Instead, Harney met the leader of the Missouri State Militia, the South-supporting General Sterling Price, and agreed that Price could police the state whilst guaranteeing that there would be no movement of Union troops.

Lyon and Blair were aghast. Harney, it seemed, was intent on undoing all the work they had achieved. Blair, however, had a secret weapon. The Secretary of War, with the approval of Lincoln, had issued the congressman with a document authorising him to remove Harney if he felt it vital to do so. Blair, nevertheless, held his hand at the personal request of the President who, on hearing of the Harney–Price agreement, wrote:

I do not write now to countermand it [the authorisation to dismiss Harney], but to say I wish you would withhold it, unless in your judgement the necessity to the contrary is very urgent. There are several reasons for this. We had better have him a friend than an enemy. It will dissatisfy a good many who otherwise would be quiet. More than all, we first relieve him, then restore him, and now if we relieve him again the public will ask 'Why all this vacillation?' Still, if in your judgement it is indispensable, let it be so.

Yours very truly, A. Lincoln.

The situation failed to improve as Price's militia (now called the 'State Guard') drove Unionists from their property. As a last warning shot, Thomas, the Adjutant-General, wrote to Harney. After complaining of the actions of Price's men and the untrustworthiness of the state's administration, Thomas wrote:

> You will therefore be unceasingly watchful of their movements, and not permit the clamors of their partisans, and opponents of the wise measures have already taken, to prevent you from checking every movement against the government however disguised under the pretended State authority. The authority of the United States is paramount, and whenever it is apparent by a movement, whether by color of State authority or not, is hostile, you will not hesitate to put it down.

But Harney did hesitate, and took no action against Price. For Blair, the time had come and, on 30 May, the congressman ordered Harney to stand down from the command of the Western Department. The following day, Lyon was promoted to brigadier-general, appointed as Harney's replacement and let loose on the secessionists.

Six days after his dismissal, Harney wrote to Thomas. Most of the complaints about secessionist activities were, he believed, 'without foundation.' His confidence in General Price remained 'unimpaired.' The hardest thing to take, however, was his dismissal by Blair, 'in a manner that has inflicted unmerited disgrace upon a true and loyal soldier.' He continued:

> During a long life, dedicated to my country, I have seen some service, and more than once I have held her honor in my hands; and during that time, my loyalty, I believe, was never questioned; and now, when in the natural course of things I shall, before the lapse of many years, lay aside the sword which has so long served my country, my countrymen will be slow to believe that I have chosen this portion of my career to damn with treason my life, which is so soon to become a record of the past, and which I shall most willingly leave to the unbiased judgement of posterity. I trust that I may be yet spared to do my country some further service that will testify to the love I bear her, and that the vigor of my arm may never relax whilst there is a blow to be struck in her defense.

After this plea on behalf of his reputation, Harney went on to suggest a way in which the 'vigor' of his arm might be put to service:

I respectfully ask to be assigned to the command of the Department of California, and I doubt not the present commander of that division is even now anxious to serve on the Atlantic frontier.

But, no matter how keen the 'present commander' was to move to the fighting, it was not to be. No one was convinced of Harney's loyalty, and many were suspicious of his sympathies. He was never employed again in a military role, but, in his retirement, he was given the brevet promotion to Major-General in recognition of a long and distinguished career. He was also recalled to serve on the 1867–68 Peace Commission that negotiated with the Plains Indians. Finally, Harney, the man who nearly brought about a war between the United States and Great Britain, died in May 1889. He had undoubtedly served his country well, but it had not always been the same country.

20

Great Britain Aids the South

For the Royal Marines on San Juan Island, life continued with orderly calm. From his house on high ground, Captain Bazalgette could look across the open space to the water's edge where his Marines drilled, stood guard and tended to the circular garden. Buildings took the place of tents and a wharf was constructed for ships bringing in supplies. Bazalgette had also established a lime kiln by an attractive bay just to the north that had been surveyed by Lieutenant Roche of HMS *Satellite*. The 'Roche Harbour' lime was used to whitewash the newly erected buildings.

Relations with the Americans continued on the same friendly course, despite the fact that, with the Union and the Confederacy at each other's throats, it would have been a simple matter for British ships to have turned up in Griffin's Bay and ordered the Americans to leave. There may have been a brief resistance, but even that is doubtful. When, in November, Captain English received orders that his company was about to be relieved by Captain Augustus Robinson and Battery D of the 3rd Artillery, many of his men promptly deserted rather than risk going eastwards towards the fighting. Had the British removed the American troops, it is highly unlikely that such a minor irritation would have featured anywhere near the top of President Lincoln's list of urgent issues. At most, a letter of protest would have been sent before the matter was pushed aside to be settled later. In fact, the first shot to be fired between the two nations came from the Americans at sea off the coast of Cuba.

The 13-gun sloop USS *San Jacinto* was under the command of Captain Charles Wilkes – the same Wilkes who had 'discovered' non-existent land in the Antarctic and who had carried out a survey of the San Juan islands. Steaming up to the unarmed British mail ship *Trent* on 8 November, Wilkes fired a solid shot across her bows. Captain Moir of the *Trent*, with the British colours clearly flying, refused to stop, so this time Wilkes fired a shell across her bows. As the shell exploded ahead of him, Moir gave the order to close down steam and come to a halt. Two boats full of armed men were sent alongside the British ship and Lieutenant Donald Fairfax clambered aboard, demanding to see the ship's passenger list. Moir refused and objected loudly to the Americans stopping his ship. He was joined in his vociferous complaints by Commander Wilson, a naval officer responsible for the security of the mail. Finally, Fairfax declared that he was on board to arrest two Confederate commissioners, John Slidell and James Mason, along with their secretaries, all of whom were known to be taking passage to Europe in the *Trent*. At this, the commissioners and their secretaries, Eustis and McFarland, stepped forward from a gathering crowd of hostile passengers. Fairfax called up his armed men and sent to the *San Jacinto* for reinforcements. Eventually, with the loudly abusive passengers held back at bayonet point, and after a token resistance from the commissioners, Fairfax left the ship with his prisoners.

On his arrival at Boston, Wilkes was vehemently hailed as a hero, a bright light amongst the poor performance of the Union army in the field. The press heaped adulation upon him as the House of Representative passed a resolution honouring his achievement. From the British point of view, however, things looked rather different.

For some time, the Unionist press had been suggesting that action should be taken against England for the apparent sympathies being expressed in favour of the Southern states. In July 1861, an embargo on British trade was urged on the grounds that $70 million of British goods came into America annually, and $175 million of cotton, tobacco, flour, corn, etc., were bought by the British in return. This peculiarly self-defeating suggestion prompted an immediate run on the banks. The popular press continued to bluster:

> If the embargo led to war it could not injure us much more than active British sympathy with the rebels would. England has not enough men to effect a landing on our coast. In the Crimean War she could not raise an army of 50,000 men. New York alone could take care of any army she might send out … We might inflict more serious injuries on our antagonist if we secured the alliance of France, or aroused an insurrectionary movement among the Irish or the Chartists.

Then came a glimpse of the glittering prize:

> On the other hand a war with England would this time insure the annex-
> ation of Canada – no mean gain to us in view of the future.

The British press looked for a different reason. It was convinced that the
war had gone so badly for the North that the Unionists were on the verge
of accepting that the old Union could never be put back together again.
On the other hand, an outbreak of war with Great Britain would provide
a perfect excuse for letting the South go:

> … such an opinion has secretly taken root in the minds of the Cabinet at
> Washington, and that a contest with England is adopted as a policy out
> of which may spring a pretext for the ultimate acknowledgement of the
> independence of the South.

Few, whether from the North or the South, were prepared for Britain's
reaction to Wilkes's boarding of the *Trent*. In addition to a strongly
worded letter of complaint demanding both the handing over of the
Southern commissioners and an apology, the British Government began a
mobilisation, the like of which had not been seen since the Crimean War.
Warships, including modern ironclads from the Mediterranean fleet, were
sent to the Gulf of Mexico, with the Pacific and North Atlantic fleets in
support. Batteries of artillery joined the 1st Battalion of the Grenadier
Guards, the 2nd Battalion of the Scots Fusiliers and several companies of
the Royal Engineers on transports bound for Canada. Each soldier was
issued with:

> Two pairs of woollen drawers, one jersey, two merino under-vests, two
> pairs of worsted stocking, one comforter, one chamois leather waistcoat,
> one sealskin cap with ear mufflers, one pair of sealskin mitts, one pair of
> Canadian boots, and one sheepskin coat.

The 15th, 17th, 36th, 47th, 62nd, 63rd and 96th Regiments were raising
men and preparing to follow.

As the Scots Fusiliers sailed from Southampton, they passed a Confederate warship, the CSS *Nashville*. The Southern sailors waved and cheered
as their band struck up 'I'm off to Charleston so Early in the Morning.'

In Canada, the militia was being replaced by volunteer regiments, with
men flocking to the colours. At the same time, the defences of Toronto and

Quebec were being strengthened and companies of Royal Engineers were sent to the Bahamas, the obvious base from which to break the North's blockade of the Southern ports. Even worse, the much-vaunted possibility of French support for the American case evaporated, as the Emperor gave his support to Great Britain along with the Austrians and the Prussians.

The Secretary of State, William Seward, was suitably unimpressed:

> It causes us no concern that the [British] government sends a naval force into the Gulf and a military force into Canada. We have no designs hostile to Great Britain so long as she does not, officially or unofficially, recognize the insurgents or render them aid or sympathy.

By the time Lord Lyons presented Seward with the British Government's note, American opinion of Wilkes's action had undergone a sea change. The brash, bullying captain had turned the possibility of war with Great Britain into a likelihood. The Secretary of State's lawyers searched for a way out and eventually came up with the suggestion that Wilkes should have brought the *Trent* into an American port. Once there, a formal Government representative could have gone on board to make a decision whether or not Slidell and Mason could be legitimately removed from the vessel. Instead, Wilkes had acted as his own judge in the matter, thus rendering his actions illegal. This, then, was the straw that Seward clutched in an attempt to preserve the dignity of the Federal Government as the two commissioners were handed over to the British. Seward could not avoid adding the comment:

> I have not been unaware that, in examining this question, I have fallen into an argument for what seems to be the British side of it against my own country. But I am relieved from all embarrassment on that subject. I had hardly fallen into that line of argument when I discovered I was really defending and maintaining, not an exclusively British interest, but an old, honored and cherished cause …

In other words, the British did it first in 1812, causing America to go to war – the *Trent* incident merely proved that America was right all along.

The possible diplomatic activities arising from secession of the Southern states had been seen as a bone of contention between the United States and Great Britain for several months. Even before war had broken out, the Secretary of State, Seward, had written to his minister in London with the blatant threat:

Would it be wise for her Majesty's government, on this occasion, to set a
dangerous precedent, or provoke retaliation? If Scotland and Ireland are
at last reduced to quiet contentment, has Great Britain no dependency,
island or province left exposed along the whole circle of her empire, from
Gibraltar through the West Indies and Canada till it begins again on the
southern extremity of Africa?

It was, however, to be maritime matters that rose to the fore as the most
likely source of conflict. Jefferson Davis, the President of the Confederate
States, with the prospect of a blockade of Southern ports and without a
navy of his own, issued 'letters of marque' to ship-owners, authorising
them to arm their vessels and wage war on Northern ships. These
'privateers,' protected by their letters of marque, became, in every sense,
the Confederate Navy. The Union, on the other hand, considered them
to be pirates.

At the Declaration of Paris in 1856, the major powers had signed an
agreement that privateers should be outlawed. Unfortunately for the
North, the United States had not signed the declaration on the grounds
that some countries did not have navies and, therefore, the deployment
of privateers was their only form of naval defence – exactly the situation
with the seceding states. Not unsurprisingly, the Unionists were suddenly
keen to sign the agreement. The British, on the other hand, were not
quite so eager.

The Foreign Secretary, Lord John Russell, seeing the approach of an
armed struggle between the North and South, with the North about to
impose a blockade on the Southern ports and President Davis issuing
letters of marque, had 'come to the conclusion that civil war existed in
America, and her Majesty had thereupon proclaimed her neutrality in
the approaching contest.' To support Washington's application to sign the
agreement now would not be the act of a neutral. It would justify the
Union's insistence that the privateers were nothing more than 'pirates,'
and deny recognition of the Southerners' rights and protection under
letters of marque. Repeated changes to the proposed wording by both
sides, along with British prevarication, eventually led to the Unionist case
falling apart and the matter being dropped. The outcome of the failed
negotiations was not long in being felt.

In May, word reached Washington, DC, that the Confederacy had
purchased a British vessel, the iron-hulled *Peerless*, currently alongside
in Toronto. The plan, apparently, was for a British crew, under a
British captain, flying the British ensign, to steam the ship down the

St Lawrence and hand the vessel over to the Confederates once the open sea had been reached. The Secretary of State sent for Lord Lyons and demanded that he instruct the Governor-General of Canada to prevent the ship sailing. Lyons replied by saying that he had no authority to do such a thing. Seward then announced that he would have the US Navy capture the vessel. Lyons maintained his position but, shortly afterwards, the Canadian authorities put a stop to the ship's purchase. Interestingly enough, it was not just ships from Canada that became involved in the war; many thousands of Canadians also fought on both sides. One was a woman, Sarah Emma Edmonds, who, disguised as a man, fought with the Union cavalry at the Battle of Antietam. Her true identity was not revealed until she attended a regimental reunion in 1884.

The *Peerless* incident was followed by an attempt to demonstrate the impermeability of the North's blockade. On 9 June, the Hartlepool-based ship *Perthshire*, carrying cotton from Mobile, Alabama, was stopped and boarded by the USS *Massachusetts*, now no longer cruising the calmer waters of Puget Sound. The British ensign was hauled down and the Stars and Stripes run up in its place. Six days later, however, the commodore of the blockading fleet returned the *Perthshire* to her captain and sent her on her way. The incident cost the Federal Government £200, not only for 'the detention to which she had been subjected,' but also for the 'tea, coffee, and sugar used by the prize crew whilst on board the *Perthshire*.'

Six weeks later, on 30 July, the CSS *Sumter* steamed into Trinidad harbour. The first of the Confederate sea-raiders, the *Sumter* was under the command of Captain Raphael Semmes and her name was already beginning to cause concern in Unionist quarters. Semmes had brought her down the Mississippi, slipped past the blockade and was soon burning and sinking any Federal ship he came across. When she arrived at Trinidad she was flying the Confederate flag – an ensign not yet known around the world. Consequently, a boat from HMS *Cadmus* came out to meet her. The British officer was shown a commission signed by a 'Mr Jefferson Davis, calling himself the President of the so-styled Confederate States of America.' With no orders to the contrary, Captain Hillyar of the *Cadmus* allowed the *Sumter* entry into the harbour (Hillyar was a son of Captain James Hillyar of the *Phoebe*, who had captured the USS *Essex* nearly fifty years earlier). At the same time, the Union Flag was broken out ashore, an act the Unionists took to be a welcoming gesture, but which the British insisted was nothing more than a means of identifying the ownership of the island. Even worse, an American on the island reported to Seward that 'the officers of the British war vessel *Cadmus* appeared to be on amicable terms with those of the *Sumter*.' Faced with complaints from Washington, DC, Lord Russell swept them aside by saying there was no 'reason to believe that her Majesty's proclamation of neutrality has been violated by the governor of Trinidad, or by the commanding officer of Her Majesty's Ship *Cadmus*,' despite admitting that the *Sumter* 'was allowed to stay six days at Trinidad, and to supply herself with coals and provisions.'

The problems with the *Sumter* were as nothing compared with what was to follow. In March 1862, a newly built fast steamer named the *Oreto* sailed from Liverpool for the Bahamas. Shortly after her arrival, she was renamed *Florida* and commissioned into the Confederate Navy. For more than two years, the *Florida* harried Federal shipping, taking thirty-seven prizes. She was captured illegally whilst in neutral Brazilian waters and taken to Newport News, Virginia. There, a court demanded her return to Brazil on the grounds of violation of neutrality, but, before this could be done, an 'accidental' collision with a troop-carrying vessel sent her to the bottom.

If the Federal Government was somewhat suspicious of the supply of this ship by British ship-builders to the Confederate Navy, there was no doubt at all about hull number 290 currently on the stocks of John Laird, Sons & Co., of Birkenhead. A barque-rigged steamship with a telescopic funnel and a lifting screw, 290 had been under observation for some time when the American Minister in London, Charles Adams, the son of President John Quincy Adams, wrote to Lord Russell concerning 'a new and still more powerful war steamer' that was 'fitting out for the especial and manifest object of carrying on hostilities by sea' under the direction of 'agents and officers of the insurgents in the United States.' As a result, Russell had the ship inspected by the Surveyor of Her Majesty's Customs at Liverpool. He had no doubt what the purpose of the ship was. It was 'apparent to all that she intended to be a ship-of-war.' This finding was backed up by a sworn statement from a member of 290's crew. He had written that she had 'a magazine, and shot and canister racks on deck, and is pierced for guns, the sockets for the bolts for which are laid down.' This was all very well, but not only did the ship have no guns, it was owned by British interests.

Eventually, Russell did react to American pressure, but it was too late. As orders were being drafted to have the ship detained, 290 was on her way out of the Mersey. With her guns fitted off the Irish coast, she made her way to the Azores, where, on 24 August, she rendezvoused with Captain Raphael Semmes, the former captain of the *Sumter*. After sinking numerous Federal ships the *Sumter* had ended up in Gibraltar, where her crew were entertained by the Royal Navy, Semmes and his officers even being taken fox-hunting by the Admiral. However, Federal Navy ships were closing in on Semmes and his men and, rather than risk sinking or capture, he took the unusual step of selling his ship to the British, who used her as a blockade-runner.

Now in command of his new ship, Semmes read his commission and gave her the name *Alabama*. Five months later, having sunk twenty-two Federal ships and ransomed four others, the *Alabama* met the USS *Hatteras* off Galveston, Texas, and left her a burning wreck. This, in some measure, made up for the *Alabama*, much to Semmes' outrage, being called a 'British Pirate' by the Unionist press. For the next eighteen months, the *Alabama* sailed far and wide in search of Federal vessels, sinking over sixty ships with a total value of almost $6 million. Worn out and in need of repair she arrived at Cherbourg, where the USS *Kearsarge* caught up with her. In the ensuing battle, a shot from the *Kearsarge* entered the *Alabama*'s stern at the waterline and she began to sink rapidly. As she went down, a British yacht, the *Deerhound*, closed with the stricken vessel and rescued Semmes and forty-two men, taking them all safely to England. The day produced one remarkable hero: Surgeon David Llewellyn from Wiltshire, one of many British men on board the *Alabama* (fifty-eight came from Liverpool alone), refused the chance to escape the sinking vessel and chose to stay with his wounded patients. He became the only Englishman to be awarded a posthumous Confederate Medal of Honor.

Whatever the outcome, no one on the *Alabama* would have guessed that their exploits would play an important part in the story of a small island thousands of miles away at the southern end of the Gulf of Georgia.

21

The Island Settles Down

During the protracted, and ultimately futile, negotiations between Great Britain and the Federal Government regarding the latter's belated attempt to sign the 1856 Declaration of Paris, there was a disagreement over a particular clause the British wanted to include. When challenged by the Americans, Lord Russell defended the addition on the grounds that:

> On some recent occasions, as on the fulfilment of the treaty of 1846, respecting the boundary ... serious differences have arisen with regard to the precise meaning of words, and the intention of those who framed them.

On San Juan Island itself, the 'serious difficulties' were not reflected in the rapport that had grown up between the British and the American troops. In February 1862, Captain Lyman Bissell and Company C of the 9th Infantry took over from Captain Robinson and his men. Once again, on being introduced by the outgoing commander, the officers and men on both sides settled down to a routine of social and military harmony.

Bazalgette had little to concern him beyond the day-to-day difficulties at Garrison Bay. Bissell, on the other hand, found he had problems with the local natives. In the June after his arrival, a band of Indians arrived and set up a camp on the south beach, close to where Pickett had established his second camp. Not trusting the Indians' motives (which was possibly little more than to carry out their tradition of fishing on that part of the coast, although some Indians had found that prostitution was a well-paid occupation), Bissell ordered a patrol to be sent out to fend off their canoes. If the newcomers refused to put to sea again, the patrol was 'to fire at them.' For some reason, however, the soldiers were not over-keen to shoot at the Indians and, by October, Bissell had to modify his orders, which now read:

> Hereafter any soldier of this command, caught, or recognized, at the Indian ranch (without authority), on the beach near the spring after Tattoo, will be confined at hard labor in charge of the Guard, with chain and ball attached to his left leg, for the period of sixty days.

All of which suggests that the soldiers had not been visiting the Indians to help with the fishing.

Whilst Bissell was attending to his local problems, Major-General Isaac Stevens, the former Governor of Washington Territory who had stood up to Governor Douglas's demands over the sheep-rustlers, but had been instructed by the Secretary of State to calm things down, was taking part in the Battle of Chantilly in Virginia. Seeing the men around him falter, Stevens picked up the fallen colours of a regiment in which he had earlier served. Holding the colours aloft (the colours were in the design of a St Andrew's cross and had given the regiment the nickname 'The Highlanders'), Stevens called out 'Highlanders, my Highlanders, follow your general.' As the soldiers dashed at the Southern troops ahead of them, Stevens was hit by a bullet and killed instantly.

On the far-off waters of the Atlantic, an old spectre reared his head once again in an effort to test the tense relationship between the Federal Government and Great Britain. In the afternoon of 20 November, look-outs on the Bahamas guard-ship HMS *Barracouta* alerted their officers to the sight of a propeller-driven barque and a paddle-steamer moving slowly past the entrance to the harbour – well within British territorial waters. Both ships were flying the ensign of the United States. The barque was also flying the flag of a rear admiral: she was the USS *Wachusetts*, flagship of none other than Rear Admiral Charles Wilkes.

Commander Malcolm of the *Barracouta* promptly sent a boat out under the command of Lieutenant Cochrane to board the intruder and enquire after its purpose. Flying a large white ensign, the boat closed with the *Wachusetts* and was clearly seen by a large number of people on her upper deck. Despite being seen, and its intentions being obvious, the American ignored the boat and left it in her wake, only to anchor close inshore further up the coast.

Malcolm, outraged by this behaviour, stormed ashore, tracked down Mr Whiting, the American consul, and gave him a full broadside, saying that he 'considered the manner in which the boat had been treated as most uncourteous.' Furthermore, he added that to anchor without permission was 'a violation of her Majesty's regulations.' To drive the point home, Malcolm assured the consul that if 'Wilkes should anchor without permission, and, when officially and distinctly informed of her Majesty's regulations, should refuse to move, he would fire into him.' The commander then reported to the senior officer of the station, Vice-Admiral Sir Alexander Milne, who, in turn, informed Lord Lyons at Washington, DC.

After Wilkes had tried and failed to bluster his way out of the situation, the Secretary of State, Seward, informed Lyons (after heavily mentioning Malcolm's 'verbal communication' with the American consul) that:

> … instructions have been given to Rear-Admiral Wilkes to render, on all occasions of intercourse with naval officers of Great Britain, the courtesies due from naval officers of one nation to those of a friendly power.

The Secretary of State then went on, rather pompously, to propose:

> If similar suggestions shall be given to the officers of her Majesty's service in the Gulf, I trust the irritations which have recently existed there, so much to the regret of both governments, will come to an end.

Vice-Admiral Milne, however, confined himself to reporting that Commander Malcolm's outburst at the consul may have been 'injudicious,' but that:

> … he [the vice-admiral] was bound to express his belief that in making that communication that officer was unconsciously influenced, to a certain degree, by those feelings of irritation which Rear-Admiral Wilkes's marked discourtesy in not communicating with the boat of the *Barracouta* was calculated to excite, as his conduct had generally been discreet and deserving of approbation.

Early the following year, at the south end of San Juan Island, Captain Bissell found himself faced with a problem that could have led to difficulties with the British. Whatcom County officials, wishing to re-establish themselves over the civilians on San Juan, sent their Justice of the Peace over to the island. He, in turn, wishing to stamp his authority, promptly tried to eject a British subject from the man's property. On discovering this, Bissell acted with commendable speed and dismissed the magistrate. When the inevitable complaint arrived at the desk of Brigadier-General George Wright (the former Commander of the Oregon Department who had replaced General Harney and was now Commander of the Department of the Pacific), he came down firmly on Bissell's side. Peaceful co-existence continued to reign over the island.

On 3 July 1863, far to the south-east, 'peaceful co-existence' was as far from many men's minds as could possibly be. General Lee and the Confederate Army were at Gettysburg facing the Army of the Potomac under the command of Major-General George Meade. Lee decided that a full-blooded assault should be made against the centre of the Union lines and ordered Lieutenant-General James Longstreet to carry out the attack with three divisions. The leading division was to be under the command of Major-General George Pickett, who had yet to be engaged in the battle. In all, around 12,000 men were to advance for more than half a mile over open ground against massed infantry, using rifled muskets and supported by artillery.

Following a hard pounding of the Union position by the Confederate artillery, and with the Union artillery return fire falling away, Pickett was handed a note from the artillery commander informing him that the guns were running out of ammunition and the artillery bombardment would soon have to stop. Reporting to Longstreet, Pickett asked for permission to start. Deeply depressed by the order he had to give, and totally unsure that the outcome would be successful, Longstreet sadly nodded his head in reply.

Returning to the head of his division – almost entirely made up of men from his native Virginia – Pickett gave the order to advance. Within minutes, nine brigades of gray-uniformed men, their front ranks stretching for almost a mile, were marching directly at the enemy, 1,000 yards away. They had not got far when the casualties began to mount. The advancing ranks were constantly sprayed by devastating small-arms fire and, surprisingly, the Union artillery opened up with a cannonading that ripped through the Confederate ranks.

As the advance reached the Emmitsburgh Road, Pickett, as divisional commander, halted and waved his men on. He had to be in a position to control the assault, something he could not do from the front. From the road, he watched as the mighty Confederate wave broke against the Union line. Cold, raw courage led to a shock of arms unlike anything else that had happened in the war; but courage alone was not enough for either side. The Confederate survivors, now less than half the number that had set out fifty minutes earlier, retreated over the 'crimson field,' as the Union men were too dazed and exhausted to mount a counter-attack. Pickett's three brigadier-generals and all the commanders of the thirteen regiments in his division were dead or wounded. The Union artillery, which had been assumed to be either destroyed or out of ammunition, had, in fact, been waiting for just such a frontal attack. The commander of the Union artillery was Colonel Henry Hunt, the older brother of Lewis Cass Hunt, who had taken command of the American camp after Pickett's removal at General Scott's suggestion.

When General Lee rode across to Pickett's position, he gave the order to regroup the division so they could receive a possible counter-attack. Pickett replied bitterly, 'General, I do not *have* a division.' He did, however, have an imperishable memorial. 'Pickett's Charge' was etched indelibly into the record of the Civil War.

The following day, as word of the battle at Gettysburg was still on its way, the American troops on San Juan Island celebrated 4 July. The Company mess was decorated with branches of fir and with muskets arranged to form stars edged with glinting bayonets. Above the door was written the words 'Welcome All' – a welcome that was extended to the Royal Marines on the island as well as 'a number of the fair sex.' Before the lunch began, Sergeant Jones of Company C read out a portion of the Declaration of Independence, following which 'the "Star Spangled Banner" was sung in excellent style.' After the meal, everybody went outside, where a number of sporting events took place. The Americans took first place in the Hop, Step and Jump; the High Leap (both standing and running); the Long Leap (standing and running); the 100 Yards Running Backwards; the 100 Yards Blindfolded; and Throwing the Shot. As impeccable guests, the Royal Marines settled for just Marine Newberry winning the 100 Yards Foot Race.

As the summer progressed, the Americans were almost overwhelmed by the arrival of the steamer *Enterprise*, which brought 180 lady and gentlemen 'excursionists' from Victoria. Backed up by the Royal Marines, they entertained their visitors during a picnic held beneath the shade of trees close by the American camp. Afterwards, dancing took place on the grass until the sun proved to be too hot for continued 'terpsichorean indulgence.' The party then adjourned to the quarters of the camp doctor, where the dancing continued until the steamer's whistle eventually demanded their return.

It was not only the Americans who had to endure such visits. 'Excursionists' also turned up at the British camp, where they were entertained just as courteously as they were by the Americans. The Royal Marines also had to suffer a number of high-profile visitors who required Captain Bazalgette's diplomatic attention.

One such visitor was the saintly George Hills, the first Bishop of British Columbia: A kindly man who remained undaunted by the prospect of working amongst the toughest of gold-miners, and surely welcomed being 'comfortably housed in the quarters of Captain Bazalgette commanding the detachment of 80 marines in the very snug and very beautiful cove at the north part of the island.' On one occasion, although at the camp for less than twenty-four hours, the bishop held four services and found time to attend the camp hospital to read the Bible to a feverish Roman Catholic private. For this he was rewarded by the lavish hospitality of his hosts:

> The Dinner at the mess today proved the value of the island so far as support life is concerned. There was excellent mutton fed upon the downs and shapes[?] around. Venison which is always to be had for a walk in the early morning. Salmon and a rich small member of the tribe Oulachan [Eulachon or candlefish] in size between a smelt and a herring caught in the bay of the settlement and duck shot nearby – all produced on the island.

Two other visitors were William Fitzwilliam, Viscount Milton; and Dr Walter Butler Cheadle. The two men had just made a unique crossing of the mainland from Fort Garry to Victoria, via the Yellowhead Pass through the Rocky Mountains and the Cariboo goldfields. Others had done the journey before them, but what made their passage unique was that, while others had travelled for exploration, settlement or in search of fortunes, they were 'a party of mere pleasure' – in fact, the first 'tourists' to visit that part of the world. Their journey had been fraught with difficulties, including the company of an unwanted Irish freeloader who was terrified of everything from wild bears to doing his share of the work. They had been forced to eat two of their horses to survive and had arrived at Kamloops in rags. Their good fortune had been the acquisition of a one-handed Assiniboine guide, who insisted on bringing his family along.

In his journal, Cheadle described the camp as:

> ... a beautiful little spot, with neat barracks & officers' quarters. The men's quarters on a pebbly flat, the officers' ditto on the slope of a hill. You enter the harbour by a narrow inlet, round a promontory, into a small bay.

Upon their arrival they met Bazalgette, who:

> … had just come in from shooting, having got some 200 ducks & geese in
> 3 days. Deer (small fallow) are common, & brought in frequently by officers.
> Sheep & cattle do well on island altho' it is rocky and herbage scanty in
> most places; some productive little farms. Fruit trees & strawberries flourish
> in an astonishing manner, as in all this region.

Bazalgette was described as:

> … a merry fellow of rather affected manner, but his genial nature soon
> causes one to forget this.

Milton and Cheadle had been brought to the British camp on board
the gunboat HMS *Forward*, commanded by the Honourable Lieutenant
Horace Lascelles, the son of the 3rd Earl of Harewood and brother of the
4th Earl. Lascelles had earned a reputation as the leader of a number of
punitive expeditions against the Indians. The previous April he had found
himself in Lamalcha Bay on Kuper Island in pursuit of Indians accused of
killing white settlers. The Indians, hidden amongst trees lining the shore,
opened fire, killing a sixteen-year-old seaman. After destroying most of
the Indians' village, Lascelles withdrew to avoid more pointless casualties.
When the proprietor of a Victoria newspaper was less than complimentary
about this event ('He who fights and runs away, lives to fight another day'),
he was invited to sea in the *Forward* and, somehow, ended up in the water
of Victoria harbour. He sued Lascelles for false imprisonment, the costs
of which the *Forward*'s captain paid without a second's thought. Joining
Milton and Cheadle for dinner with Bazalgette and the other officers,
Lascelles returned to his ship and, in typical high spirits, let loose with his
cannons and 24-pound Hale rockets, which flew through the air with a
spectacular, nerve-tingling howl. Those ashore returned the 'salute' with
revolvers and rifles. Cheadle then noted: 'After dinner had grog & pipes
& retired at 12.' The following day, Bazalgette accompanied them on a
'pleasant & picturesque voyage to Nanaimo.' Four days later, the *Forward*
brought them all back to the British camp, where they played skittles
in the afternoon before an evening entertainment was provided in the
officers' mess, '"Gus" Hoffmeister with guitar, Sparshott with tambourine,
& McBride (the doctor) with bones.'

Some years later, Viscount Milton, by then a Member of Parliament,
took up the San Juan cause with vigour and produced a book explaining

in detail why the island should not go to the Americans. Cheadle was more pragmatic:

> The island has a considerable number of settlers, consisting of white men who care not under which Government they may eventually be.

Earlier, Bazalgette had a narrow escape when Jane, Lady Franklin, and her niece, Sophia Cracroft, sailed passed the island. Lady Franklin was the indomitable widow of Sir John Franklin, the discoverer of the North-West Passage, and an energetic traveller in her own right. Both ladies were furious at the American presumptions regarding the island ('They have no possible pretext for claiming it'), and may well have pointed this out with some force, given a chance to get ashore. As they cruised past the island, they found it 'tantalising not being able to land.'

Captain Bissell, at the American camp, did not escape the occasional dignitary, and in September 1864 was visited by none other than the Commander of the Pacific Department, Major-General Irvin McDowell, the most senior officer to visit the Americans. McDowell had commanded the army forced into retreat at the First Battle of Manassas and, apart from a brief moment of glory at the Battle of Cedar Mountain in 1862, achieved little else. Appointed to the West, into what was little more than an administration post, McDowell at last found his ideal situation and settled comfortably into the job. He had taken over from General George Wright (who was to die at sea the following year), found the department in good order and intended to keep it that way.

With the exception of some civilian muttering over military authority, McDowell found the American camp, and the island in general, to be well maintained and run. There was little for him to do in that region. The British had behaved extremely well under the circumstances and had not tried to take advantage of the situation (and opportunity) presented by the Civil War. But, just as all good things, as well as all bad things, must come to an end, so the end of the war was in sight.

22

Attempt to Take Canada

The Civil War finally came to an end in April 1865. General Lee was forced to surrender to General Grant at Appamotox, and General Sherman accepted the surrender of General Johnston in North Carolina. The nation that was almost torn apart had held itself together at an appalling cost. From a combined population of 31 million, a total of 4,198,000 men had enlisted for the fight. Over 600,000 had died on the field of battle or from disease – more than the combined total of the First and Second World Wars, Korea and Vietnam. The Southern economy had been wrecked and the merchant and whaling fleets devastated. The newly re-United States needed a scapegoat, someone on whom it could place the blame for the suffering and loss. There was only one candidate: Great Britain. After all, the British had treated the Confederacy as a *bona fide* belligerent rather than a rebel faction. British ships had constantly breached the blockade to buy Southern cotton and tobacco. British dockyards had supplied the Confederacy with warships that had wrought havoc amongst Unionist shipping, and had allowed them the facilities of British ports around the world.

As if to underline the grievances, and with exquisite timing, the CSS *Shenandoah* steamed into Liverpool harbour on 6 November 1865. Originally launched at Glasgow as a troopship, the *Sea King* was purchased by Confederate agents, taken to Madeira, armed and commissioned as the *Shenandoah* under the command of Lieutenant James Waddell. Her new captain had orders to hunt down Federal ships in parts of the world that were not already covered by other Confederate ships – essentially, that meant the Pacific. On his way through the Atlantic and Indian Oceans,

Waddell took six prizes before arriving at Melbourne, Australia, where he and his (mainly British) crew were feted by the locals. He then set off to the north and fell upon the whalers in the Arctic seas. In the ensuing months, Waddell created havoc, sinking and burning so many ships that the New England whaling industry was never to completely recover. Then, on 2 August, he learned from a British ship that the war had been over for almost four months. By that time, the *Shenandoah* had destroyed thirty-eight vessels.

On his arrival at Liverpool (becoming the only Confederate ship to circumnavigate the world), Waddell handed his ship over to the Royal Navy, from whom she was sold to the Sultan of Zanzibar.

Even before this event, Charles Adams, the American Minister to London, had applied to the British Government for compensation for the damage done by the *Alabama* and other Confederate ships built and given refuge in British harbours. The '*Alabama* claim' was rejected out of hand. Great Britain was a free and independent country who had every right to sell ships to whomsoever she wished. In point of fact, she had not sold a single vessel to the Southern states, merely to individual purchasers who, if they so wished, might have sold them on to the Confederacy. That, nevertheless, was no concern of the British. Adams then appealed to British honour, an appeal that fell upon stony ground as an outraged Lord Russell stiffly replied that 'Her Majesty's Government are the sole guardians of their own honour.' To make matters worse, in October 1865 Russell was appointed Prime Minister. Any further considerations of such nonsense as the '*Alabama* claim' would be pointless.

In the United States, however, the 'claim' was being taken very seriously indeed, with some hotheads advocating the seizure of British Columbia. But that was nothing compared to the complicity of the President, Andrew Johnson, and the Secretary of War, Edwin Stanton, in an actual attack against British North America itself.

Irish political agitators, known as 'Fenians,' had organised themselves into a Government of Ireland in exile in New York. They planned to establish themselves in British North America and either exchange the land they had captured for Irish independence, use it as a base from which to attack British commerce, or even to use it for an attack on Ireland itself. They had thousands of volunteers with battlefield experience gained in the Civil War, a 'Secretary of War' who was a serving general in the United States Army and were well armed thanks to Stanton ignoring the transfer of weapons and ammunition to the Fenians. Their leadership had met the President, who had assured them that he would 'recognise the accomplished facts.' In other words, if they achieved their aims, he would not interfere.

Unfortunately for the Fenians, they were riven by factions, and had within their ranks many spies, some at the highest level. Consequently, the British were aware that something was about to happen. It was expected that St Patrick's Day, 17 March, would be chosen, but the day passed without incident and the militia raised to defend the border stood down.

Three weeks later, a large number of men were noted massing at the Maine coastal town of Eastport. It did not take long before word reached the British that the Fenians intended to land on Campobello Island, just off the Maine coast. Word had also reached President Johnson, and he sent General Meade north in a warship to keep an eye on things. Meade was not to interfere if it looked as if the planned invasion had every chance of success. If, on the other hand, it looked as if the possible damage to the United States outweighed the opportunities that might arise, he was to try and persuade the Fenians not to go ahead.

It did not take a man of Meade's abilities to see that there was a disaster in the making. The British had not only put the militia on alert, but had also sent six warships to patrol the coast. As the Fenian weapons and ammunition were arriving by sea (in a former United States warship supplied by Stanton), it was clear that the Royal Navy could easily stop the supply ship, allowing all the arms and equipment to fall into the hands of the British. Meade ordered the ship to be intercepted and sent back to New York, where its cargo was handed over to another Fenian faction. The intended attack never materialised and became known as the 'Campobello fizzle.'

May the 31st, however, was to reveal a plan of an entirely different nature. This time, over 24,000 men (including 500 Mohawk Indians and 100 black veterans of the Union Army) were to launch an attack across the border in a three-pronged assault. The main thrust, under the command of General John O'Neill, a former colonel with the 7th Michigan Cavalry, was to be across the Niagara River at Buffalo, New York. Once across, O'Neill was to advance on Toronto with the aim of taking that city before moving on to Montreal. Another 3,000 men would cross over from Detroit to aid in the attack on Toronto, whilst an army of 5,000 would leave from Cleveland in support. For the attack on Montreal, the Fenians could depend upon French radicals still nursing grievances from more than a century earlier.

The chief problem proved to be that, while the plan might have been imaginative, even likely to succeed, the Fenian rank and file were not only unimpressed – they failed even to turn up. Instead of 16,800, Neill found himself with numbers estimated at anywhere between 800 and 1,800. Undeterred, he set off and found Fortune's favour. A small force at Fort Erie was swept aside and, when he came under attack from the militia at Ridgeway, his luck continued to hold out. The militia commander, seeing horses and hearing bugles, assumed he was about to be attacked by cavalry and formed his men into squares. When the experienced Fenians attacked with bayonets instead, the militia was easily driven from the field.

The next day, O'Neill found that his luck had run out. Facing him were 10,000 militiamen, stiffened by 5,000 British soldiers. Even worse, his supporting troops from Detroit and Cleveland had not even left their camps. Falling back to the Niagara River, the Fenians boarded their barges and set off to cross over to the United States, only to find their way blocked by the USS *Harrison*. Meade and his superior, General Grant, had arrived on the scene and decided to put a stop to the whole event. Rail wagons arriving from New York containing arms and ammunition were stopped and confiscated, and O'Neill and his men arrested.

Four days later, 1,000 Fenians crossed into Quebec and vandalised two small villages before retreating. They had learned not only that the United States authorities had seized all their supplies, but that President Johnson had, at last, ordered the application of the Neutrality Act.

The result of the raids was not that anticipated by either the Fenians or the Americans. For some time there had been talks regarding the union of the Province of Canada with the colonies of New Brunswick and Nova Scotia. The original reason had been the withdrawal of the United States from a trade agreement between it and the colonies. The Fenian raids now injected a note of urgency into the matter and, on 29 March 1867, Queen Victoria signed the British North America Act. The Act came into force the following 1 July and the Dominion of Canada came into being with the four provinces of Ottawa, Quebec, New Brunswick and Nova Scotia. Instead of capturing a British colonial outpost, the Fenians had created a nation.

23

Alaska and British Columbia

For Captain George Bazalgette, all had gone well at Garrison Bay. Relations with the Americans had been entirely amicable, his Marines were contented, a minor limestone business was flourishing (although, already under the eye of American entrepreneurs) and the balls and levées at Victoria provided a welcome diversion. Then, in October 1865, the Americans replaced Captain Bissell with Captain Thomas Grey.

Grey, a man of little imagination, and to whom the meaning of the term 'diplomacy' was utterly lost, was cast in the mould of General Harney. He also had the misfortune to be appointed to San Juan just as the American structures, so carefully tended by his predecessors, showed signs of beginning to unravel.

To start with, his men (Battery I of the 2nd Artillery) numbered no more than forty-four, about half that of the Royal Marines at the British camp. His demand for more men led, amongst other soldiers, to the posting of a bugler named George Hughes. Astonishingly, four years earlier, Hughes had been a private in the Royal Marines and had deserted from the British camp on the island. Once Bazalgette learned of this, and after gaining the approval of his superior officer, he wrote to Grey formally requesting that Hughes be handed over as a deserter. The American camp commander replied stiffly:

> Not recognising that you have any legitimate grounds for requesting this soldier to be turned over to you as a deserter, I therefore decline to comply with your request.

Grey continued with a strange logic:

> I am not aware of your having returned to this command a deserter,
> therefore no one would regret the interruption of the good understanding
> which has always existed between the two camps more than I and I cannot
> but express my surprise at your anticipating, in the case of Hughes, any
> such result.

Rather than take the risk of a direct confrontation, Bazalgette once again
reported the matter to his superiors. Before long, word had reached
the US Army's Department of the Pacific, and the commander of the
department, General Henry Halleck, ordered that the bugler be discreetly
and promptly re-posted. Astonishingly, despite acting with the support
of his superior (Captain R.B. Oldfield, RN, the senior naval officer at
Esquimalt), Bazalgette managed to fall foul of the gloriously named
Richard Plantagenet Campbell Temple-Nugent-Brydges-Chandos-
Grenville, 3rd Duke of Buckingham & Chandos. Recently appointed as
Secretary to the Colonies, his grace, for reasons known only to himself,
decided to pontificate on Bazalgette's actions several thousands of miles
away, and a million miles away from any of his own personal experiences:

> On this allegation, without rendering any proof of the identity or of the
> desertion Captain Bazalgette demanded not enquiry or investigation,
> which would have enabled him to send home a report for consideration
> by Her Majesty's Government, but the surrender of an enlisted soldier of
> the United States Army ... His Grace considers it necessary therefore to
> draw the serious attention of their Lords Commissioners of the Admiralty
> to the case in order that they may direct such instructions to be sent to
> Captain Bazalgette as they may deem fit to prevent reoccurrence of any
> similar proceedings.

The Admiralty, noticing that Bazalgette had been away from England
for many years, deemed it 'fit' to appoint his replacement. Incidentally,
Richard Plantagenet Campbell, etc., etc., 3rd Duke of Buckingham &
Chandos, was the last of his line.

As if Fate decided to demonstrate with Grey the folly of his action
in snubbing Bazalgette's reasonable request for the return of Hughes,
several of his own men decided to desert. They achieved this by stealing
unsecured boats from the shores near the American camp. At this, Grey
demanded that all boats be locked and that any found to be unlocked

were to be destroyed. Unfortunately, one of his patrols came across such an unsecured boat and, obeying their orders, smashed in the sides and bottom. The boat, however, belonged to a British subject named Daniel McLachlan, whose loud protestations saw him being dragged off to the American camp and locked up. He was only released some weeks later after protracted diplomatic negotiations by Bazalgette, desperately trying to keep the situation from toppling out of control. But topple out of control it did, not with British involvement, but American.

Not long after the Royal Marines had celebrated the Queen's Birthday with blindfold wheelbarrow races, sack races and a greasy pole, Grey found that a one-time postmaster named Higgins had decided to turn to farming for an income. Not that the choice of occupation was a problem, but the fact that Higgins had chosen to set up his farm between the American camp and San Juan Town, thus cutting off access to the supply jetty. When told to take his fences down (by a possibly drunken Lieutenant Graves, Grey's second-in-command), Higgins refused. Asked for a second time, Higgins again refused, only to see the fences torn down by Grey's soldiers. The would-be farmer stormed up to the camp and confronted Graves, who promptly locked him in the camp's gaol. A week later, Higgins was released and immediately banished from the island. Enraged at his treatment, Higgins turned to law in an effort to obtain redress for his humiliation, and soon found he had very powerful allies.

The Government of Washington Territory had long felt the annoyance of having part of its region under military rule, and word went out that an opportunity had now presented itself for a correction of the situation. Accordingly, Grey and Graves were charged with malicious trespass and a sheriff sent to arrest them. The two officers, however, refused to be arrested and sent the sheriff away with a dusty answer. At this, a judge ordered the sheriff's return, backed up by a posse of armed men. This time the sheriff found himself up against Grey's men, armed and ready for action: again he withdrew.

Consequently, Captain Grey and Lieutenant Graves were tried in their absence, with the result that Higgins was awarded $6,000 for his troubles. The fine was, of course, ignored, causing Higgins (with the support of the territorial legislature) to petition William Seward, the Secretary of State, for redress. Seward did not take long in replying. The law on San Juan Island, he declared, must remain 'exclusively military.'

A controlling military presence on the island was, in fact, a small but nonetheless important part of Seward's strategy in his moves against Great Britain and the British presence in North America. He knew that

American opinion, certainly in the North, was virulently anti-British, and had been so for some years. As far back as 1864, the Reverend Charles Boynton spoke for many of his fellow countrymen when he urged an alliance between Russia and America in opposition to the British and the French. Because of American support during the Crimean War, Russia, he claimed:

> ... felt deeply, and is still grateful for American sympathy in her own great struggle with France and England; and, because of common perils from a common enemy ... the Great Empire of the East and the Great Republic of the West are very likely to be not only friendly, but allied powers in the not remote future ... The United States desire peace with England, if she will do us justice; but Americans have been forced, by her own conduct, into a position where they regard her good opinion far less than before. They know her power, and yet they do not fear her, and are by no means, at present, in a mood to court her favor. Great Britain must wipe out not only the stain, but the memory of her conduct in this rebellion, before the United States will court her favor.

Just in case there was any concern over a conflict with Great Britain, the reverend gentleman went on to assure his readers by informing them that the entire land area of their potential enemy was:

> ... less than that occupied by our three States of Ohio, Indiana, and Illinois, and less than half the size of Texas. England, alone, is not quite as large as the single State of Alabama ... it will do us no harm to remember that, ere this century closes, she will see here a hundred millions of people, who will be at least her equal in everything pertaining to either peace or war, and outnumbering her nearly three to one.

Should anyone be unclear as to the reason why the British should be vigorously opposed, the foaming cleric reminded them that they had hastened:

> ... with all aid and sympathy to the rebels; hastens to send fleets with Enfield muskets, rifled cannon, and arms, and sends forth piratical ships, under the Rebel flag, to plunder and burn our ships.

Boynton's reviewer demanded that his book should '... be put into the hands of every intelligent man in the nation.' And, as a direct result of his publication, Boynton was first appointed to the Naval Academy and then, shortly afterwards, made Chaplain to the House of Representatives. Against such a background of anti-British sentiment, Seward could expect an easy ride in his post-war demands from the British.

With any direct demand for compensation over the '*Alabama* claim' falling upon deaf ears, Seward tried to be a little more subtle. He told Adams, still the American Minister in London, and easily contactable via the new Atlantic Telegraph, that the United States would be prepared to forget about the claims if the British would sell the Bahamas to America. If not the Bahamas, possibly British Columbia, or even the new Dominion of Canada? Entirely predictably, the British refused even to consider such ideas. Seward then tried another tack: this time he would both purchase territory *and* pursue the '*Alabama* claim.'

Alerted by a flurry of speculative telegrams, the British Government had its fears confirmed by a letter to the Prime Minister, Lord Stanley (who had taken over on Lord Russell's retirement). The letter came from the British consul at New York, Frederick Wright-Bruce, who reported:

> The Russian Government have entered into a treaty ceding the whole of their possessions in North America to the United States for seven million dollars.

Seward had bought Russian North America for $7.2 million, unaware that the Russians would have settled for a mere $5 million. Even worse, as the money was to be paid 'in coin' (i.e. in gold), the actual value against the currency was more than $10 million. The purchase had not been popular, and had only succeeded in the Senate by one vote. Leading the opposition in the Senate, Cadwalader Washburn considered the acquisition to be nothing more than gaining a territory 'absolutely without value,' along with the 'responsibility and never-ending expense of governing a nation of savages.' On the other hand, Senator Leonard Myers supported Seward's proposal on the grounds that, if they did not obtain the territory, it would go to Great Britain:

> The nation which struggled so hard for Vancouver and her present Pacific boundary, and which still insists on having the little island of San Juan, will never let such an opportunity slip. Canada, as matters now stand, would become ours some day could her people learn to become Americans; but never, if England secures Alaska.

James Gordon Bennett, writing in the *New York Herald*, suggested that any impoverished monarch wishing to sell a piece of worthless land should simply apply to 'W. H. Seward, State Department, Washington, D.C.' The bombastic Senator Charles Sumner, eager to support Seward's anti-British initiative, had suggested the name 'Alaska' for the new territory, from a native word 'Alashka' meaning 'Great Land.'

The Russians had, on the whole, been keen to sell. The fur market was falling and attempts at agriculture in the region had failed. To sell to the Americans would serve to bring the two countries closer together in an alliance against the British. There was, however, no doubt in anyone's mind as to the real reason why the Americans had made the purchase. The British consul at New York drew attention to it in his letter to Lord Stanley:

> The United States will find means of evading a settlement of the questions arising out of the late war with Gt. Britain, they will base claims for cession of British Columbia or other territory as satisfaction for what Mr. Seward calls the political wrong and material injury done to the United States by the recognition of the Confederates as belligerents ... Unless a great change takes place in public opinion, I regret to say that this policy will meet with general support in the United States ... and it only remains to humiliate Great Britain to complete the self satisfaction of these people.

The Minister to St Petersburg, Sir Andrew Buchanan, adopted a superbly sour grapes attitude when he met the Russian Chancellor, Prince Gorchakov. Although, no doubt, fuming inside, he airily told the prince:

> ... it might have been considered a friendly act on the part of the Russian Government if She had afforded Her Majesty's Government or the Government of Canada an opportunity of purchasing the territory which has been sold, but that their not having done so, was materially unimportant as I felt assured as it would not have been bought.

The Foreign Office glowed with approval:

> Sir, – I have to acquaint your Excellency: that H.M. Government approve the language you held in your conv. with Prince Gortchakow, on the subject of the Sale of the Russian territory to the United States: you were quite right in saying that if the territory had been offered for sale to this Country it would not have been bought; the offer might have been an act

of courtesy on the part of the Russian Govt. but it would certainly have
been declined.

It is unlikely that anyone really believed that, given the opportunity, Great
Britain would not have grabbed the chance to secure her North American
territories by the possession of all the land north of the 49th Parallel. Now
it was too late. The Americans held the land both north and south of British
Columbia. Hemmed in by the Rocky Mountains to the east and the Pacific
Ocean to the west, the colony was ripe to fall into the hands of the United
States, and there was no doubt that the Americans intended that it should. It
was reported to Adams that Seward had said:

> The *Alabama* claims would soon be settled, but now they could only be
> settled in one way, by such acquisition from England as to enable us to
> round off our North-Western territory.

Even the British Government faced up to the appalling possibility that
British Columbia could end up as part of the United States; much to the
outrage of Lady Franklin's companion, Sophia Cracroft:

> It makes me so indignant that our Government can accept even as a
> possibility the loss of our only possession on this side of the Pacific.

Much worse, however, than the possible loss of British Columbia was
in the air. On 2 July 1866, Nathanial Banks was given permission to
introduce to the House of Representatives proposed legislation entitled:

> A Bill for the admission of the States of Nova Scotia, New Brunswick,
> Canada East, and Canada West, and for the organisation of the Territories of
> Selkirk, Saskatchewan, and Columbia.

In his bill, Banks demanded that Great Britain, and the provinces and
colonies north of the 49th Parallel, accept that:

> … the proposition hereinafter made by the United States, to publish by
> proclamation that, from the date thereof, the States of Nova Scotia, New
> Brunswick, Canada East, and Canada West, and the Territories of Selkirk,
> Saskatchewan, and Columbia with limits and rights as by this act defined,
> are constituted and admitted as States and Territories of the United States
> of America.

The United States would pay $85.7 million for the privilege of annexing British North America, and the Hudson's Bay Company would be bought off with $10 million. In the end, the proposed bill never got past a second reading in the House, and was never actually voted on, but British Columbia began to look seriously at joining the Dominion of Canada.

24

A New Commander

Captain George Bazalgette was relieved of his command on 24 July 1866. He had served on San Juan Island for over six years and had maintained the harmonious relations with his American counterpart demanded by his instructions. Throughout his time on the island, the Royal Marines had performed their duties well, and the British camp had never failed to earn praise for its appearance and condition. One report arising from a flag officer's inspection read:

> Inspected the Detachment of Royal Marines landed at San Juan, and found the Camp in a most satisfactory state. The admiral afterwards visited the American Camp accompanied by Captain Bazalgette … and reports that the most cordial and amicable relations exists.

Bazalgette was stationed at Stonehouse Barracks, Plymouth, until February 1870, from where he was appointed as recruiting officer for the Royal Marines at Exeter. Two years later he was put on the retired list. In accordance with the custom of the time, in which Royal Navy and Royal Marines officers were advanced one rank on retirement, Bazalgette was appointed Major in June 1872. He lived until August 1885 and was buried in Kensal Green cemetery in London.

Bazalgette's replacement was Captain William Delacombe, an experienced officer who had served in the Baltic during the Crimean War and had survived the explosion on board HMS *Bombay* in 1864: out of ninety-seven of the ship's company who lost their lives, thirty-four were Royal Marines. Delacombe also brought his family; consequently, a rather smart, five-room cottage was built to accommodate them. Another, smaller building was built for Delacombe's deputy, Lieutenant James Inman and his family. Both of the officers' quarters were built on a ledge overlooking the main camp. They also looked down upon the vegetable garden, and Mrs Delacombe, in the knowledge that fresh vegetables were easily available from Victoria, transformed the plot into the curiously English concept of the formal cottage garden.

It was not long before Delacombe found himself faced with a tricky question of protocol. The American camp commander, Captain Grey, had been relieved by Major Harvey Allen of the 2nd Artillery. It had always been assumed that the relative ranks of the two commanding officers on the island would be equal, thus enabling a more relaxed relationship between the two men. Although not obliged to accept any form of authority from the senior American officer, Delacombe felt that the difference in rank could provide an obstacle to that relationship, even if only arising from the courtesy needed to be shown to a senior officer. Accordingly, when the opportunity arose, he mentioned the difficulty to the governor.

Edward Seymour had been governor since 1866, when he had taken over from the aging, but still combative, Sir James Douglas. The new governor soon found himself overseeing a new region named 'The United Colonies of Vancouver Island and British Columbia,' a merger forced by political and economic necessity. Seymour supported Delacombe and wrote to Edward Thornton, the current British Minister to the United States. Thornton could see no difficulty and agreed that consideration should be given to a temporary promotion for the Royal Marine officer. Unfortunately, like Douglas before him, Seymour had forgotten who was really in charge of the British forces on San Juan Island. The Commander-in-Chief in the Pacific, Rear Admiral George Fowler Hastings, the second son of the 12th Earl of Huntingdon, did not take kindly to civilians, governors or not, arranging for the promotion of his officers. Seymour, on being sharply reminded by the admiral of this fact, wrote to the Colonial Office demanding to know who was in charge. His demand was ignored, and Delacombe never received his promotion. Hastings, on the other hand, appeared to hold no grudge against Delacombe and, after an inspection of the British camp, reported:

I visited the Island of San Juan in HMS *Sparrowhawk* and inspected the Detachment of Marines and the Camp generally. And am glad to report that everything was proceeding satisfactorily as regards the relations between the British and American occupation.

Clearly, the attempt to obtain promotion for Delacombe had been unnecessary.

For Charles Adams, however, the American Minister to London, it was not promotion that concerned him – it was resignation. He had tired of the pressure from the Secretary of State to get the British to agree to the '*Alabama* claim.' The British were proving obdurate and, if anything, were even more fixed in their opinion than before. Adams left for America in May 1868 and was replaced by Reverdy Johnson.

The seventy-two-year-old Johnson was an experienced lawyer who had served in Government as attorney-general. Known for his extremely courteous and obliging manner, he was almost certainly unaware of the existence of a possible plot involving Seward and others in which he was to play a significant part.

The British Government had just undergone a major change when Johnson arrived in London. As a result of the 1867 Reform Act, the Liberal Party had obtained a massive majority and William Gladstone became Prime Minister in place of Benjamin Disraeli. The new Foreign Secretary was George Villiers, 4th Earl of Clarendon, a vastly experienced diplomat who had served in Russia and Spain before being appointed as Secretary of State for Foreign Affairs in 1853. During the Crimean War he had been instrumental in holding together the difficult alliance between the British and the French, helped, no doubt, by his friendship with the French Empress, who he had known since she was a child in Spain. Clarendon did further service at the Foreign Office in 1865 and had now returned under Gladstone.

Both Johnson and Clarendon were keen to put aside the differences between their two countries and set about their negotiations almost immediately upon assuming their offices. Surprisingly, the discussions went extremely well, with Johnson being guided by Seward using the Atlantic Telegraph. The Americans retreated from their firm stand and agreed that the claims made by the nation should be removed and only private, individual claims should be considered. In response to the American private claims, the British made claims of their own, including the stopping of ships during the Northern blockade. The claims were to be dealt with by a joint commission, who could select an arbitrator 'by lot,' and no fault was to be accorded to either side. The results of the convention would be a 'full and final settlement' and any later claims would be 'barred and inadmissible.' Extraordinarily, even British holders of Confederate bonds would be compensated. All in all, the British had come out of the 'Johnson–Clarendon Convention' negotiations extremely well – suspiciously well, in fact.

Not surprisingly, when the convention reached the Senate for ratification, the house reacted with outrage. Chief amongst the protestors was the Chairman of the Senate Committee on Foreign Relations, the Massachusetts senator Charles Sumner. In his early years, Sumner had been considered to be a strong Anglophile, but now, possibly as a result of serious brain damage he had received during a savage physical attack upon him in the Senate itself, he was ready to launch his part in the plot with Seward and Johnson, the unknowing dupe.

Rising to his feet on 13 April 1869, Sumner raged at the convention:

A treaty which, instead of removing an existing grievance, leaves it for heart-burning and rancour, cannot be considered a settlement of pending questions between two nations. It may seem to settle them, but it does not. It is nothing but a snare! … The massive grievance which our country suffered for years is left untouched; the painful sense of wrong planted in the national heart is allowed to remain. For all this there is not one word of regret or even of recognition; nor is there any semblance of compensation.

On the subject of British blockade-runners, Sumner loudly declaimed:

From the beginning they went forth with their cargoes of dead; for the supplies which they furnished contributed to the work of death. When, after a long and painful siege, our conquering troops entered Vicksburg, they found Armstrong guns from England in position; and so, on every field where our patriot fellow-citizens breathed a last breath, were English arms and munitions of war, all testifying against England. The dead spoke also, and the wounded still speak.

Eventually, Sumner arrived at the point of his speech: how much should the British pay to compensate the United States? Dealing with the loss of seaborne trade, he shocked the house with his demand for reparations of $110 million. That, however, was 'only an item in our bill.' The war itself had cost the United States $4 billion and, thanks to the British, had certainly doubled in both time and casualties. That being the case, the British should pay the United States $2 billion in compensation. Whereas the house had previously been shocked, it was now stunned beyond belief. Everyone knew that such a figure would be beyond the capability of Great Britain to pay without crippling its economy. There was only one way in which such a matter could be settled: by the handing over to the United States of all the territories in British North America. The Senate rejected the Johnson–Clarendon Convention by a vote of fifty-three to one.

Three days later, a Michigan senator, Jacob Howard, jumped on the bandwagon and delivered a speech to the Senate about the current state of affairs on San Juan Island. He explained that the dispute had grown out of an argument over a dead pig between a 'Scotchman' and a 'Yankee settler,' which had, in turn, caused General Harney to:

> … post troops on San Juan to protect the American settlers from such outrages, as well as from the depredations of marauding Indians from the north … thereupon three British ships of war approached the island in a menacing manner. But this attempt to intimidate did not move Captain Picket.

Then General Scott had been sent out by the President and had:

> … without attempting to settle, or even inquire into the merits of jurisdiction, entered into an agreement with Governor Douglas for a joint military occupation of the island by the United States and Great Britain, to the exclusion of the civil authorities of either, temporarily, and until it would be settled by the two Governments. And such is its present status.

The senator then firmly championed the Canal de Arro as the channel intended by the 1846 treaty, even resorting to the dubious legal tactic, used in cases where international boundaries are formed by rivers, of explaining that the depth of his passage of choice was 118 fathoms (708 feet), whereas the Rosario Strait was a mere 93 fathoms (558 feet). As the depth required by even the largest ship afloat was unlikely to be much more than a mere 5 fathoms, it is hard to see what bearing such measurements had upon the issue.

Searching for a means to stiffen his case, Senator Howard harked back to the letter sent by Lord Lyons to the Secretary of State, Lewis Cass, in December 1860. Lyons had suggested that the question of San Juan should be submitted to international arbitration. Howard told the house that Lyons had named:

... the king of the Netherlands, the king of Sweden, and the president of the Federal Council of Switzerland as the persons from whom the arbiter should be selected ... Strange to say, he passed by our old friends the king of Russia, the king of Prussia, the emperor of Brazil, the president of the republic of Mexico ...

The senator then revealed his view of international arbitration by declaring that the future of San Juan Island should never be put 'in the keeping' of someone like:

... the 'President of the Swiss Confederation,' the temporary head of a feeble State without permanent official position or responsibility, possessing in small measure the dignity of head of a State; a man without known eminence as a jurist, a man unfamiliar with our language and institutions, representing a small nation: it places in his feeble hands both the honor of our country and its indubitable territorial rights; and invites him, if he can be induced so to do, to tarnish that honor and to transfer those rights.

No, Senator Howard was not prepared to allow foreign heads of state to meddle in the affairs of the United States. Instead, direct action had to be taken. 'It is time,' he ranted, that the British Government:

... should understand that the people of the United States are no longer to be trifled with; that treaties made with that people are not to be broken but kept; that we are able, willing, determined, that the faith of England given to us in her treaties shall be kept. I say it without boasting, but she knows and we know that we have it in our power easily to compel her to do justice. Why, then, omit to warn her to surcease her usurped occupation of this island? Why permit the 'joint occupation' agreed upon by General Scott in 1859 to endure longer? It may be replied, it will be followed by war. I do not believe it. But should she choose war, should she lift her weapon in attempting to enforce her claim, we must accept the issue. We must reckon with her hilt to hilt; we must then mark down the future boundaries of this country with the point of the sword.

Needless to say, the bold senator had never served in the armed forces of his country.

In Great Britain, Sumner's threat of economic ruin or the loss of British North America, and the bombastic speech by Howard, were treated with dignified indifference. There was talk of war in some quarters, but government observers knew that there was already a significant change on the American scene that could affect everything.

Even as Sumner and Howard had been speaking, a new president had already taken office. Ulysses S. Grant, the most outstanding general of the Civil War, was inaugurated president on 4 March 1869. Seward, whose last great attempt to grab Canada and British Columbia still stood in the balance, had been replaced, firstly by Elihu Washburne and, shortly afterwards, by Hamilton Fish. The gentle Reverdy Johnson was replaced as Minister to Great Britain by John Motley, an artist and historian who had served in the same capacity in Austria.

In his first annual message to the Senate and House of Representatives, given in December 1869, Grant explained the problems with Great Britain arising as a result of perceived British actions during the Civil War. He was, however, entirely pragmatic in his approach:

> The rejection of the [Johnson–Clarendon] treaty was followed by a state of public feeling on both sides which I thought not favourable to an immediate attempt at renewed negotiations. I so accordingly instructed the minister of the United States to Great Britain, and found that my views in this regard were shared by Her Majesty's ministers. I hope that the time may soon arrive when the two Governments can approach the solution of this momentous question with an appreciation of what is due to the rights, dignity, and honor of each, and with the determination not only to remove the causes of complaint in the past, but lay the foundation of a broad principle of public law which will prevent future differences and tend to firm and continue peace and friendship.

The British Government could only – and with great relief – agree. The Americans had consigned the bluster and threats of rabid senators to the bottom of the pile. There was, after all, a crisis shortage of British investment in the United States affecting both post-war reconstruction and expansionism. With the immediate pressure taken off, the British could keep a closer eye on events across the English Channel that were causing deep concern.

25

The Politicians Grow Restless

President Grant's annual message of December 1869 contained an important item of news. It read:

> The commissioners for determining the northwest land boundary between the United States and the British possessions under the treaty of 1856 have completed their labors, and the commission has been dissolved.

The American commissioners under Archibald Campbell, and the British led by Colonel John Hawkins of the Royal Engineers, had completed their monumental task of surveying the boundary along the 49th Parallel from the Gulf of Georgia to the Lake of the Woods. On 10 May 1869, Hawkins wrote to Lord Clarendon at the Foreign Office to inform him that:

> I now have the honour to inform your Lordship that on the afternoon of the 7th instant our labours were brought to a conclusion, which will I hope be quite satisfactory to you and Her Majesty's Government, and meet with the approval of Her Majesty.

It had been a considerable achievement. The boundary had stretched along 9° of longitude – about 410 miles, although over 800 miles had actually to be covered due to the nature of the terrain. Astronomical points had been set up along the route, each point marked by an iron pillar or a stone cairn, and each marker was further identified by having half a mile of forest cleared on either side following the direction of the border, the clearance being 20 feet wide.

Campbell described the effort involved in his report to the Secretary of State:

> The work of running the land boundary was carried on through a country previously almost unknown. The 49th parallel extends over rugged and precipitous mountains that attain great elevation, and in the Cascade range, on and near the boundary, perpetual snow covers many of the peaks, whose northern gorges are filled up with immense glaciers. The timbers on the western slope of the Cascade mountains is dense, being a heavy growth of pine and fir, that in many places stands over a fallen forest not yet decayed.

Astonishingly, after all the effort, shortly after the reports and maps had been presented to both governments, they disappeared in the quagmire of bureaucracy. No one seemed terribly excited about their disappearance, and it was to be many years before anyone gave them a second thought.

The same might have been said about the soldiers and Royal Marines on San Juan Island. Captain Delacombe and his men at the British camp found that, apart from the occasional visit by senior officers, life continued with little difficulty or disturbance. The Americans, on the other hand, by now under the command of Captain Joseph Haskell, were facing the usual problem of the Washington Territory authorities trying to wrest back their legal responsibilities.

The limestone diggings, started by Bazalgette, had fallen into the hands of an unsavoury bunch of individuals who included none other than Lyman Cutler, the pig-slayer who had started all the international trouble now affecting the island. Before long, they were at each other's throats, until one was shot dead. At this, with the backing of the acting Attorney-General of the United States, the United States Attorney for Washington Territory, supported by a deputy marshal and a posse, turned up on the island demanding the alleged killer. Two problems then presented themselves: not only did Haskell refuse to hand over the man until authorised by his superior officer, but the man himself was British. The latter problem was soon dealt with: no British official was prepared to prevent the Americans taking the man away and trying him for murder. With this question out of the way, Haskell was ordered to deliver the man up to the Washington Territory officials. In the end, and after murdering a fellow prisoner, the man was sentenced to hang – only to escape just before the sentence was due to be carried out. He was never seen again.

As if he had not suffered enough, Captain Haskell was faced with a visit from Lady Franklin and her niece, Sophia Cracroft, back in the area for a second visit. They had hoped to land at the British camp to meet Captain Delacombe, '… as he is a particularly nice person.' But that had not been possible. Landing on the beach of Griffin Bay, the two ladies then visited one of the houses close by:

The room was exceedingly nice & tidy, but the hostess was truly Irish (her brogue betrayed her at once) with a dirty cotton gown tucked upon one side, displaying unlaced boots – hooks and eyes in at irregular distances & bare arms, completed the characteristic picture. She welcomed us by shaking hands & we remained a few minutes, during which we learned not at all as a joke that we were in the *City* of San Juan, & that the population consisted of *2 families*!

The pair then made their way to the American camp, which Sophia was to describe as:

… an orderly collection of wooden buildings, with gardens & other small enclosures, arranged after the usual military fashion, the regularity of which is very pleasing,

On their arrival, Captain Haskell took them to his quarters:

… where his wife recd us very kindly in a nice little drawing room. They have 2 fine little boys … The youngest was delighted to shew my Aunt his picture books … We like Captn & Mrs Hescoll [*sic*], they were so cordial & certainly much pleased to see my Aunt. The English & American officers seem to be on the most amicable terms …

Miss Cracroft then turned her attention to the question of who owned the island, which was:

… occupied by both American & English tho' in fact & in honour, *ours*. The Boundary agreed upon by Treaty included as ours, the Straits of Hara [*sic*], and this was understood (by obvious geographical interpretation) to give us the Isd of San Juan, a most important position as commanding the only available entrance to our western (Pacific) sea board … a certain American General Harney, commanding lower down the coast, took upon himself to land 500 soldiers here, hoist the American Flag, and take possession! …

> the Island is clearly ours by Treaty, as implied by the terms of it and the
> longitude agreed upon. But the Americans still maintain their ground with
> about 70 men and 3 or 4 officers & so keep up their occupation of it!

It did not help that Sophia was distinctly unimpressed with the American officers' feathered uniform hat which, she thought, was 'exactly the hat of a Spanish muleteer.'

Whilst the British Government would, no doubt, have supported Sophia's spirited stand against American encroachment upon British territory, it had other matters that were giving it cause for concern. The French had looked uneasily at the rise of Prussia as a powerful state. The Prussians had recently defeated the Austrians and were beginning to look like a cause for the unification of the German states. When it appeared that a German prince was about to be set upon the vacant throne of Spain, the French demanded that the idea be dropped immediately, along with an apology for even thinking of such an idea. The Prussian Chancellor, Otto von Bismarck, was disinclined to agree, and soon French and Prussian armies were lining up to oppose each other.

The French had managed to alienate all of their possible allies. The Russians, still sullen after their defeat in the Crimea, remained neutral, but could not be trusted to keep out of any conflict. The British, alarmed by earlier French demands for possession of Belgium and Luxembourg, avoided involvement and merely watched as, on 31 July, Napoleon III led his army across the Saar River. It was not long, however, before someone pointed out a serious danger to Great Britain. If the French were defeated, and Germany united, the balance of power in Europe would have shifted dramatically – and who knew what that could lead to? If, for example, the Germans and the Russians became military allies, they would create a formidable combination that could attack whomever they wished, and neither owed any favours to the British. If the French defeated the Prussians and began to grab the small countries they had recently had their eye upon, would Britain be dragged into a European war? Even further, what would the United States do, bearing in mind the bullish American attitude towards Great Britain as a result of British actions during the Civil War? Was a United States–Germany alliance possible?

In an effort to forestall these questions, the Foreign Officer proposed to Gladstone that a joint commission be set up with the United States to look for ways to get out of the impasse remaining over the '*Alabama* claim' and any other difficulties between the two nations. To find out if the Americans had any interest in such an idea, Gladstone sent Sir John Rose to Washington, DC. Rose, a Canadian of Scottish ancestry, already had an amicable relationship with the Secretary of State, Hamilton Fish, and had discussed with him such matters as the '*Alabama* claim' and the question of fishing rights off Nova Scotia and Newfoundland. Furthermore, some years earlier, Rose had actively considered the possibility of Canada joining the United States and had been a member of the short-lived 'Annexation Association.' Now, however, he was a firm friend of the Prime Minister of Canada, Sir John MacDonald, and could be depended upon to put the British–Canadian case across to the American. The purpose of Rose's visit was kept secret from all but the President and Fish, for fear of alerting Senator Sumner, who would be bound to launch a fierce campaign of opposition. Nevertheless, Sumner turned up at a dinner being attended by Rose and, on learning that Rose was a Canadian, loudly informed him (and the rest of the table) that any differences between the two countries could be easily remedied. The Canadians only needed to 'Haul down that flag and all will be right!'

Despite their ability to get on with each other, Rose and Fish lost none of their desire to see the best for their respective nations. Rose, for example, wanted the damage caused by the Fenian raids to be included in the negotiations of the joint commission. Fish refused. In turn, when Fish wanted to include the 'indirect claims' connected with the '*Alabama* claim' (i.e. the vague, but inherently costly, financial damage caused to the United States as a nation), Rose rejected the idea. In the end, it was agreed that the commission could examine the private '*Alabama* claim,' fishing rights, the navigation of rivers and canals that formed or crossed the border between the two countries, the free navigation of Lake Michigan, the duty-free transit of goods across one country when intended for the other, the meaning of neutrality with regard to the supply of ships to belligerents and, almost as an afterthought, the question of the San Juan water boundary.

With the groundwork done, the two countries assembled their respective commissions and met in Washington, DC. The American commission was led by the Secretary of State, Hamilton Fish, who was assisted by Robert Cumming Schenk, Envoy Extraordinary and Minister Plenipotentiary to Great Britain; Samuel Nelson, an Associate Justice of the Supreme Court of the United States; Ebenezer Rockwood Hoar, of Massachusetts; and George Henry Williams, of Oregon. When listed, these distinguished Americans looked almost drab when compared to the list of British commissioners. They were led by the Rt Hon. George Frederick Samuel, who also held the titles Earl de Grey and

Earl of Ripon, Viscount Goderich, Baron Grantham, Baronet, Peer of the United Kingdom, Lord President of Her Majesty's Most Honourable Privy Council, Knight of the Most Noble Order of the Garter, etc. He was supported by the Rt Hon. Sir Stafford Henry Northcote, Baronet, CB, MP; Sir Edward Thornton, KCB, Her Majesty's Envoy Extraordinary and Minister Plenipotentiary to the United States of America; Sir John Alexander MacDonald, KCB, a member of Her Majesty's Privy Council for Canada, and Minister of Justice and Attorney-General of Her Majesty's Dominion of Canada; and Mountague Bernard, Esq., Chichele Professor of International Law in the University of Oxford.

Some parts of the negotiations were easier than others. The question of fishing rights was soon dealt with, the only problem being that the United States was gaining considerably more than the British. To inquire into this imbalance a commission was to meet at Halifax. The commission was to be comprised of one commissioner from each side, with a third agreed by both sides. If agreement could not be reached regarding the third commissioner, he would be appointed by the London representative of His Majesty the Emperor of Austria and King of Hungary. The international laws of neutrality were agreed, with the British further agreeing that, although clearly not in force at the time of the Confederate ships, the new laws could be used as a basis for negotiating the '*Alabama* claim.' The transit of goods question and the use of rivers, canals and Lake Michigan presented no difficulty and were mutually agreed upon.

No agreement could be made on the '*Alabama* claim' and, consequently, it was decided to offer the question up to a court of international arbitration. This tribunal would be made up of five members, one of each to be proposed by the Queen of Great Britain, the President of the United States, the King of Italy, the Emperor of Brazil and (no doubt to a howl of horror from Senator Jacob Howard) the President of the Swiss Confederation. If a reserve was needed, he would be selected by the King of Sweden and Norway. The *Alabama* Claims Commission was to meet in Geneva.

Private and corporate claims from both sides were to be dealt with by a commission comprising one member from Great Britain, one from the United States and one appointed conjointly. If no agreement could be found on the third member, he would be appointed by the American representative of the King of Spain. The commission would meet in Washington, DC.

The comparative harmony of the joint commission was then, suddenly, torn apart. Facing the question of the San Juan water boundary,

Hamilton Fish was adamant that the island belonged to America. The boundary could only go through the Straits of Haro – any other route was unthinkable. The British, on the other hand, were quite certain, beyond any doubt, that it went through the Rosario Strait. The debate became so heated that, at one time, the British commissioners were on the verge of walking out. After repeated attempts to get each other to change their minds, the British offered a solution. A compromise channel existed between San Juan and the islands to the east, and the British were prepared to put such a compromise on the table. The Americans flatly refused, but managed to turn the proposal around in order to make progress. They would agree to go to arbitration if, and only if, the arbitrators were offered just the choice of the Haro and Rosario passages: there was to be no compromise channel.

Consequently, when the joint commission's draft treaty appeared before the Senate on 24 May 1871, Article XXXIV, after referring to the 1846 Boundary Treaty, declared:

> … whereas the Government of Her Britannic Majesty claims that such boundary line should, under the terms of the Treaty above recited, be run through the Rosario Straits, and the Government of the United States claims it should be run through the Canal de Haro, it is agreed that the respective claims of the Government of Her Britannic Majesty and of the Government of the United States shall be submitted to the arbitration and award of His Majesty the Emperor of Germany who, having regard for the above-mentioned article of the said Treaty shall decide thereupon, finally and without appeal, which of those claims is most in accordance with the true interpretation of the Treaty of June 15th, 1846.

The Emperor of Germany, it should not be forgotten, was, according to Senator Jacob Howard, one of a group of 'old friends' of the United States. The Senate ratified the treaty, and the ratifications were exchanged in London the following June.

26

British Columbia Joins Canada

Just as the Washington Treaty ratifications were being exchanged, the colony of British Columbia was taking an important step to secure its future. With continuous threats from the United States of possible annexation, a number of leading citizens were pressing for entry into the Dominion of Canada. The chief opponents of such a proposal rested their case on the fact of the huge distance between the Pacific coast colony and the dominion itself. However, the year before, Manitoba had joined the confederation and the gap had been much reduced. Even more importantly, the colony found itself in considerable debt due to a large increase in its population and the end of the gold rush. Consequently, when the Canadian Government offered to pay the debts and link the colony to the rest of Canada by a railway, British Columbia became the sixth member of the dominion on 20 July 1871.

The new status of British Columbia had little effect upon the occupants of the camps on San Juan Island. The Americans, still under Captain Haskell, continued to fend off attempts to establish a civilian legal authority whilst trying endlessly to clamp down upon whisky-sellers and Indian prostitutes. The death of Private Garloch in May 1871 was followed a few months later by the suicide of Sergeant Whetston, the third suicide at the camp since it had been established.

The Royal Marines at the British camp had suffered a few deaths since it was founded eleven years earlier. Five men had died from drowning, one from unknown causes and one accidentally shot by his brother. Their graves and memorials were placed in a quiet glade on the slope of Young Hill.

Both the American and the British camps were visited by Mrs Phelps, a lady singer who entertained the soldiers and Marines with songs such as 'Beautiful Snow' and 'Captain Jinks of the Horse Marines.' On New Year's Eve 1871, the Royal Marines gave a ball. The barracks were decorated with evergreens and bunting and a large number of 'rustic belles' from Victoria were entertained to supper before dancing until the break of dawn. The guests were then escorted to their waiting ferry by the Marines and a band.

Not all visitors were quite so jolly, although an inspection by the Commander-in-Chief of the Pacific Fleet, Rear Admiral Farquhar, had him commenting that:

> I found the men in efficient order and their Quarters neat, clean, and comfortable. Captain Delacombe has taken great trouble to render the men contented, and their quarters comfortable, many improvements have been carried out with this view.

Meanwhile, at scattered points around the world, thousands of miles from the tranquillity of San Juan Island, politicians and jurists began their work of removing the grievances that existed between the United States and Great Britain. In general terms, the British and Canadians were doing rather well. The commission meeting at Halifax to discuss the fishing dispute restored the American fishing rights for the next twelve years, at a cost of $5.5 million to the United States. In Washington, DC, the commission considering the question of private and corporate claims surprised everyone by dismissing the American claims and awarding the British claimants almost $2 million.

The *Alabama* Claims Commission held at Geneva, however, was a very different matter. The Americans had chosen Charles Adams, the former Minister to Great Britain, to be their representative. This upset the British, who considered Adams (who had been closely involved in much of the earlier negotiations) to be far too prejudiced to make an objective assessment. The British selected the Chief Justice of the Queen's Bench, Sir Alexander Cockburn, a prickly blusterer who had no experience of having his opinions challenged. Furthermore, Cockburn treated the commission like a court, where witnesses could be browbeaten rather than have their expert assessments closely, but courteously, examined.

The Italian representative, Count Frederic de Sclopis, was elected as chairman and upset Jacob Stampfli, the Swiss representative, by having a larger chair. Baron d'Itajuba of Brazil had poor command of the English language (as did Stampfli), and it was decided that the proceedings should be conducted in French. At this, Cockburn tried to persuade Adams that the other commissioners should be dismissed and the differences between the two English-speaking nations be debated in their native tongue. Adams not only refused, but, in presenting the American case, included the potentially hugely costly 'indirect claims' that had previously been agreed would be dropped. When it became clear that the British were on the verge of walking away from the commission, Adams, rather than lose any opportunity to settle the issue, arranged for the other arbitrators to reject the indirect claims. If Adams was to come under any American criticism for the loss of the indirect claims, he could merely shrug his shoulders and point at the rest of the commission.

Finally, on 14 September 1872, the commission announced its decision. The British Government would pay the Americans $15.5 million. Cockburn refused to sign the arbitration and stormed out of the building to the sound of church bells and guns as the rest of Geneva celebrated. He was guilty of over-reacting. The amount awarded was nothing compared to the $2 billion demanded by Senator Sumner, and had hardly any effect on the national economy. Indeed, not only would it be easily recovered by the re-opening of British investment in the United States, the British had recently spent more than double that amount on rescuing a few of their diplomats from the clutches of an Abyssinian despot.

With his victory in the Franco–Prussian War, the German Emperor, Wilhelm I, could afford to spend a little time on the question of ownership of a remote island far away to the north-west of North America. Not, of course, that he would do the necessary study and research into the question of selecting the channel that had been intended in the 1846 treaty. Instead, he would be granted the honour of making the announcement when the decision had been made.

To make that decision, the Emperor chose as commissioners three eminent German scholars with international reputations. Professor Heinrich Kiepert of the University of Berlin was a geographer and cartographer who had worked on maps of California, Mexico and Texas, amongst other places. Professor Levin Goldschmidt was a renowned jurist with vast expertise in commercial law. They were joined by Dr Ferdinand Grimm, the Vice-President of the Supreme Court in Berlin.

Many Americans had been worried by the selection of the Emperor. He was, after all, the father-in-law of Princess Victoria, Queen Victoria's daughter, and, during the revolutionary riots of 1848, as King of Prussia, he had fled to the safety of England. The United States, however, riposted by appointing George Bancroft as their representative to the commission. Bancroft, a diplomat, politician and historian, had studied in Germany, where he had made many highly connected German friends. He had been the Minister to Great Britain during the 1846 treaty negotiations and knew every facet of the debate intimately. In 1867, Bancroft had been appointed as Minister to Prussia, then Minister to the North German Federation and then, finally, in 1871, as Minster to the new German Empire. He was well acquainted with both the Emperor and the Chancellor, Otto von Bismarck, and had once commented that the latter 'loves to give the United States prominence in the eyes of Europe as a balance to Great Britain.' Unacknowledged support came in the form of John Motley, recently the American Minister to Great Britain and now in the same role at The Hague. Motley and Bismarck had gone to school together.

The British were to be represented by Admiral James Prevost, the same man who, as captain of HMS *Satellite*, had led the water boundary commission negotiations against the unyielding Archibald Campbell, and who was unknown in German high society. The British Ambassador to Berlin, Odo Russell, a nephew of Lord Russell, was well connected with the Chancellor. He was, however, still smarting from a reprimand given by Gladstone in the House of Commons after he had told Bismarck that Great Britain would go to war 'with or without allies' against Russia. This was a result of the Russians – now that France had been defeated by the Prussians – threatening to tear up the 1856 Treaty of Paris which had ended the Crimean War. Gladstone had told the House that their Ambassador in Berlin had acted 'without any specific instructions or authority from the government.' Consequently, Russell was not keen to get involved in a squabble over a small island thousands of miles away in the Gulf of Georgia.

For the most part, Prevost did a good job in presenting the British case. Using earlier correspondence and contemporary testimonials, the admiral laid the facts before the commission with admirable clarity. Firstly, at the time of the signing of the 1846 treaty, the only channel 'generally known and commonly used by sea-going vessels' was the channel known later as the Rosario Strait. Secondly, the southward-running boundary line should enter 'the head-waters of Fuca's Straits.' This could not be done if the line ran through the Canal de Arro. Thirdly, the proviso guaranteeing free navigation 'of the whole of Fuca's Straits' only makes sense if free navigation was granted as far as the Rosario Strait. To have cut it off at the Canal de Arro would have rendered the proviso both unnecessary and meaningless. Fourthly, as the Rosario Strait was not named at the time of the treaty, it could have been the only route intended by the treaty. The Canal de Arro, on the other hand, *had* been named prior to the treaty and, if *that* channel had been intended, it would have been so named in the treaty. It was not. Fifthly, a boundary line running through the Rosario Strait would have been 'favourable to both parties.' But a line running through the Canal de Arro 'would have deprived her Britannic Majesty of a right of access to her own possessions through the only then known navigable and safe channel.'

However, for reasons best known only to himself, Prevost did not cause attention to be brought to the numerous American maps, drafted subsequent to the 1846 treaty, which showed that American geographers and cartographers agreed with the British view that the boundary line ran southwards through the Rosario Strait.

George Bancroft attacked the British case with both vigour and rancour. Firstly, the British, despite centuries of being a maritime power, did not understand the meaning of the word 'Straits.' By his definition, 'Straits' could only mean 'a narrow passage connecting one part of the sea with another.' Therefore, the Straits of Fuca could only extend as far as the south-east cape of Vancouver Island, and did not stretch as far east as the shores of Whidbey Island. This, in turn, meant that the southern end of the Canal de Arro did, in fact, meet the 'headwaters' of the Straits of Fuca, thus answering the requirements of the treaty. And secondly, the claim by the British that the Canal de Arro was not known to be navigable at the time of the treaty was both 'irrelevant' and 'ignorant,' and depended upon the testimony of 'Obscure men.' Indeed, such a claim 'must be classed among the dreams that come from the realms of shades through the ivory gate.'

Just in case brusque language did not meet the case, Bancroft then resorted to pathos:

> The American Government cannot offer the rebutting testimony of American mariners, for their fur-trade on the northwest coast had been broken up before 1810, and when at a later date they attempted to renew it, they had been forcibly compelled by the officers and servants of the Hudson's Bay Company to give up the field. The American sailors, therefore, who were familiar with those regions have long since gone to slumber with their fathers.

Both the British and the American cases were laid before the commission in June 1872. Four months later, on 21 October, their decision was presented to the Emperor for his signature. The final conclusion read:

> Most in accordance with the true interpretations of the treaty concluded on the 15th of June, 1846, between the Governments of Her Britannic Majesty and of the United States of America, is the claim of the Government of the

United States that the boundary-line between the territories of Her Britannic Majesty and the United States should be drawn through the Haro Channel.

The British had lost the argument, and lost an island. Bancroft noted that:

> The award was a grievous disappointment to Admiral Prevost, the very amiable high officer in the British Navy, who had for twenty-one years participated in the management of the case. Up to the last moment he confidently expected a decision in his favour.

In fact, it could have been Prevost's amiability that lost the case in the face of Bancroft's aggression. It had, in the end, been a close-run thing. There is every reason to suspect that the final result had verged upon a more equitable outcome. Bancroft, with the firm backing of the Secretary of State, Hamilton Fish, would not allow a compromise channel to be put before the commission. Neither Sir John Rose during the talks leading to the Washington Treaty, nor the Earl of Ripon at the treaty talks themselves, nor Admiral Prevost subsequent to the treaty, had responded with equal determination to allow such a channel. The commission, faced only with the choice between the Canal de Arro and the Rosario Strait, finally voted two to one in favour of the Canal de Arro. Professor Levin Goldschmidt refused to be led down such a route when there was a clear compromise available, a cause he strongly advocated. If such a compromise had been open to discussion, there is every probability that he would have been able to persuade the other commissioners to arrive at the same conclusion.

There was little reaction to the lost cause in Britain, but, far away in British Columbia, the ageing Sir James Douglas, on hearing the news, wrote to his daughter:

> We have just heard that the San Juan question has been decided against England and we have lost the Island. I cannot help thinking that our case has not been fully or clearly represented to the Emperor of Germany, or he could not have arrived at so unjust a decision, which is utterly at variance with the rights of the relative parties. Well, there is no help for it now, we have lost the stakes, and must just take it easy.

But he found it difficult to 'take it easy.' A few days later he wrote:

> The island of San Juan is gone at last. I cannot trust myself to speak of it, and will be silent.

27

Decision and Aftermath

After thirteen years of joint military occupation, with, for the most part, a general accord between the opposing troops, Lieutenant Jacob Ebstein, one of the United States officers, was able to describe their situation thus:

> The duties of the two commanding officers were manifold and delicate; they were not only military commanders, but also judges, notaries, customs officials, land commissioners, registrators, and even coroners. There was no other authority on the islands of the archipelago, than that of these officers. The population exclusive of the garrison was about 600, nearly equally divided in national adherence. All British subjects were required to register their land claims at the British camp, and in like manner American settlers made their registry at our camp. Breaches of the peace and misdemeanours were tried before the commander of the power whose protection the offender claimed. If the offense involved citizens of both nations, the two commanders sat in joint court. The punishments were imprisonment in the guard house, fine, or in aggravated cases, banishment from the island.

Once General Harney had been dispatched to other duties, political bravado and diplomatic blustering had played little part in the lives of the men expected to take up arms and risk their lives in their countries' quarrel. They had recognised the situation for what it was: a squabble over the inexact wording of a treaty leading to opposing claims for a small archipelago at the southern end of the Gulf of Georgia. Both sides could have adopted an aggressive attitude and faced each other with sullen belligerence, yet neither chose to do so.

On 21 October 1872, the signature of the Emperor of Germany put an end to the need for British troops on the island. Captain Delacombe had been the first to receive the news in the form of an order from the Commander-in-Chief of the Pacific Station. The order was delivered on 18 November by Captain Ralph Cator of HMS *Scout*. Delacombe was told he had four days to close the camp down and embark 'the Garrison, with all stores, naval, colonial, etc.' There was to be no prolonging the process of withdrawal. With his men gone, Delacombe was to remain on the island to oversee any difficulties for the British settlers resulting from the removal of the Royal Marines. Early the following morning, Delacombe sent a messenger over to the American camp to inform the commanding officer, First Lieutenant James Haughey, of the developments.

When a former Secretary of War, General John Schofield, currently serving in San Francisco, heard of the Emperor's decision, he telegraphed an instruction to Haughey ordering him 'to pay the usual compliments to the British Flag on the withdrawal of the garrison from San Juan.' When General Edward Canby, Commander of the Pacific Northwest, saw a copy of the telegram, he was obliged to reply to Schofield that 'the usual compliments' would be impossible, as there was no artillery on the island – thanks to the joint occupation agreement – to fire such a salute. 'The only compliments,' he continued, 'that can be paid will be verbal between the commanding officers.' Instead, Canby telegraphed Haughey:

> Please express to Captain Delacombe my regret that the short notice of his removal makes it impossible to send a public vessel to the island to salute the British Flag upon withdrawal of British Garrison.

Haughey delivered the telegram in person to Delacombe on the 22nd, and returned with a reply:

> Sir, I have the honour to return you my grateful acknowledgement of the high compliment (contained in your message received through Lieut. J.A. Haughey USA this day) it was your intention to have bestowed had our withdrawal been less hurried, and on behalf of the officers serving under my command, and myself, to express how fully we appreciate and value the personal expressions you have been pleased to forward …

Delacombe also informed Haughey of his orders to remain on the island to look after the interests of the British settlers. The American replied that Delacombe's delayed departure was entirely acceptable, but that he would inform General Canby.

That morning, the Royal Marines had assembled on the clear ground fronting the water and were inspected for the last time. On completion, Captain Cator stood to their front and, above a rising wind, shouted in his best quarterdeck manner:

Marines! You are a credit to your country!

At this, the Marines marched to the beach, where they boarded ship's boats waiting to ferry them to the *Scout*.

The following day, Haughey arrived with another telegram he had received from Canby:

Your action approved, please extend to Captain Delacombe any assistance he may require while on San Juan.

The courteous offer of assistance was, however, no longer needed. Delacombe's orders to remain on the island had been withdrawn and he was to embark on board HMS *Peterel* with his family, his second-in-command, Lieutenant Herbert Schomberg, and the few remaining men left with them. Before they departed, Cator, with no instructions from London to guide him, was concerned that squatters might descend upon the camp the moment it was vacated. He decided instead, that Delacombe should hand the site, complete with its buildings, over to the American army.

Delacombe wrote to Haughey:

Sir, I am directed by Captain R P Cator RN of HMS *Scout*, Senior officer of HBM Navy present, to inform you that the Detachment of Royal Marines lately serving under my command on this Island are withdrawn, and he having determined to abandon this camp, is desirous that I should hand over the buildings etc. as they now stand to the Government of the United States as soon as you can make it convenient to receive them.

I am also directed to request you will present to General Canby, Captain Cator's thanks for his cordial offer of assistance to me, on hearing of its being the intention that I should remain on the Island for a time which is now cancelled.

I now beg to express to you personally my warmest thanks for your ready co-operation with me at all times, and permit me to subscribe myself with feelings of the highest order.

On the 24th, Lieutenant Ebstein rode into the camp with a troop of mounted soldiers. Having been sent to accept the camp from the British, he had brought with him a large Stars and Stripes flag. His dismay might be imagined when, just as he reigned in his horse, the massive 80-foot flagpole which dominated the waterfront, slowly toppled to the ground. Delacombe assured him that the mast was needed as a spar to replace a defective one on board one of the ships, but Ebstein later recalled that 'a young subaltern' (almost certainly Schomberg) told him:

> … with much more candor than judgement … 'You know we could never have any other flag float from a staff that had borne the cross of St. George.'

Within hours, the last of the Royal Marines had left the island. From the American point of view they had been an occupying force – but no such force has ever been more welcome. From the British perspective, they had held the line against American expansionist aggression – but no defenders ever had more cordial relations with their potential enemy.

The following spring, a San Francisco newspaper reported:

> The appearance of red-coated soldiers – or rather marines – upon our streets yesterday, created no little astonishment to those who were aware that the harbor contained no British ships-of-war at the time. The phenomenon was explained by the fact that the steamer *Prince Alfred* had arrived from Victoria with the garrison formerly in occupation of San Juan Island, lately awarded to the United States by arbitration. The detachment numbers seventy-six men of the Royal Marine Light Infantry … the men are fine, healthy, sturdy looking fellows, and seem quiet and well-disposed.

Captain Delacombe retired from the Royal Marines as a Lieutenant-Colonel in 1876, and was appointed Chief Constable of Derbyshire, an appointment he held with great distinction for the next twenty-two years. He died in 1902.

The British settlers who had been left stranded on San Juan Island took an entirely pragmatic view of their situation and took United States citizenship. In reality, the most dramatic change in their life was the tax they suddenly had to pay, an imposition they had escaped as subjects of the Queen.

Life for the American soldiers continued as before, but without their British guests. On 4 July 1873, soldiers and civilians held the 'first national celebration proper of the Islanders.' They celebrated with sports, music and fireworks; dined and danced under 'extensive bowers'; and cheered as guns boomed out a national salute. The event was, no doubt, attended by many with British accents still learning the words to 'the Star Spangled Banner.'

And an important lesson had been learned. In 1875, the residents of Thurston County (on the mainland to the south of San Juan Island) petitioned the 'Hon. Members of the Council and House of Represent-atives of Was. Territory now assembled … to enact a law to prevent hogs from running at large.' If only Lyman Cutler had attempted to get a law enacted rather than shooting Griffin's pig, how different might things have been.

Whatever the outcome of the San Juan incident, the cold war between the United States and Great Britain continued to be waged, with Canada as the main prize. When the Emperor of Germany awarded the island to the Americans, George Bancroft told Odo Russell, the British Ambassador to Berlin:

> … that since George III acknowledged our independence in the late summer of 1782 to the present time, the strife about boundaries between the two Governments had known no intermission; now at last there remained no further differences; that therefore the definite friendly settlement effected by the reward of the German Emperor opened the way to a new career of reciprocal good feeling between the two countries.

Perhaps Bancroft believed in what he was saying, but others continued the unspoken conflict.

The United States abrogated its agreement over the Newfoundland fishing rights in 1885, thus engineering a political dispute between Newfoundland and Canada. An independent agreement was arrived at between Newfoundland and the United States, but Great Britain refused its ratification at the insistence of Canada, which wanted to present a united front against America. Canada wanted Newfoundland to join the confederation, having been alarmed at events in Nova Scotia. There had been an earlier attempt by some Nova Scotians to leave the confederation and join the United States. The movement had re-emerged in 1886 with American encouragement before being snuffed out. In the end, Newfoundland refused to join the confederation until 1949.

In 1886, the Americans decided that the Bering Sea was not part of the Pacific Ocean and began to arrest British ships hunting seals. Canadian vessels were also barred from sealing. After some years of failed negotiations, the matter was put to international arbitration in 1892. The following year, the commission appointed to arbitrate granted Great Britain every one of its demands and fined the Americans nearly $500,000 for the detention of British ships.

Two years later, using the Monroe Doctrine as an excuse, the United States decided to get involved in a dispute between Great Britain and Venezuela over the latter's border with British Guiana. The border problem had been simmering for some years and, in 1887, the Venezuelans asked the Americans to intervene. They did, achieved nothing and withdrew. In 1895, the Secretary of State, Richard Olney, on the grounds that the Monroe Doctrine had now been extended to the entire western hemisphere and, therefore, the border dispute affected America's interests, forced himself into the dispute with a demand that arbitration be sought. The British Prime Minister, Lord Salisbury, dismissed such a demand by reminding the United States that the Monroe Doctrine was not part of international law. The President, Grover Cleveland, pestered by economic depression and railway strikes, decided to deflect attention from his domestic problems by threatening Great Britain. In a Message to Congress, Cleveland demanded a commission, provided by the United States, to look into the border dispute, whether the British liked it or not. If Great Britain objected to the findings of the commission, it would be the duty of the United States:

> … to resist by every means in its power, as a wilful aggression upon its rights and interests, the appropriation by Great Britain of any lands or the exercise of governmental jurisdiction over any territory which after investigation we have determined of right belongs to Venezuela.

Salisbury met such sabre-rattling with mature composure. Busy contending with France over the 'Scramble for Africa' and trying to keep a lid on the Boer problems in South Africa, the Prime Minister agreed to the United States commission. If its findings did not suit his purposes, he could always put the American posturing to the test (he was unaware that the Secretary of the Navy, Hillary Herbert, had prepared a plan to seize the Great Lakes and the St Lawrence, ready for an invasion of Canada). In the end, perhaps to everyone's relief, the commission came down on the side of almost every British demand.

Towards the end of the nineteenth century, anti-British sentiment in the United States was so virulent that it almost seemed as if America was looking for a reason to go to war with Britain. A pro-British American lawyer, David Wells, wrote in 1896 of the widely held assumption:

> ... that the government and commercial policy of England is characterised by no other principle save to monopolize, through arbitrary, selfish, and unjust measures, everything on the earth's surface that can glorify herself and promote the interests of her own insular population, to the detriment of all other nations and people; and that it is the bounden duty of the people and government of the United States, in behalf of popular liberty, civilisation, and of Christianity, to put an end to the further continuance of such a policy, even if a resort to war would be necessary to effect it.

Senator Joseph Hawley told an audience that:

> ...in every emergency with which the United States has been confronted the British Government has been our enemy. She is pushing us on every side now ... I tell you that we must be ready to fight. Either we will float a dead whale on the ocean, or we must say to Great Britain, 'Here is where you stop!'

A college president wrote:

> There is no power on the face of the earth that we need fear trouble with except England.

Such was the atmosphere when, in 1897, gold was discovered in the Yukon. To get to the Klondike goldfields, the obvious route was by sea to the Lynn Canal, then overland from the head of the waterway. Unfortunately for non-American miners, this meant passing through United States territory known as the Alaska Panhandle, a strip of coastal land running as far south as the Portland Canal. According to the treaty Great Britain had agreed with the Russians in 1825, the Panhandle stretched no further eastwards than '10 Maritime Leagues' (30 miles) inland. If that distance was taken from the general line of the coast it would allow Canada access to the Lynn Canal and other inlets. But if it was taken to mean the entire shores of the inlets, the line would reach 30 miles inland from the heads of the inlets, thus depriving Canada of any water access to the Yukon.

After several attempts to get agreement between the United States and Great Britain failed, it was decided to create a joint commission of 'six impartial jurists of repute,' three from the United States, two from Canada, and one from Great Britain. President Theodore Roosevelt's idea of 'impartial' was to select three men whose minds had long before been made up, and were unlikely to change them. He chose Senator Henry Cabot Lodge; a former senator, George Turner; and, with a stunning lack of subtlety, the Secretary of War, Elihu Root. Just in case there was any doubt in the minds of the United States commissioners, Roosevelt let it be known that, if the decision went to the British, he would send marines to enforce the American claim.

The Canadians, just as keen to impose their opinions, sent men with equally closed minds: Sir Louis Jette, the Lieutenant-Governor of Quebec, and a barrister, Allan Aylesworth. From Britain came Lord Alverstone, the Lord Chief Justice of England, and probably the only man on the commission prepared to be impartial. The result was a victory for the United States. Faced with yet another impasse, Alverstone voted with the Americans. The Canadians were furious and considered that they had been severely let down. In fact, his lordship had done a far better job than had been expected. He had negotiated the Americans back from their original line and gained great tracts of land for the Canadians, despite their initial refusal to compromise. He had also obtained sovereignty over two small, but important, islands at the mouth of the Portland Canal. But by then it really did not matter: the gold rush was already over.

In the meantime, another front was opened up against the British. Webster Davis, an Assistant Secretary of the Interior, went to South Africa in support of Americans who had decided to join the Boers on the battlefield. Buoyed up by what he had seen, Davis returned to the United States and attempted to drum up further support for the Boers. When his own Republican Party rejected his agitation, he joined the Democrats, where he found much more support, although not enough to effect matters before the war's end.

The outbreak of the First World War in 1914 saw America presented with a perfect opportunity to weaken British influence in the world, despite claiming to be neutral. There was plenty of support for such a notion, especially from the large German and Irish communities throughout the United States. In Chicago, people from a wide variety of backgrounds campaigned vigorously in support of the Germans: meat-packers, local politicians, congressmen and the Director of the Chicago Symphony Orchestra all gave their support. Colonel Edward House, President Wilson's political advisor, was merely being pragmatic when he told Wilson: 'The best chance for peace is an understanding between England and Germany in regard to naval armaments and yet there is some disadvantage to us by these getting too close.' The United States was exporting an enormous amount of goods to Germany via adjoining neutral countries and obtaining imports from the same source. In the American-owned Philippines, fifteen German firms continued to supply the Fatherland.

The Professor of History at Washington University, St Louis, was concerned about the effect of a British victory. There were constant rumours, he noted, of the annexation of Canada; however:

> Any attempt during the war or at its close to establish a more intimate connection between the United States and Canada will not be viewed with approval in London ... The potential power of England is enormous, and in the present circumstances aught to be better understood ... all our approaches are at the mercy of her fleet once that fleet is victorious over her present enemies, and an army could invade the United States from Canada with ease and probably with success. It could not, indeed, hope to hold the country or conquer it, but a dash at New York, Chicago, or Seattle, is eminently feasible.

Despite continuing losses of American lives and ships through German action, the President continued to do little more than complain to Berlin. Extraordinarily, although most of the losses were through attacks by German submarines, the Americans welcomed without hesitation the arrival in New York of a German 'merchant' submarine carrying goods for the American market. Even more astonishing was the arrival of the submarine U-53 at Newport, Rhode Island. Members of the crew went ashore and purchased a newspaper containing the shipping departures. Within days, nine ships had been sunk by the U-53 off Nantucket Island.

The British and their allies were becoming more and more concerned at the progress of the war. Not only was there still a stalemate along the Western Front, the Revolution in Russia threatened to pull that country out of the war, thus releasing many enemy divisions that could be deployed against the British and the French. Could the Americans be persuaded to join the conflict on the side of the Allies? Apparently not, at least from the anti-British sentiment frequently expressed on the other side of the Atlantic. But then Fate stepped in to give the British the key to American involvement.

In early February 1917, a copy of a telegram from the German Foreign Minister, Arthur Zimmermann, to the German Minister in Mexico, came into the possession of British Naval Intelligence. Although in code, it was soon decrypted by Nigel de Grey and the Reverend William Montgomery, its contents revealing a plot intending that Mexico should invade the United States with German backing. This would ensure that the Americans did not enter the war on the side of the Allies, and would obtain for the Mexicans Arizona, California and New Mexico. The British held on to the telegram for two weeks, firstly to destroy any evidence of the means by which it had been obtained, and secondly to reveal the contents at the time of their choosing. On 24 February, the telegram was handed over to the American Ambassador in London. Not unnaturally, at first the message was looked upon as a hoax, but, a week later, Zimmermann himself acknowledged its contents. Suddenly, the Secretary of State, Robert Lansing, decided that it was:

> … the duty of this and every other democratic nation to suppress an autocratic government like the German because of its atrocious character and because it was a menace to the national safety of this country …

The United States declared war on Germany and the Central Powers on 6 April 1917, fighting to victory alongside their grateful British and Canadian allies.

Following the war, the Director of Canadian Military Operations & Intelligence, Colonel James Southerland Brown, decided that there was a serious possibility the United States might invade Canada. Consequently, in 1921 he produced 'Defence Scheme Number 1,' in which he decided that the best scheme of defence was to attack. His plan, in part, consisted of an invasion of the United States to capture border cities including Seattle, Minneapolis and Albany. Such a plan, he believed, would delay the Americans to such an extent that time would be provided for help to come from the rest of the British Empire.

Military plans were part of the standard training and military research carried out at the United States Army War College and (after 1921) at the US Army War Plans Division. Only one, however, was tested to the limit of actual aggression. In 1930, 'War Plan Crimson' laid out an attack upon Canada. 'Crimson' was the code name for Canada, 'Red' being for Great Britain, and 'Blue' for the United States (although, oddly, the planners constantly forgot to employ the code names). In strategic terms:

> Newfoundland, while not a part of the Dominion of Canada, would undoubtedly collaborate in any Crimson effort.

After describing the topography of Canada in great detail, the planners observed:

> Any extensive military operations in Canada between November 1st and April 15th would be extremely difficult, if not impossible.

Attention was drawn to the main railway systems of Canada:

> From a military point of view, these railroads provide excellent transportation facilities for Blue, if invasion of Crimson is decided upon, and being located in close proximity to the border are, from the Crimson viewpoint, very liable to interruption.

Not unexpectedly, 'Crimson' communications were a target:

> Interruption of Canada's trans-oceanic telegraph and radio service will seriously handicap Red–Crimson co-operation.

After listing Canada's economic assets, the planners noted:

> In case of war with the United States, Canada's coal imports from this country will be cut off and her railroads and industrial activities seriously handicapped. If Blue controlled the Quebec area and Winnipeg, Canada's railroads and industries dependent upon 'steam power' would be crippled.

The five main areas to come under initial attack were to be (without a single code name being provided): Halifax, Quebec and Montreal, the Great Lakes, Winnipeg, and Vancouver and Victoria. Three years later, the plan was modified to include the use of poison gas and strategic aerial bombing.

In early 1935, Congress approved the spending of $57 million for the construction of three airfields near the Canadian border as bases for a pre-emptive strike; the one built near the Great Lakes was to be disguised as a civilian airport, yet had to be 'capable of dominating the industrial heart of Canada, the Ontario Peninsular.'

Later the same year, massive military manoeuvres, deploying 36,000 troops along the border south of Ottawa, and with another 15,000 held in reserve in Pennsylvania, tested the system. The army recorded these exercises as 'The Greatest Peacetime Event in US History.'

Then help came from an unexpected quarter. With the outbreak of the Second World War, the American Ambassador to the Court of St James was Joseph Kennedy. According to the departing German Ambassador, Kennedy was 'Germany's best friend' in London, although he was known more widely as 'Jittery Joe' from his habit of experiencing German bombing from the safety of his retreat in Windsor. To the Under-Secretary at the Foreign Office, he was 'a very foul specimen of a double-crosser and defeatist.' Kennedy had not endeared himself to the British people by informing the Americans that Great Britain would easily succumb to a German invasion. When asked by the *Boston Sunday Globe*, 'Then what about Canada if the worst comes to the worst,' Kennedy replied, 'Well, we're sucked in on that one, and the Monroe Doctrine and all.' So 'Crimson' might not have 'Red' available to help in any case.

The plight of Great Britain during the first few months of the war proved to be of immense benefit to the American economy, which was still recovering from the Depression. Thanks to pre-war short-sightedness, the British armed forces lacked modern weaponry (the Royal Navy's main aircraft was still a biplane) and munitions. The Americans were keen to supply such materials, but only under the 'Cash and Carry' system. This meant that British ships had to cross the Atlantic and pay cash for anything that was needed for the war. By mid-1940, however, it became clear that to continue with this system of supply, it was necessary for the Royal Navy and the Royal Canadian Navy to have more ships to escort the merchant convoys. Accordingly, in August 1940, with Britain almost bankrupt, Phillip Kerr, Marquis of Lothian and the British Ambassador to the United States, made Cordell Hull, the Secretary of State, an offer. In return for 'naval and military equipment and material' (in practical terms, ships), the British would grant the United States naval and air bases on Newfoundland, Bermuda, the Bahamas, Jamaica, St Lucia, Trinidad and British Guiana. The bases would be granted rent-free for ninety-nine years. The Americans jumped at the chance and supplied the British with fifty obsolete destroyers. Thus, at a single stroke, not only had the British gained the needed ships, but had arranged for the armed forces of a neutral power to be based on its North American and Caribbean colonies. Not only would any enemy be very reluctant to attack such territories and risk the wrath of the United States, the bases would also supply (and fund) much-needed employment. Furthermore, if the United States did enter the war, the complete and ready-to-operate bases would be exactly where the British wanted them – on the Atlantic side of the United States.

In March 1941, Congress passed the 'Lend-Lease Act,' which allowed for the free supply of war materials to the Allies (including, after June 1941, the Soviet Union). Neutrality complications were avoided by requiring the supplies to be sent only to those governments 'whose defense the President deems vital for the defense of the United States.' The apparently generous gesture had, however, cold calculation at its heart. The supply of war materials would keep Britain in the war at the risk of British lives, while America watched from the sidelines as its economy boomed.

Clearly, it would have been in Britain's interest if the United States entered the war on the side of the Allies. Then, in October 1941, it looked as if the Americans were given just the push needed to get them involved. A car crash in Buenos Aires led to a British secret agent snatching the contents of a German courier's bag. Amongst the papers was a map drawn to show how the Germans would divide up South America once they had won the war. Somehow, the map ended up on the desk of President Roosevelt, who, appalled at this breach of the Monroe Doctrine, declared in his Navy Day speech, broadcast on 27 October 1941:

> Hitler has often protested that his plans for conquest do not extend across the Atlantic Ocean. I have in my possession a secret map, made in Germany by Hitler's government – by the planners of the new world order. It is a map of South America and part of Central America as Hitler proposed to reorganise it. This map makes clear the Nazi design, not only against South America, but against the United States as well.

The only problem was, there had been no car crash in Buenos Aires, no German courier, no British secret agent and even no German map. The 'map' had been created by the British secret service and leaked to the Americans. However, before this fire could be stoked to an even hotter temperature, an earlier exploit by the British brought the United States into the war almost by accident.

For some years, Japanese planners had thought that the best way to attack the American fleet would be by submarine, and all their planning stemmed from that conclusion. Then, in November 1940, twenty-four outdated Royal Navy bi-planes fell upon the Italian fleet in its harbour at Taranto. In less than an hour three battleships had been torpedoed, shore installations bombed and a cruiser badly damaged. It was to be months before the Italian fleet could get to sea again. In Japan, the planners switched from submarine attack to an attack by naval aircraft, but the Americans appeared not to have noticed the significance of the Taranto raid.

Almost four years later, on the day that Germany surrendered, the Lend-Lease scheme was cancelled. Any goods in the pipeline, and any subsequent supplies, had to be paid for. Almost instantly, Great Britain found itself with a bill for £1,075 million. Unable to pay, the British Government were forced to negotiate a loan from the United States at a 2 per cent interest rate. By now the world's richest nation, with more food, clothing and steel than it needed for its own use, the United States squeezed its most loyal ally, a nation still reeling from the cost of victory. The nation that had never known rationing ensured that food and fuel rationing continued in Britain for several more years. The loan was finally paid off in December 2006.

Eleven years after the defeat of Hitler's Germany, British troops had withdrawn from Egypt, leaving the Suez Canal in the hands of Colonel Nasser. Searching for arms for national defence, Nasser asked the United States to supply him, but was turned down after strong lobbying by American supporters of Israel. Nasser then promptly turned to the Soviet Union who, very keen to get a foothold in the Middle East, supplied Egypt with arms via Czechoslovakia. Seeing that this move could admit Soviet influence into the region, the British suggested to the United States that they counter the arms deal by offering to provide funding for the Aswan Dam project. After some delay, the Secretary of State, John Dulles, agreed. But when the Egyptians accepted the offer, Dulles promptly withdrew it. Nasser responded by nationalising the Suez Canal, Great Britain's (and Europe's) oil lifeline. With Nasser ignoring British attempts to get a settlement that would allow an international body to run the waterway, Great Britain, France and Israel launched an attack to regain control of the canal. All went well for the first few days (despite dangerous interference from the US 6th Fleet, whose Commander-in-Chief had to signal Washington, DC, with the plea 'Whose side are we on?'), until the United States, standing against two NATO allies and a young nation it had helped to found, attacked the British economy to such an extent that, with the pound plummeting in value, the British had to pull out. It was a master-stroke by the United States. Great Britain's standing in the world fell and, in effect, signalled the end of the British Empire. The ramifications, however, were enormous. Egypt let in the Soviets, Israel was seen as vulnerable, Arab nations began to fall into the hands of extremists, France withdrew from the military wing of NATO and the European Union took root. Middle Eastern nations, thrown off balance, began to attack one another as religious extremism flourished and the supply of oil became a diplomatic weapon. The Soviets invaded Afghanistan, causing the United States to sponsor a detestable dictatorship in Iraq, who used the American support to attack Iran, etc., etc., etc.

But the British were not finished. Less than a decade after the humiliation over Suez, the Prime Minister, Harold Wilson, was playing the American President, Lyndon Johnson, like an angler with a sluggish trout. Desperate for the British to send troops to Vietnam, Johnson continued to use the dollar to prop up a failing pound. Wilson, in the meantime, mainly for the benefit of his own image at home, made great play of attempts to get international mediation, none of which bore any fruit, and proved more of an irritant to the Americans than anything else. Equally, and for the same reason, he made prestigious visits to Washington to call upon an increasingly surly Johnson. The President's patience finally came to an end with the Wilson Government's 1966 Defence Review, which imposed severe cut-backs on the British armed forces. The dollar support for the pound was halted and Wilson was forced to devalue the pound in November 1967. As a result, the following year Wilson declared that Great Britain would withdraw its forces east of Suez. Although this would clearly take some time to achieve, it sent a clear signal to the Americans that there was no longer even the slightest chance of British involvement in Vietnam. From then on, Great Britain watched from the sidelines as widespread civil unrest grew on the other side of the Atlantic to match the falling morale of the United States forces in Vietnam. So bad was the effect on national morale that, nine years later, when a clear case for the enforcement of the 'Western Hemisphere' version of the Monroe Doctrine presented itself, the United States merely stood and watched as British forces re-took the Falkland Islands. The United States Ambassador to the United Nations was, nevertheless, dispatched to the Argentinean Embassy to offer congratulations at a banquet thrown to celebrate the invasion of the islands. Some retaliation was made by fostering American support for Irish terrorists – even to the extent of inviting Irish Republican representatives to the White House. A further opportunity for a small revenge occurred in 1983 when, outnumbering the enemy by at least seven to one, the United States invaded the tiny

Commonwealth island of Grenada – whose Head of State was none other than Queen Elizabeth II.

After British and American forces served alongside each other in the 1990–91 Gulf War to free Kuwait from an Iraqi invasion, another perfect opportunity presented itself for Britain to remind the United States that, despite facing a future as a province of Europe, the country still retained some vestiges of dignity and authority of its own.

Following the awful, harrowing attack on the World Trade Centre in New York in 2001, President George W. Bush decided to retaliate with the bizarre concept of declaring 'War on Terror.' To do this, he intended to invade Iraq, a country ruled by a cruel despot who had nothing to do with the New York attack, and Afghanistan, a violent and unstable country where it was possible, but only *possible*, that the leader of the terrorists was in hiding. At this point, if the rules of the centuries-old Anglo-American Cold War had been observed, the British Prime Minster, Tony Blair, should have refused to have anything to do with such pointless actions. Instead, he should have advised Bush that such ill-founded concepts such as the 'War on Terror' was no basis for putting at risk thousands of his own people's lives, the lives of his allies and the lives of non-combatants. Equally, it was clearly obvious that such actions would prompt widespread support for religious extremists, not all of whom were living in the Middle East. But Blair did not understand the great game that had been played by his predecessors, and the dire consequences became plain for all to see.

It did not take long after the attack on New York for farce to rear its head again. Twenty-first-century technology, in the shape of the global positioning system, discovered that the border along the 49th Parallel was actually some hundreds of feet to the north of the Parallel itself. Consequently, when suspected criminals were charged by Washington State at the actual border, they claimed that, as the northern limit of the state was 'along said forty-ninth parallel of north latitude,' they were actually north of the state's jurisdiction and, therefore, unaccountable to its system of law. As a result, in 2002, the Washington State Supreme Court pored over the treaties of 1846, the joint survey ending in 1869, the maps showing the boundary markers, the 1870 declaration between Great Britain and the United States that the ground survey was, in fact, the boundary, and the 1889 admission of Washington as one of the states in the Union. In the end, rather than recognise that there existed a strip of land north of the treaty border, the Supreme Court decided that – regardless of modern surveying technology – the markers erected by Hawkins and Campbell in 1869 were the actual border.

Canada, represented by the triangle hovering over the unfinished pyramid on the Great Seal of the United States, is no longer a colony of Great Britain. It is a great country in its own right, a country that can make its own decisions and take action on its own behalf. It is unlikely, however, that its future will be at a more grave risk over such a tiny incident than when an American settler shot a British pig on a small island in the Gulf of Georgia. An act that found governors and generals eager for war, politicians and diplomats vying for position, presidents and prime ministers posturing, whilst sailors, soldiers and marines, from both sides, learned the value of co-operation and common sense – a lesson still to be learned by their leaders.

Appendix: Maps

Detail of Captain Vancouver's chart, showing his route through the Rosario Strait.

1858 map made for the US Secretary of War, showing the border passing through the Canal de Haro.

Detail from Wilkes's chart, showing the Canal de Haro and ignoring the Rosario Strait.

Detail from Charles Preuss's map produced for the United States Senate, showing the water boundary passing to the east of the San Juan Islands.

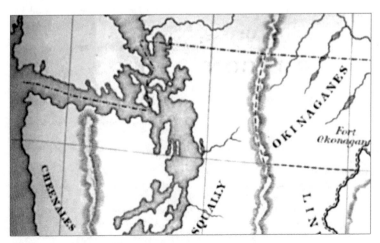

Detail from the 1852 American 'Map of Oregon showing the location of Indian Tribes.' It also shows the 'Compromise' water boundary, which the Americans refused to accept.

Select Bibliography

Carter, James H. *Canada–US Dispute Resolution: Some Lessons from the Past.* Paper given to the
   Canadian Council on International Law, Ottawa, Canada, 27 October 2005.

Coleman, E.C. *Captain Vancouver: North-west Navigator.* Tempus Publishing, Stroud, Glos., UK, 2006.

DeKay, Tertius James. *The Rebel Raiders.* Pimlico, London, UK, 2004.

Delgado, James P. *The Beaver: First Steamship on the West Coast.* Horsdal & Schubart Publishers,
   Victoria, BC, Canada, 1993.

Dent, John Charles. *Canadian Notabilities,* Vol. I. BiblioBazaar, Charles ton, SC, USA, 2007.

Department of the Interior, Office of the Chief Astronomer. *Certain Correspondence of the
   Foreign Office and of the Hudson's Bay Company copied from original documents, London, 1898.*
   Government Printing Bureau, Ottawa, ON, 1899.

Efrat, Barbara S. & Langlois, W.J. (editors). 'Captain Cook and the Spanish Explorers on the
   Coast.' *Sound Heritage,* Vol. VII, No 1. Aural History, Provincial Archives of British Columbia,
   Victoria, BC, 1978.

Evans, Lynette & Burley, George. *Roche Harbour.* B & E Enterprises, Everet, WA, USA, 1972.

Foreign Office Correspondence: International Boundary, 49th Parallel, British Columbia,
   1869–1870. US Correspondence, 1861–1863. Foreign Relations, 1896. North-West Coast
   America–Alaska. Hudson's Bay Company Correspondence, 1825.

Fowler, Albert G. 'The Other Gulf War.' In *The Beaver: Exploring Canada's History,* Vol. 72, No 6.
   Dec. 1992–Jan. 1993.

Gough, Barry M. *Gunboat Frontier: British Maritime Authority and Northwest Coast Indians,
   1846–1890.*

Gough, Barry M. *The Royal Navy and the Northwest Coast of North America, 1810–1914.* University
   of British Columbia, reprinted 1974.

Government Papers, Northwest Boundary Arbitration. II. *Case of the Government of Her
   Britannic Majesty, Submitted to Arbitration and Award of His Majesty The Emperor of Germany
   in accordance with Article XXXIV of the Treaty between Great Britain and the United States of
   America, signed at Washington, May 8, 1871.* III. *Reply of the United States to the case of the
   Government of Her Britannic Majesty presented to His Majesty The Emperor of Germany as
   Arbitrator under the provisions of the Treaty of Washington, June 12, 1872.* IV. *North American
   Water Boundary. Second and Definitive Statement on behalf of the Government of Her Britannic
   Majesty, submitted to His Majesty the Emperor of Germany, under the Treaty of Washington of May*

8, 1871.V. *Governor the Earl of Cathcart's Speech to the Legislature of the Province of Canada, 20 March, 1846.*

Haller, Granville O. 'San Juan and Secession.' In *The Tacoma Sunday Ledger*, 19 January 1896.

Howard, M. Jacob. Speech to the Senate, 16 April 1869. Appendix to the *Congressional Globe*, 16 April 1869.

Howay, Judge, Scholefield, E.O.S. & others. *Cariboo Gold Rush*. Heritage House Publishing Company, Surrey, BC, Canada, 1987 & 1999.

Kaufman, Scott & Soares, John A. '"Sagacious Beyond Praise"? Winfield Scott and Anglo-American-Canadian Border Diplomacy, 1837–1860.' *The Society for Historians of American Foreign Relations, Diplomatic History*, Vol. 30, No 1. Blackwell Publishing, Malden, USA, and Oxford, UK, Jan. 2005.

Latane, John Holladay. *From Isolation to Leadership Revised: a Review of American Foreign Policy*. Doubleday, Page & Co., New York, NY, USA, 1922.

Longacre, Edward G. *Pickett: Leader of the Charge*. White Mane Publishing Company, 1995.

Mason, General Edwin C. *How We Won the San Juan Archipelago*. From a paper read to the Executive Council of the Minnesota History Society, 9 November 1896. Minnesota History Society.

Masters, D.C. *Reciprocity, 1846–1911*. Historical Booklet No 12. Canadian Historical Association, Ottawa, ON, Canada, 1969.

Morgan, C.T. *The San Juan Story*. 16th edn. San Juan Industries, Friday Harbor.

Murray, Keith. *The Pig War*. Pacific Northwest Historical Pamphlet. Washington State Historical Society, Tacoma, WA, April 1968.

New York Times, 17 October 1900.

North Pacific History Company of Portland, Oregon. *Biographical Sketch of Col. Granville O. Haller, USA, History of the Pacific Northwest, Oregon and Washington, 1889*, Vol. II. North Pacific History Company of Portland, OR, USA, 1899.

O'Neal, Bill. 'The Holy Sanction of "Manifest Destiny."' In *True West*, Vol. 42, No 12. Dec. 1995.

Putnam's Magazine. 'The Northwest Boundary Dispute' *Putnam's Magazine of Literature, Science, Art, and National Interests*, Vol. VI, No XXXIII. Sep. 1870.

Richardson, David. *Magic Islands: a Treasure Trove of San Juan Islands Lore*. Orcas Publishing Co., Eastsound, WA, USA, 1964, 1965, 1970, 1995.

Richardson, David. *Pig War Islands*. Orcas Publishing Co., Eastsound, WA, USA, 1971.

Smith, Dorothy Blakey (editor). *Lady Franklin Visits the Pacific Northwest: Being Extracts from the letters of Miss Sophia Cracroft, Sir John Franklin's Niece, February to April 1861 and April to July 1870*. Memoir No XI. Provincial Archives of British Columbia, 1974.

US Government. *The Northwest Boundary: Discussion of the Water Boundary Question*. Government Printing Office, Washington, DC, 1868.

US House of Representatives. *Northwest Boundary Commission. Message of the President of the United States Concerning the Northwest Boundary Commission*. Executive Document No 86. Ordered to be printed 13 February 1869.

US Senate. *Message of the President of the United States, Communicating, In compliance with a resolution of the Senate of the 9th instant, the correspondence of Lieutenant General Scott, in reference to the Island of San Juan, and of Brigadier General Harney, in command of the department of Oregon*. Executive Document No 10. Ordered to be printed 7 February 1860.

Vouri, Mike. *Outpost of Empire: the Royal Marines and the Joint Occupation of San Juan Island*. Northwest Interpretive Association, Seattle, WA, USA, 2004.

Vouri, Mike. *The Pig War: Standoff at Griffin Bay*. Griffin Bay Bookstore, Friday Harbor, WA, USA, 1999.

Walbran, Captain John T. *British Columbia Coast Names*. Second Reprinting by J.J. Douglas. Douglas & McIntyre, Vancouver, BC, Canada, Dec. 1971.

Watkin, Sir E.W., Bt, MP. *Canada and the States: Recollections, 1851–1886*. Ward, Lock & Co., London, UK, 1887.

National Archive Sources:

Admiralty Documents: ADM1/5720 US Navy 1854 Chart of the vicinity of Vancouver Island and the Mainland around San Juan Island; ADM12 Digests: 1855–1862: Vancouver's/San Juan Island; ADM54 Supplementary Ships' Logs 1808–1871; ADM201/38 Settlements: Papers from Nine Oversees Posts 1809–1878; ADM352/58 Hydrographic Department: Original Surveys.

Foreign Office Documents: FO5/809-816B North-West Boundary and Island of San Juan 1846–1869; FO5/1466–1474 North-West Boundary and Island of San Juan 1849–1873; FO14/414 Correspondence pertaining to San Juan Island; FO414/16 Correspondence: Occupation of the Island of San Juan by US Troops, 1859–1860; FO93/8/34B Arrangement: Joint Occupation of Island of San Juan, October 25th, 1859; FO881/808 Memorandum: Island of San Juan, Despatch to Lord Lyons, August 24th, 1859; FO881/816 Despatches: Occupation of Island of San Juan by US Troops, 1859; FO881/817 Correspondence: Occupation of Island of San Juan by US Troops, Part 1, August to October, 1859; FO881/818 Despatches: Occupation of Island of San Juan by US Troops 1859; FO881/844 Despatches: Occupation of Island of San Juan by US Troops, 1859; FO881/912 Correspondence: Occupation of San Juan Island by US Troops, Part 2, 1859–July, 1860; FO881/1769 Water Boundary Correspondence; FO925/1884 Maps and Plans. Boundary Lines 1872; FO925/1651 San Juan Boundary 1872; FO925/1656 San Juan Boundary 1873; FO881/1769 Correspondence: Water Boundary, North-West Coast of America, Island of San Juan, 1857–1859.

Government Correspondence: PRO 30/22/31; PRO 30/22/34; PRO 30/22/35; PRO 30/22/96; Lord John Russell, San Juan Island, 1859.

Index